UNDERSTANDING

ASSISTED SUICIDE

Nine Issues to Consider

JOHN B. MITCHELL

The University of Michigan Press / Ann Arbor

Copyright © by the University of Michigan 2007
All rights reserved
Published in the United States of America by
The University of Michigan Press
Manufactured in the United States of America
⊚ Printed on acid-free paper

2012   2011   2010   2009   5   4   3   2

A CIP catalog record for this book is available from the British Library.

Library of Congress Cataloging-in-Publication Data

Mitchell, John B. (John Barry), 1944–
    Understanding assisted suicide : nine issues to consider / John B.
Mitchell.
        p.   ;   cm.
    Includes bibliographical references and index.
    ISBN-13: 978-0-472-09996-2 (cloth : alk. paper)
    ISBN-10: 0-472-09996-5 (cloth : alk. paper)
    ISBN-13: 978-0-472-06996-5 (pbk. : alk. paper)
    ISBN-10: 0-472-06996-9 (pbk. : alk. paper)
    1. Assisted suicide.   2. Euthanasia.   3. Terminal care—Moral and
ethical aspects.   I. Title.
    [DNLM: 1. Suicide, Assisted—ethics—Personal Narratives.   WB 60
M681u 2007]

    R726.M565   2007
    179.7—dc22   2007008826

Understanding Assisted Suicide

To Mom and Dad . . . . Wish you were here.

Acknowledgments

When I go over my notes, it is striking how many people helped me and how pivotal their respective contributions were. Without the assistance of many of these people it is unlikely there ever would have been a book at all.

First, and always first, my wife, Eva, who helped in every way imaginable. Renee Lock got me going on this project when so long ago she sent me a pack of provocative newspapers clippings on the topic. My friend Bruce Firestone strongly encouraged me to bring my personal experience throughout the book. John Harris, world renowned philosopher and bioethicist, and his Manchester colleagues took me through the rudiments of formal philosophy and got me started in my education. Annette Clark guided me in taking page upon page of ideas and turning them into a book and then just kept on helping me and helping me. Jonathan Eames got me to the center of Oregon's health care world. Linda Ganzini generously shared her extensive research on physician-assisted suicide and the Oregon health care profession. Dr. Greg Hamilton spent time educating me about the anti-euthanasia position. Jim Bond, Erwin Chemerinsky, Sandra Johnson, Michael H. Shapiro, and Kathryn L. Tucker pushed me to expand the intellectual scope of my work. My colleague Marilyn Berger and Michael Ames, editor at the Vanderbilt University Press, made me clearly see the book I was *not* writing and so led me to the one I was. David Skover, my workplace neighbor, educated me about how to craft a good proposal and unfailingly encouraged me throughout. Martha Nussbaum coached me in being aggressive in order to get my book moved through the contract process. Nanette Cardon took indexing to a level I never conceived. Endless word processing was done by Nancy Ammons, Phyllis Brazier, and Erin Espedal. And the law school's incredible librarians—Kelley Kunsch and Bob Maniteaux endlessly guided and assisted my research, while Susan Kezelle spent half her days obtaining interlibrary loans for me. Finally my amazing editor, Mary Erwin, and the rest of the University of Michigan Press gang—Raphael Allen (my first editor), Anna Szymanski, and Christina L. Milton—who made this book a reality.

Contents

Introduction

HOW I CAME TO WRITE THIS BOOK:
THE END OF MY FATHER'S JOURNEY
AND THE BEGINNING OF MY OWN

This is a book about ideas. It was born, however, out of deep emotion. My father was diagnosed with fourth-stage pancreatic cancer in 1995. For the last six weeks of his life, we brought him and my mother home to live with us. While staying at our house, my father asked my sister and me to help him commit suicide. I wouldn't do it. Part of me thought it was wrong. Part of me was afraid to get caught and have to face criminal prosecution. (My sister and I are somewhat bumbling when dealing with very practical things, and I did not wish to involve my exceptionally competent wife, who probably could have gotten away with it.) My father died several weeks later after suffering excruciating pain, which was only intermittently brought under control by the most powerful pain medications available.

My mother had Alzheimer's and Parkinson's diseases. My father had been her life companion and her caretaker during the last portion of her life. After his death, her dementia took over. At some point in 1997, she had to be taken to the hospital to be treated for several extremely painful pressure sores, gaping wounds filled with fetid, rotting flesh. When she arrived by ambulance, she was unconscious. She had a living will and had given me durable power of attorney for health care. When she had not regained consciousness by the second day, I ordered all artificial feeding and hydration terminated. My mother died within a few days. My decision is documented in the report of the attending physician.

> PLAN: I have discussed quality of life issues with the son, John Mitchell, in detail. He has many concerns about his mother's quality of life. He does not wish to prolong her life in any manner that would require tube feeds or artificial hydration. He states that she would not have wanted that, indeed, she has signed written declaration stating that any procedures that artificially would prolong the dying process should be withheld or withdrawn and she be permitted to die naturally with only the administration of medication with medical procedures deemed necessary to provide her with comfort care or to alleviate pain. Owing to her severe level of dehydration and decreased p.o. intake, as well as no desire for feeding tube and poor quality of life with her severe Alzheimer's disease and her down-going mental status, the son wishes to have a hospice consult and comfort measures only to give his mother quality ending to life other than prolonging her to be in continued pain.

> I have talked to Dr. —— about this and he agrees totally as I do. We will arrange hospice visit for the patient. In the meanwhile we will provide her with intravenous fluids at 88 cc an hour as well as intravenous antibiotics for infection, also providing her with pain medication as needed. Would expect transfer to an extended care facility for comfort care only in the near future.

After my father died, I did not think too deeply about the request he had made of my sister and me. I missed him terribly, but there was so much to do to take care of Mom, let alone raise two children and handle the rest of the day-to-day life, that I did not engage in much reflection. But, after Mom died, my decision haunted me. Perhaps I should have helped my father to die even though it would have been illegal and I could have gone to prison. What was the real basis of my initial reaction that suicide was immoral and uncourageous? Maybe the truth was that I was a coward.

And so it went: guilt, shame, uncertainty—what had I done? Then a funny thing happened. Without even knowing it, without apparent thought let alone a dramatic moment of decision, I slowly began a journey. This journey eventually would lead me to accept what I had done, whether good or bad, courageous or cowardly, right or wrong, or possibly somewhere along a spectrum between these absolutes. This book is in large part a chronicle of that journey.

As I said, it began without me even knowing it. I'd be waiting in a doctor's office and a few fragments of some article about dying in America would pop out. *A century ago, people died at home, surrounded by family. Death was a public matter, not something to be feared, or denied.*[1] Or I'd be flipping through the newspaper looking for the sports section and my eyes would rest on another article about dying. *Once death happened at all times; at all ages.*[2] *Now most die when elderly after a long bout with some chronic illness.*[3] Then I'd be browsing in a bookstore. *Death has been transformed from an existential to a medical reality.*[4]

Suddenly, all around me were books, articles, news programs, speaker's series, and such about assisted suicide and euthanasia and particularly about the debate over physician-assisted suicide (PAS). I don't think a psychologist would be surprised at this new framing of my awareness. My mind was taking me where I needed to travel.

Prior to my parents' deaths, I was vaguely aware of assisted suicide movements, the Hemlock Society, and various state initiatives for PAS. But these concepts were no more part of my reality than the suicide practices of the ancient Greeks[5] and Romans,[6] the self-inflicted deaths in the face of dishonor I'd seen in Japanese movies,[7] or the self-sacrificing suicides of the elderly in Eskimo, Samoan, and Crow Indian cultures about which I had once read in college.[8] Those were just tales to me, like the one somewhere in the back of my memory about the villages in ancient Brittany where there was a holy hammer in each village chapel and the oldest living relative would take the hammer and crush the skulls of the dying who were suffering.[9]

But I also began to learn that an openness to the possibility of suicide, and more particularly assisted suicide and euthanasia, was not new to American soil. In the 1930s, there was a serious debate about euthanasia in the United States and England.[10] This debate resurrected an intense interest in euthanasia that had been expressed in American medical journals and meetings in the late 1800s under the sway of social Darwinism[11] and great advances in medicine.[12] The 1930s debate came to a screeching halt after the close of World War II with the discovery of the nightmare that was the Nazi eugenics program.[13]

I did not need to read deeply to come to realize that the idea of assisted suicide for the terminally ill had reemerged as a legitimate topic of discussion in America and many other parts of the world.[14] What I did not realize is that my initial feelings that it would be wrong for my father to kill himself, with or without my aid, likely placed me in the minority in this nation.

Over the past decade, surveys have consistently shown that approximately 70 percent of Americans believe that the terminally ill should have the assistance of a doctor should they choose to end their lives.[15] A recent survey at Eastern Texas Christian College shows how stable this belief is. Intuitively, you would expect overwhelming disapproval from this pocket of the Christian subculture. Yet the survey came up with the same results as all the others—72 percent approval.[16] It seems that Americans approve of the concept, at least in principle. Indeed, one state—Oregon—has actually passed legislation to legalize physician-assisted suicide.[17] Some, on the other hand, have pointedly argued that the polling method used in the surveys overstates the magnitude of public support for assisted suicide.[18] Perhaps the fact that, other than in Oregon, statewide ballot measures to legalize some forms of assisted suicide have failed reflects a gap between attitudes toward the concept, on the one hand, and adoption of that concept when manifested in a concrete proposal on the other.[19] Nonetheless, whatever one can conclude from these surveys, it is plain that the issue of assisted suicide and euthanasia is in the wind in our culture and hardly my issue alone.

I don't know when, but at some point I acknowledged my journey and commenced it in earnest. In this private journey, I read everything I could get my hands on relating to suicide, assisted suicide, and euthanasia. These works ranged from those expressing religious views to moral and political philosophy, law, and medicine.

Other than my expertise in law, which I have practiced and taught for nearly 35 years, most of my reading involved fields with which I was not very familiar. I was back in school, often struggling to merely comprehend what I was reading. Eventually, I learned the jargon and themes and could grasp what was at the core of each position. From there I slowly began to develop my own critique.

As I journeyed through the literature of so many different fields, I began to see that there was an odd structure to the assisted suicide debate in our culture. While superficially divided into pro and con, the sides were not drawn along single lines. Rather, each side was comprised of a coalition. And the members of the respective coalitions staked out their ground based on their conclusions drawn from one or more of *nine separate, discrete issues.* Moreover, whether in scholarly or popular literature or op-ed pieces in newspapers, no one relied on more than a few of the nine and often disagreed with a fellow coalition member on an issue that the other person had relied on. For example, the coalitions opposed to assisted suicide are further delineated by the members' beliefs about suicide itself. For some, suicide is immoral, so any discussion of assisted suicide on its own terms is a nonstarter. Others make no moral claim denying individuals the choice of killing themselves but do have moral and/or pragmatic objections to the addition of a third party to the equation, that is, they object to assisted suicide. Further, those arguing opposing positions rarely countered their adversaries' reasoning or data in all but the most superficial or conclusionary manner, rather relying on their conclusions from their own set of debates as determinative.

Therefore, I concluded that to participate in the important cultural discussion of this extraordinarily complex issue, a discussion that will become increasingly significant over the next decade as the baby boomers age and state legislatures consider assisted suicide laws like Oregon's, one must ponder all nine issues.

It is not the casual use of language that leads me to call each of these nine areas contested "issues" rather than "arguments." While plainly employed in argumentation, each of these nine areas possesses its own (often extensive) literature and value structure and is fundamentally self-contained. While I recognize that the various issues borrow pieces from the others to form their arguments, they are nonetheless rhetorically distinct, although the opposing arguments within each issue might be interrelated and logically connected.[20] These nine issues can be fairly characterized as:

Issue 1: Our culture does/does not subscribe to the notion of the "absolute sanctity of life."

Issue 2: Western religion does/does not plainly forbid suicide (and a fortiori assisted suicide or euthanasia).

Issue 3: Assuming that a particular suicide or assisted suicide might be justified, condoning such a suicide or assisted suicide would/ would not result in overall harm to the society.

Issue 4: Permitting physician-assisted suicide would/would not result in a "slippery slope," ending in involuntary termination of our most vulnerable and powerless citizens.

Issue 5: Assisted suicide is/is not morally supported by the principle of "autonomy."

Issue 6: Individuals can/cannot be mentally competent and/or rational if they choose suicide (and a fortiori assisted suicide or euthanasia) as the best choice for themselves.

Issue 7: Physician-assisted suicide is/is not morally supported by the combined concepts of "medical autonomy" and "mercy."

Issue 8: One does/does not have a constitutional right to suicide, assisted suicide, or euthanasia.

Issue 9: Legislation permitting physician-assisted suicide would/would not be sound social policy.

As I indicated, there are some interrelationships between the issues, as core elements of one will play a role in another. Thus, culturally based morality (issue 1), carries religious undertones (issue 2) and echoes many of the concerns about risks to the most vulnerable and marginalized, which appear in the discussion of the "slippery slope" (issue 4). Religion (issue 2), on the other hand, adds force to the notion of the absolute sanctity of life found in issue 1 and offers a counterclaim in reliance on one's individual autonomy (issue 5).

The analysis based on utilitarianism (issue 3) offers a "cousin" in form to the slippery slope (issue 4) and a counter to the claims of individual autonomy (issue 5). The slippery slope (issue 4) in turn looks back to utilitarian balancing (issue 3) and depends heavily on the concerns underlying the fear of moving away from the position that life has absolute sanctity (issue 1).

Autonomy (issue 5) plays a central role in legal arguments (issue 8) and finds that its ultimate benefits are utilitarian (issue 3) in nature. The debate about whether one can choose some form of suicide and still possess mental competency (issue 6) weaves through debates about the slippery slope (issue 4), concerns that underlie abandonment of the absolute sanctity of life (issue 1), and questions about whether autonomy is possible under these circumstances (issue 5).

The combination of medical autonomy and mercy (issue 7) finds a place in discussions of the legal rights to assisted suicide (issue 8) along with autonomy (issue 5) and the slippery slope (issue 4). Finally, autonomy (issue 4), mercy (issue 7), and the slippery slope (issue 4) appear throughout the discussion of the advisability of legislation (issue 9) permitting assisted suicide.

Rhetorically, however, the nine issues do not blur into one another, even though they may share common elements or building blocks. Obviously there are many ways to organize and conceptualize this complex, overarching metaissue of assisted suicide of which the "nine issues" are subcomponents. Standing back, I can imagine viewing the issue as one that is principally moral (though not necessarily religious) and concerned with the tension between maintaining lines, on the one hand, and alleviating recognizable human suffering on the other. I can then imagine an author who chooses to organize a book around these concepts. Yet that is not how people—whether in buses, restaurants, family kitchens, or classrooms—discuss the issue. They select among the nine issues and align themselves with coalitions constructed of them. Structuring this book to reflect how people actually talk and argue thus seemed to be most useful for those who seek to understand, and perhaps even enter the public discussion about, assisted suicide.

While there certainly are strong emotional commitments in the substrata of this issue, at bottom its acknowledged complexity is a function of the fact that we are dealing with nine separate, sophisticated issues that appear, disappear, and reappear in the rhetoric. What follows is organized around these nine issues and offers my analysis and conclusions as to each.

One last point: In our culture of expertise, there are people who have devoted a lifetime to studying a single passage of Genesis or the philosophies of John Stuart Mill. In fact, an expert on Mill might stake his or her career on a single one of the philosopher's works. It's therefore likely that there does not exist a single person who is an expert in all the fields discussed in this book. With that in mind, I am offering my best understanding, based on my own analysis and personal experience, of the vast spectrum of theories, ideas, and information about assisted suicide.

A BRIEF NOTE ON THE CHOSEN ORDER FOR DISCUSSION OF THE NINE ISSUES

The order in which I treat the nine issues reflects the sequence of my personal and intellectual journey. Although there was some back and forth, my reading progressed in a relatively straight line. Interestingly, although my life's work has been in the law, I did not really focus on this aspect of assisted suicide until the last part of the journey. Rather, what occupied me were questions of morality: is or is not assisted suicide immoral? I guess, under the circumstances, my priorities made sense. My anguish did not result from some legal interpretation; my pain resided in issues of right and wrong.

I began by exploring moral systems that purportedly justified an absolute moral bar against suicide, assisted suicide, and euthanasia, regardless of specific circumstances, situations, or consequences (formal philosophers call these *deontological* moral theories). Obviously, had I been convinced by any of the following it would have been the end of my journey:

1. the cultural philosophy that it is always wrong to kill an innocent person
2. religion, specifically the Judeo-Christian tradition
3. the cultural philosophy that lives perceived to be of less "quality" nonetheless must be perceived as of equal value with all other lives

I next considered moral systems that purportedly justified an absolute moral bar against assisted suicide based on specific circumstances, situations, or consequences (formal philosophers call these *consequentialist* moral theories). I should note here that from the perspective of an academic philosopher my small distinction between moral theories that consider consequences and those that only focus on abstract principles would appear simplistic. Obviously, at some point deontological principles are formed based on some conception of the consequences of adhering to those principles. A deontological system that routinely leads to consequences a society would not wish to experience would not likely find many followers. For my purposes, however, my admittedly oversimplified distinction provides a clarity for this discussion that is beneficial.

1. utilitarian balancing
2. the "slippery slope," including the experiences of the Netherlands and Oregon

From there, I considered the principal moral theory from which one could deduce that suicide, assisted suicide, and euthanasia are affirmatively moral.

1. autonomy

And from there I progressed through other theories from which one could purportedly deduce that suicide, assisted suicide, and euthanasia are moral under the appropriate circumstances.

1. utilitarian balancing
2. the combination of autonomy and mercy

Only after all my thoughts on these debates in moral philosophy and bioethics took shape did I at last look at law—first at assisted suicide and the courts and then at whether assisted suicide should be legalized through legislation.

Issue 1

Our culture does/does not subscribe to the notion of the "absolute sanctity of life"

Cultural Arguments That Assisted
Suicide Is Always Wrong

There are concepts embedded within our culture that would find any attempt to end my father's suffering by ending his life morally wrong. In this regard, I believe certain ideas run through our society that are not proclaimed by formal philosophers but are philosophical nonetheless.[1] These ideas reflect our sense of life and its meaning.[2] One such idea is at the core of any discussion of suicide or euthanasia: life is sacred and has absolute sanctity.[3] Here I should be clear that when I discuss the absolute sanctity of life I do not mean that concept in the sense of vitalism, where life is to be maintained at all costs.[4] While some may believe that, most who use the sanctity of life as an argument against suicide recognize that although life has incommensurate value it is not the only thing of value. Rather, life does not need to be maintained at all costs. It is, however, inviolable.

This sense of life's sacredness certainly finds support in religion, but it can also reside in the heart of an agnostic or atheist. It is deeply embedded in our culture, and it is deeply embedded in me. It was there the day my father asked my sister and me to help him kill himself. He was suffering, but he was still alive. His life was sacred, inviolable. This idea of absolute sanctity provides the basis for holding suicide, assisted suicide, and euthanasia to be immoral regardless of circumstances or consequences.

Yet we do condone taking lives. We condone war, self-defense, and capital punishment. In the medical context, we allow lives to be shortened by pulling the plug, not providing "disproportionate" treatment, giving pain medication when we know that there is a substantial risk that the medication will kill the patient, permitting the patient to refuse lifesaving medical treatment, and allowing terminal sedation. My father stopped the provision of food and hydration (other than sponging his lips) to accelerate his death. I requested the same for my mother to achieve the same end. I wanted her to die. So, as I went through this part of the journey, my focus was on whether these seeming exceptions to the absolute sanctity of life could be explained or whether, in fact, we do not really believe in life's absolute sanctity. If the latter were correct, the notion of the sanctity of life could not provide the basis for an absolute moral claim against suicide, assisted suicide, and euthanasia.

IT IS ALWAYS WRONG TO INTENTIONALLY TAKE A HUMAN LIFE

In our culture, life's sanctity manifests itself in a moral prohibition against intentionally taking human life.[5] This serves as a powerful claim against suicide, assisted suicide, and euthanasia. Prior to delving into this aspect of our cultural philosophy, like most of us, I accepted that this belief in the wrongness of taking life could somehow coexist with the acceptance of war, self-defense, and capital punishment. It's not that I have supported all of this nation's military adventures. I have not. Nor do I support capital punishment. But my objections have not rested on the notion of the sanctity of life. I was, therefore, curious in my reading about how the proponents of an absolute sanctity of life objection to assisted suicide found war, self-defense, and capital punishment to be legitimate exceptions to the ban against taking life.[6] I concluded that they do so based on the rationale that the individuals who are killed have somehow forfeited the right to have their lives treated as inviolable. This forfeiture is expressed within what is, in effect, a coded phrase, a term of art—*noninnocent*. But, as I read and thought, it became clear to me that we do condone intentionally taking lives that are "innocent."[7] While this may be justifiable from the perspective of a consequentialist moral theory (i.e., one that considers contexts, circumstances, and costs and benefits), it hardly supports an absolute moral claim that it is *always* wrong to take innocent life. To the contrary, our willingness to take innocent life undercuts the use of any claim that it is "always wrong to kill the innocent" as an absolute moral basis for condemning suicide and assisted suicide in all circumstances.

A Just War

War, which is filled with intentional killing, has been a constant in all recorded history and our own lives over the past century.[8] Our country has gone to war in World War I, World War II, Korea, Vietnam, Iraq, and Afghanistan. And throughout we have killed civilians; although we call it "collateral damage,"[9] they are just as dead. Unless we want to say that no one in the enemy population is innocent, including babies, young children, and the elderly infirm, we make the decision to take actions that we know will kill innocents. We may wish it were otherwise and would be happier to just kill official combatants, but the point is that no modern army will forgo a strategically desirable military action just because of the certain knowledge that there will be noncombatant deaths. The very methodology of modern warfare makes killing innocents a necessary (accounting-type) cost of the military enterprise.

As I was considering war and the killing of innocents, I came across a traditional touchstone for assessing the morality of a particular war that I found useful, the Catholic "just war" doctrine.[10] The doctrine provides norms and criteria that place a moral framework around war. The just war doctrine applies one set of criteria to determine whether a government's decision to go to war is moral (*ius ad bellum*). Another set of criteria assesses the morality of the conduct of the war (*ius in bello*).

The criteria for the conduct of war consist of "proportionality" and "noncombatant immunity." *Proportionality* in this context means that military violence should be constrained by what is "necessary" to obtain military objectives. Intentionally destroying nonmilitary infrastructure, with the obvious result being that daily civilian life is severely compromised, violates this principle. *Noncombatant immunity* reflects the church's overall respect for life and the position of the New Testament of loving one's enemies. In modern warfare, however, this norm appears to be all but irrelevant.

Beginning with the Vietnam War, however, concerns were also stirred about the rising number of civilian casualties in conventional conflicts. During World War II, civilian casualties amounted to 45 percent of casualties. By the time of Vietnam, they counted for 65 percent of the total. By the 1990s, they constituted more than 90 percent.

Much of the increase in noncombatant, civilian casualties was due to the rise in guerrilla warfare, civil wars, terrorism and counter-terrorism, and ethnic cleansing. A significant portion, however, was also attributable to shifts in the war-fighting styles of developed countries' militaries, especially that of the United States. The growing lethality of conventional weapons, strategies like air dominance and the use of overwhelming and decisive force, as well as the practice of force protection (giving primacy to guarding the safety of one's own troops), contributed to this trend in civilian vulnerability.[11]

When we move our analysis to consider Hiroshima, Nagasaki, and Dresden,[12] can one say anything but that in those three instances the killing of masses of innocents was the precise and intended consequence of the action? Whatever might have been the truth about the enormity of allied casualties that would have resulted from a land invasion of Japan, the point is that our nation made no pretense that it was doing anything other than intentionally killing innocents as a calculated strategy of war. Again, while this surely might be justified by some form of consequentialist morality, it hardly supports an absolute moral claim that it is always wrong to take innocent life and, thus, always wrong to kill yourself.

Self-Defense

When I looked at self-defense, I was on my home turf. I have both practiced and taught in the area of criminal law. In contrast to war, self-defense seems clear. Someone is trying to kill you, and it's you or them. Your life is given priority over your opponent's because, as the aggressor, he or she has forfeited (at least at the moment) the sanctity of his or her life.[13] By trying to take an innocent life, attackers lose their membership in the universe of the innocent (i.e., those whose lives may not be intentionally taken). The problem is that, under modern notions of self-defense, you can kill an innocent person. You're not supposed to, but it can happen, and under the right circumstances, you'll be absolved.

A person has the right to use deadly force if he or she "reasonably believes" that another person is about to inflict life-threatening harm.

Notice that you only have to reasonably believe that you're in such danger. The danger does not have to be real.[14] Imagine you get into a fender bender. The other driver gets out and starts screaming at you, saying things like "I should kill you." He's huge, covered with prison gang tattoos, and walks to the back of his car muttering "You're a dead man . . . you're a dead man." You're terrified. You reach into your glove compartment for your registered firearm just as he goes into his trunk and pivots, pointing what looks like the barrel of a gun at you. In that instant, you react with your gun, and he falls, dropping the road flare he had in his hand.

If that's how it happened, you have killed an innocent person, albeit an extremely unpleasant one. Admittedly, you did not know he was innocent. But you did intentionally kill someone who, in fact, was innocent, and the law will condone that killing. In casual conversation, we may say that it was the deceased's fault, that he was not innocent in his own death. And I would agree in that type of conversation. But here we are talking within the context of an exception to the general rule against intentionally killing where the moral basis for finding the deceased not to be "innocent," and thus subject to intentional killing, was that, by trying to take another life, he sacrificed the sanctity of his. Here the decedent, awful as he was, did no such thing. In this context, he was innocent. Because you acted reasonably, however, your conduct will be considered justified, even though your reasonable perceptions were wrong.

Capital Punishment

This is historically the third exception to the moral rule against intentional killing. To begin with, there are certainly those who do not find this a legitimate exception and hold the death penalty immoral no matter what its subject.[15] I share that view but will take a different tack, one that brings me into my world of law.

To begin with, we know that currently we likely are mistakenly executing some unidentified innocent persons and but for DNA testing and the Innocence Project we would be killing even more.[16] This is unavoidable. In carrying out any program of state-sponsored executions, those innocent of the capital crimes for which they were convicted have been, and will continue to be, killed due to the inevitable vagaries of jury trials.[17] We would like to have a system that would not allow this to happen, but we never will. Eyewitnesses will make mistakes, witnesses will lie, jurors will have their biases, and incredible coincidences will occur. Our society knowingly accepts this "collateral damage," an acceptance that is not consistent with an absolute moral stance in contrast to a consequentialist position.

Assuming we are executing the right person, the justifying moral argument is that the condemned person has sacrificed the right to have his or her life treated as sacred by intentionally taking an innocent life. There are, however, a few problems with this rationale. Initially, throughout history the death penalty has been carried out in cases other than murder. Stealing would earn you the gallows in Merry Olde England. In the United States, at the time the Constitution was drafted in 1787, the death penalty was a common punishment in the various states for a wide variety of personal offenses, including murder, rape, fraud, and theft.[18]

Further, here the state is the one taking the life, not someone avenging a death as part of some blood feud. Of course, that's the point. By entering the picture in the form of law, the state can break the endless cycle of a blood feud in which a family avenges the death of one of its own, the other family responds in kind, and on and on.[19] This is a practical use of power, but is the state's disruption of this cycle of revenge by killing a person morally justified by the concept of noninnocence? The condemned is not now a direct threat to the state or any of its citizens. Whatever the prisoner did, he or she can't do it now. Why, now that he or she is helpless and no longer a threat, is the prisoner not again innocent for purposes of being protected from an intentional killing? If all lives are inviolable, if all lives have equal worth, it is hard to see how one can be said to forfeit this innate quality by any particular act no matter how vile.

At the end of my thinking about war, self-defense, and the death penalty, I saw a society committed to protecting life. But that society was also willing to permit exceptions to the absolute sanctity of life when those exceptions both had consequentialist benefits and could be circumscribed and cabined so that the exceptions did not permit a moral rationale that could be further expanded into other aspects of our lives. What all three exceptions have in common is that they maintain their boundaries, thereby ostensibly not permitting any moral rationale for allowing intentional killing to further intrude into our lives in the broader society, by means of spatial narratives. The boundaries are constructed in our cultural imaginations out of narratives that are confined to very narrow *physical spaces*.[20] War is on the battlefield. Self-defense takes place within the space of a person-to-person encounter (inches, feet, yards at most). The death penalty is carried out in a room in a prison. Again, this is in our imagination. Wars today are not confined to battlefields such as Gettysburg or the Somme. Nonetheless, the story remains.

What does this mean for assisted suicide? On the one hand, it cannot be limited by any spatial narrative because it can be done at any place, any time. On the other hand, when I think of all the circumstances under which we condone the killing of an innocent, the thought of an old, sick person like my father taking his own life seems by far among the least troubling or tragic.

THE ABSOLUTE SANCTITY OF LIFE: ALL LIFE HAS EQUAL WORTH, WHICH MAY NOT BE BALANCED AGAINST THE "QUALITY" OF THAT LIFE

Unlike the broader cultural arena in which the moral bar against killing innocents provides the articulation for the sanctity of life principle, in the medical context, the sanctity of life principle is articulated in terms of not considering "quality" of life in medical decisions. If one starts with the idea that life is sacred, it seems to follow that, while among us mortals there may be better or worse individuals, no one's life is more or less sacred than any other's.[21] Sacredness does not work in increments. This notion is deeply embedded in our culture: "All men are created equal." Sometimes when I would see prisoners brought into court in their orange jumpsuits or pass persons sitting in a doorway with their life's belongings beside them in a trash bag I would be struck by the idea that we were all once children and wonder what had happened to them. Because, in essence, we all are the same.

Obviously, people are born with different social and genetic assets and then make different things of their lives. But all are entitled to be treated according to the same societal standards or principles. They may not have the right to the same treatment, but they have the right to be treated equally under the law. That is the basis for a just society. No matter what your fate in the social lottery, whatever your race or gender, great athlete or physically disabled, genius or mentally challenged, everyone has to stop for you when you're in the crosswalk.

Those who strongly subscribe to this idea of the absolute sanctity of life are concerned about the establishment of a hierarchy (or "lowerarchy") in which certain lives have less value than others. They fear for those most vulnerable in our society[22] (the elderly, severely disabled,[23] poor, or disadvantaged minorities)[24] if we begin to distinguish among lives based on their quality.[25] Floating in front of those committed to this notion of the *absolute* sanctity of life is the specter of the Nazi eugenics program,[26] in which the German government began killing the insane, then the mentally disabled, then the "useless feeders" (the elderly infirm and severely disabled), and eventually six million Jews, as well as Gypsies and others.

The risk of this nightmare is seen as inherent in any ethic that considers the subjective quality of individual lives, even if that type of judgment is, to begin with, only made by the individuals themselves. Under this view, once the line is crossed from the absolute sanctity of life to a morality based on individual contextual judgments, the so-called slippery slope toward the Nazi experience is inevitable. I am not unsympathetic to this view. Most of my father's family died in German death camps during World War II. It's difficult for me to think about the Holocaust without feeling a tide of rage rise in my body. But when I look closely the fact seems to be that we consistently incorporate "quality of life" decisions in medical care.[27]

Pulling the Plug

When to stop treatment, when to give up and say goodbye to the person, is as profound and emotion-laden a choice as it is a common, everyday decision in medical care facilities in America.[28] That's what I did with Mom, although I did not agonize over the decision until much later. Within this image of "pulling the plug" are two separate concepts to which those who try to simultaneously maintain both the legitimacy of the procedure and the sanctity of life resort: letting the disease take its natural course and ordinary versus extraordinary treatment.

Letting the Disease Take Its Natural Course

One common rationale is that when we pull the plug the doctor is not killing the patient, the disease is. We're merely "letting nature take its course."[29] And if the patient is in the dying phase and the machine is interfering with the process, or if the machine alone is moving the patient's heart or lungs, then I agree. But that wasn't my mother's situation, and that's not what we're generally talking about. We are generally dealing with situations in which, due to the machine, the person could go on for half a day or days. His or her life, every moment of which in the view we are now considering has absolute sanctity, is being shortened by pulling the plug. Saying that we're merely stepping aside to let nature (in the guise of the disease) take its course does not change the reality of what we're doing or the implicit importation of quality of life considerations.

Much of the human endeavor is to mitigate and limit the day-to-day impact that the natural/physical/biological world has on our choices. We dam rivers, create irrigation systems in arid land, develop clothing that allows us to survive in the Arctic, and invent scuba-diving equipment so we can spend time under water. Most of medicine is aimed at curtailing nature—antibiotics, immunizations, cataract surgery. For individual disabilities, we've created glasses, wheelchairs, artificial limbs, and heart pacemakers.

In thinking about this "letting the disease take its natural course," I thought about glasses and people who literally cannot see anything without them but blurred, indistinct shapes. Now let's put one such person in an ice age tribe, of course without his or her glasses. Chances are that person would be dead meat—falling into some ravine or blithely walking into a saber-toothed tiger. That's letting nature take its course.

Back to the twenty-first century. If I am hiking with a bespectacled friend, and, as we are traversing a narrow, extremely precarious ledge, I grab his glasses, knowing that this will result in his taking a false step and plummeting to his death, I will be said to have caused the death and likely be facing homicide charges. In the ensuing trial, I don't believe the jury would be terribly moved if my defense was that I didn't kill him but merely returned him to a natural state in which "his disease [visual infirmity] killed him." The point is that by using a heart or other machine doctors can delay the disease that is killing the person. Their accepted choice to turn off the machine and let the disease ultimately hold sway is only comprehensible within a context in which the value, the quality of the moments that could be gained by continuing to use the machine, is not worth it.

Futile, Disproportionate, Ordinary-Extraordinary Treatment

In the world of medicine, it is accepted that doctors are not required to provide "futile" or "disproportionate" treatment.[30] *Futile* means that further medical intervention will not restore the patient's health,[31] though it could provide a few more days of sacred life.[32]

Disproportionate,[33] like the more recently adopted metaphorical dichotomy *ordinary-extraordinary,*[34] also is at bottom contextually circumscribed, its context infused with notions of quality of life. Is fighting pneumonia ordinary or extraordinary? For an otherwise healthy 20 year old, realizing that the likely result of nontreatment for some extremely virulent form of flu would be death, the doctor would be held responsible and playing in the homicide ballpark. But for a very ill, demented, 94-year-old patient who is in constant agony, nontreatment for pneumonia (resulting in the patient's death)[35] will be morally acceptable, as it will be labeled extraordinary.[36] Plainly, this does not reflect the application of an absolute moral principle exalting the sanctity of life but, rather, a balancing of factors in which subjective quality of life judgments weigh heavily.[37]

The same type of analysis applied to not providing Mom with feeding or hydrating through tubes. A finding that the procedure need not be done because it is extraordinary or disproportionate will always be tied to a narrative in which the remaining quality of life of the patient is extremely low. For a young person temporarily in a coma following an accident, a feeding tube may be ordinary; for an 81-year-old person, demented, sick, and in pain, it would be extraordinary.

Giving Pain Medication under Circumstances Such That There Is a High Risk That It Will Kill the Patient

Morphine is a wonderful pain controller. All that stopped my father's agony was morphine pumped directly through a surgically implanted shunt. He had a control button, and within certain time frames and regulated dosages, he could push the button whenever he felt the need. I remember him constantly pushing that button, often counting the minutes until the machine would let him have more. Perhaps as much as once a day, true angels, the nurses from Home Care Hospice, would recalibrate the dosage to increase the level. It never seemed to be enough.

Morphine also lowers the respiration rate, which means that at some dosage it will stop the patient's breathing altogether.[38] That's what seemed to happen to my father. At one point, a few minutes after the hospice nurses raised his dosage to try to control what had by then become weakly muttered agony, he stopped breathing. I am not saying it was that last dose of morphine that finally gave him peace. I think so, but I can't be certain. Nor am I implying that the hospice nurses were silently practicing euthanasia under the guise of pain control. From discussions I had with medical professionals and from what I've read, I know that happens and not infrequently. But I can't say that's what happened in my father's case.

Assuming the nurses were not trying to kill him, one would ethically justify my father's death as a paradigm case of the ethical concept called the "principle of double effect" (PDE).[39] You give a patient morphine to stop their pain, realizing that there is a real risk that in the process the morphine will kill the patient. You aren't trying to kill the patient. You just want to stop the pain. Of course, you could stop the pain by cutting out the middleman and just directly killing the patient. But that's not the principle of double effect (PDE). Intentionally killing someone is not a legitimate action even if the ends are good (i.e., cessation of pain). Thus, it is not a morally good action under PDE regardless of your good motive.[40] Giving pain medication under my father's circumstances, on the other hand, is a morally legitimate action.

Thus, PDE gives moral sanction to well-intended, good actions that turn out to have bad effects. This is a familiar concept in medicine. Without surgery, there's a 95 percent chance you'll die, while the chances of surviving the surgery are fifty-fifty. Under PDE, death as the result of choosing this surgery would not be seen as the product of a moral wrong. It would be seen as an intentionally good act (surgery to save a life) that had a bad result. There would be no moral blame.

The principle values life. You don't try to kill the person. You take an acceptable risk to stop the screaming pain. My father was almost 80, cancer spread throughout his body, wracked with pain. Give him the morphine. Stop the pain. To do otherwise would be inhuman. But in his place put a 20-year-old man. Having fallen from a rock he was climbing, our young man has broken numerous bones, torn ligaments, and may have damaged his kidneys. When the rescue workers find him, he is in excruciating pain. Because of the terrain, they will have to carry him for four hours to get him to a hospital where they know the doctors will be able to bring his pain under control without using morphine. All they have is morphine. To control his pain using morphine, let's imagine that the required dosage carries the same risk of respiratory shutdown as that given to my father. If they administer the morphine and the young man dies (assuming he would have arrived at the hospital alive had they not given him morphine), I think they could yell PDE to the heavens. Nonetheless, their actions would be seen as wrong, perhaps even falling within the family of homicide, as the result of their having taken an unreasonable risk.

The only difference between the case of the 20-year-old, where giving the required dose of morphine would be "evil," and that of my father, where giving the morphine was "good," is the respective quality of the lives the patients had and would have in the future: The young man had before him a long life, health, love, a future; my father faced only more suffering and death.[41]

Refusing Treatment

As I will discuss in some detail when I consider the arguments supporting assisted suicide, patients are said to have the right to refuse lifesaving medical treatment.[42] In fact, my father refused food, hydration, and a proposed surgery that would have allowed him to better digest food. In thinking about this concept, I imagined a patient who wakes after surgery to find that the doctors were forced to amputate both his legs. No one would fault the hospital staff if they stopped him from stabbing himself with a nearby pair of scissors. Yet, if before surgery the patient is told that he will die of gangrene if his legs aren't removed and the patient says, "Then I'd rather die . . . no surgery," his request will be honored. While there may be differences in assessing these two situations from a legal perspective, from one espousing the absolute sanctity of life they seem similar. Both patients are taking actions that they know will end their lives.

Certainly, the person with the gangrenous legs would be more than happy to find out that he is going to live after all, even without the surgery. But so would the person who attempted suicide if he could live life without the results of the surgery. The person refusing treatment is killing himself. I believe we only condone his refusal because of quality of life issues. Let me be clear here. I am not saying a double amputee has nothing to live for or cannot have a far better life than me. That would be beyond nonsense. What I am saying is that losing your legs does raise quality of life issues, that our society cannot judge what that means for any particular individual, and that, accordingly, we will not interfere with the individual's decision to refuse the surgery.

More commonly, the decision to refuse treatment is made when the patient has a serious illness and does not have long to live. Sometimes the cure is worse than the disease,[43] leaving the patient suffering from a surgery that adds little time to his or her life or violently ill, as can be the result of chemotherapy. While the treatment will extend the quantity of life, it will destroy the quality of the short amount of life that remains. Thus, the line between the concepts of "quality of life" and "burden of treatment" blur in such a case. Given that the person will die soon, this seems like a trade-off we should respect. Again, quality of life concerns underlie our acceptance of the patient's decision to refuse lifesaving treatment.

Instead of considering a person facing death, let's go back to our 20-year-old man. Imagine that he has an enzyme deficiency that is fatal if not treated. The treatment is a small pill (made in his favorite flavor), which he takes once a week. As long as he takes the pill, he will be a completely healthy 20 year old. The burden of treatment is low; the quality of ensuing life is high. Does anyone really believe that our society would let him refuse to take the pill and die? We would see this as a preventable attempt at suicide.[44]

Terminal Sedation

More recently, hospitals have been using a procedure called "terminal sedation" for dying patients whose pain cannot be brought under control.[45] The patient is sedated, denied artificial food and hydration, and dies in a few days.[46] Under this procedure, the patient can be revived for short periods of time to visit with loved ones and again sedated when the pain becomes intolerable.[47]

Again, quality of life considerations are implicit in this procedure. For someone like my father, it may have been an option. If we did it to our healthy 20-year-old, it would be murder.[48]

When someone considers pulling the plug, PDE, refusing treatment, or terminal sedation, I don't see how one could conclude anything other than that, in the medical context, our society has moved the line from absolute sanctity of life to considerations about quality of life. That does not say how far the line has moved or should move or how the balance with quality of life factors should be weighed. But it does show that most who take the absolute sanctity of life stance do not hold that line when dealing with end of life care.

ISSUE 2

Western religion does/does not plainly forbid suicide (and a fortiori assisted suicide or euthanasia)

Religious Arguments for Maintaining That Suicide Is Morally "Wrong"

❦

I chose to include the Judeo-Christian tradition and its opposition to suicide in my journey for a number of reasons. I am religious like my father and grandfather. My grandfather, who emigrated from Slovakia in 1906, was a practicing Orthodox Jew. Recently, my sister gave me the hand-embroidered pouch containing his father's yarmulke (skullcap) and tallith (prayer shawl). Touching the pouch, I know that I am touching something holy. There was always God in our house—Hanukkah candles, Passover dinner—but not always temple. When the family suffered a financial reversal during my early teens, it could no longer afford the dues for our temple. Whether from pride or an accurate assessment of the social realities of mid-1950s suburban America, with its preoccupation with gossip and climbing the social ladder, my parents refused to request a "scholarship" for membership dues, instead withdrawing from the temple. But God was still there.

In the last weeks of my father's life, he spent time with a rabbi in a visit arranged by either the hospital or hospice. I do not now recall. I do remember that afterward my father, though a staunch pragmatist, told me he had enjoyed "the chat" and found comfort in knowing that he was "surrounded by a spiritual realm."

I am a Reform Jew who strongly believes in a God as a moral power and consciousness in the universe and believes in the presence and immediacy of God in my everyday life. No doubt a portion of my reluctance to help my father and guilt over my role in ending my mother's life spring from those religious roots.

My choice to deal with the religious perspective on suicide (and a fortiori assisted suicide and euthanasia), however, was motivated by more than my own traditions and experiences. As I began to read, I found that the articles and books could be divided into those that credited religion in their arguments and those that did not (although some of the latter did oppose assisted suicide).

For those supporting assisted suicide, religious views are discounted or even defined from the start as carrying no weight in a "rational" discussion. Even those who support a ban on assisted suicide on nonreligious grounds take pains to emphasize that their arguments against assisted suicide are based on policy or logic and in no way depend on religious faith. America is a "pluralistic" society,[1] a nation of countless beliefs and interests. Thus, if I disagree with you, and you try to support your position by saying, for example, "but God has told us . . . ," I don't even have to consider what you are saying because it is based on the individual, the personal, the subjective—your faith.

But I could not accept that position as I began to delve into the morality of what I had done. Religion has been, and continues to be, a major influence in the life of this nation. And there are significant numbers of religious people. To hold that religious arguments have no currency in the suicide debate means that you have made a decision to exclude a huge number of fellow citizens from the discussion. Anyway, you can't really avoid the religious. It rests somewhere within the moral mix of nearly every discussion on the subject of suicide whether in an academic forum, in a living room, or at a bus stop.[2] Religious views, in fact, provide the single strongest correlation in recent surveys with positions pro and con on suicide and assisted suicide.[3]

So I had to be willing to explore what for me was a fundamental question: does a belief in God make suicide immoral in all forms and circumstances? I had never questioned that it did, but then I had never really thought about it. So I read about Christian history and tradition, carefully considered suicide and the Bible, thought about the Sixth Commandment, and delved into the classic religious arguments against suicide.

CHRISTIAN HISTORY AND TRADITION

While the Christian church has consistently taken the position that suicide is wrong, a careful look at that history does not result in as clear an answer as one would have imagined. In the first place, there is some dispute about the evolution of the ban against suicide in the Christian church. Some scholars claim the ban arose as a result of fanatical Christian groups, exemplified by the Donatists, who aggressively sought martyrdom so that they could immediately enter heaven and not take the risk of staying on earth and committing some sin that would disqualify them from entering into the Kingdom of God. Under this view of history, Saint Augustine stepped in and made suicide a mortal sin, thereby taking away the incentive for Donatist-type strategies and ensuring that the Christian population would not be depleted because Christians were resorting to suicide as a way to gain early entry through the pearly gates.[4] If this theory is correct, the ban on suicide is far more pragmatic than moral in origin.[5]

Other scholars flatly reject this claim. They contend that suicide was condemned in the early church and that the group of martyrdom-seeking fanatics was far too small and geographically remote to pose a threat to the church.[6] Unlike the fanatics who were seeking a shortcut to heaven, most martyrs during the persecutions did not seek death but let themselves be killed by pagans rather than renouncing their faith.[7]

Even those scholars who claim that Christianity was opposed to suicide from the earliest days of the Christian church, however, acknowledge that suicide by Christian virgins and married women who killed themselves rather than face rape by pagan males was accepted by the church. Suicide to avoid arrest and torture after arrest was also apparently accepted during the persecution of early Christians.[8] What do I conclude from this? I conclude that at that time and place that culture defined that violation (rape or torture by a pagan) as a "fate worse than death." Such a history, however, does not make clear to me why within our own cultural constructions we cannot similarly define situations that, from our perspective, are worse than death.[9] Thus, it is unclear to me why suicide to avoid torture by a human enemy is permissible while suicide to avoid torture by a microbe or human cell gone mad is not.

THE HOLY BIBLE AND SUICIDE

When I looked carefully at the Bible in order to determine what it said about suicide, I was quite surprised. The Bible presents a number of suicides, none of which is explicitly condemned.[10] Samson atones for abandoning God while taking vengeance on his enemies. Saul, wounded in battle, tries to kill himself rather than let himself be taken by his enemies.

Failing in his attempts, he allegedly enlists the aid of his armor bearer to complete the deed. Razis, the temple high priest, kills himself rather than let the Greeks demoralize his people, the Jews, by his capture. Zimri kills himself and his whole family when surrounded by his enemies. Ahithophel, an adviser to David and Absalom, kills himself after it is discovered that he committed an act of treason by advising Absalom to take over David's harem. Judas hangs himself, no surprise there.[11]

Now that's a lot of suicides without a single word of protest and this in a text that is not shy about telling the reader what is morally right and wrong. This is the Bible after all. Those propounding an absolute moral ban on suicide, however, seem to have a rationalization or explanation for each self-inflicted death in the Bible. They posit that God inspired or gave permission for each death.[12] But there is not a sentence in the text that bears any evidence of this. They point out that the persons committing suicide were avoiding the degradation and/or horror of capture and torture by the enemy. But what did the Philistines have on an army of cancer cells eating your pancreas or liver one cell at a time? They pronounce that many of the suicides in the Bible were the fate of those who abandoned or rebelled against God, a sign of their total alienation from God. One could contend, however, that this is just another way of saying, using theological metaphors, that a person (such as Judas) was severely depressed, as is true of so many who commit suicide.[13]

Those seeking to find a prohibition against suicide in the narratives of the Bible (in addition to the Sixth Commandment, which I discuss next) also point out that the armor bearer who allegedly carried out Saul's request for death was himself executed by David. Is that a statement against suicide (and assisted suicide)? Perhaps, but I don't think so. This person, without a single witness, comes before David and says, "Trust me. I killed the king, but I was really helping him."[14] That simply is not the type of behavior a monarchy can tolerate and still retain some sense of royal security.

The defenders of the ban on suicide also point out that in the Bible Paul discourages Christ's jailer from killing himself after the Crucifixion.[15] But how does that lead to the conclusion that suicide is immoral? No one believes that suicide is an appropriate response to guilt and depression. Anyone would suggest counseling for the jailer, which is exactly what Paul did.

Finally, not surprisingly, being a prophet is an extraordinarily stressful calling. At one time or another, Elijah, Jonah, Job, Moses, and Tabil all asked God for death. God did not heed any of their requests. But why would He? Their pain was a phase God knew they would move through. Their request for death was a way of telling God what they were experiencing. (Like my grandfather told my grandmother: "You expect me to paint the house after I've worked like a dog all week? Why don't you just bury me now, and we can skip the heart attack?") It is also a roundabout way of both telling God "You're asking too much" and saying that they need strength from God if they are to go on. If these prophets truly wanted to kill themselves, they could have done so without divine assistance.

Plainly, nothing in the Bible speaks to the desirability of suicide. Yet nothing about the suicides reported in that text explicitly indicates that suicide is even a moral issue.

THE SIXTH COMMANDMENT

We are all familiar with the Sixth Commandment: "Thou shall not kill."[16] This powerful biblical proscription has consistently served as a moral basis for condemning suicide. Not killing means not killing, including yourself. But can this properly be inferred from the Sixth Commandment? When I looked again at the Ten Commandments, I saw a unified and what at the time must have been a radical vision of deity and community. For these commandments do far more than lay down a list of rules and concepts that are now so familiar to us in Western society, so incorporated in how we see the world, that it is extremely difficult to see their conceptual unity. These commandments pronounce the vision of a different type of deity and resulting community. This is not a God responsive to discrete material interests such as rain, fertility, hunting. (In fact, the Israelis came in conflict with their God when they later began worshipping these types of household and field deities.) These commandments represent what is basically a moral God who is establishing the preconditions for a moral community.[17] Other than the duties owed Jehovah (holy times, keeping the Sabbath, the primacy of Jehovah, etc.), all the commandments have to do with relational injuries, the type of injuries that would subvert a moral community—stealing, adultery, false witness. Within this context, "Thou shall not kill" most reasonably refers to a similar type of relational injury in the community:[18] murder (i.e., killing others in the tribe) not killing oneself.[19]

Additionally, the Sixth Commandment's prohibition against killing seems to me to have obvious pragmatic roots. The fact that a society holds to the moral principle that my life cannot be unjustly taken gives me *security* in going through my day. I know that life is filled with risks and unknowns, that the door to a parallel, tragic universe is always waiting to open. I recognize that deciding to get out of a grocery line to get another stick of butter will ever so slightly change the timing of my day and that, if the fates are so aligned, that change in timing can literally be a matter of life (get on the freeway moments after a multiple car accident) or death (arrive at the spot just as a truck loses control and crosses the median or as some lunatic sniper decides to fire in my direction). I also have no doubt that out on the streets there are people who would be more than willing to hurt or kill me for my wallet or even for fun. Still, all this risk and danger in everyday modern life is nothing at all like a "lawless," junglelike world in which there are no norms about killing.

But what does this have to do with suicide? It is hard to see how my sense of security is undermined if I face death as result of a decision that is not being carried out by someone from the outside but is all my own.[20] In fact, this is as far away as one can get from a situation in which others control one's existence. It is the self deciding the ultimate fate of the self.

THE CLASSIC RELIGIOUS ARGUMENT
AGAINST SUICIDE

The classic religious argument against suicide is based on the notion that our lives are not ours to take because we were created by God.[21] I hesitate before I plunge into articulating my thoughts regarding this powerful argument, an argument that no doubt resided deep within me when I denied my father and agonized over my decision to keep my mother from food and hydration. I do not want to appear detached and analytic, a professor spinning ideas untouched by real experiences. My problem, however, is that the argument is just that, an analytic argument. The core of the argument itself does not come out of any religious or spiritual relationship with God. My belief in the existence of God is a matter of faith, of unprovable experiences. That God created me is likewise a matter of these same elements.[22] But in this argument I am dealing not with religious faith but with an argument created by a man, an argument that links the faith-based belief that God created man to the conclusion that suicide is immoral. I therefore must probe this analytic connection. Yet, in digging into the logic of this crucial analytic link between faith-based revelation and the human conclusion that suicide is immoral, I also am concerned that I will appear to be disrespectful to God, though nothing could be farther from my intent. My powers of reason are also gifts from God. I need to use those gifts to look at this argument, which has maintained such a hold on Western religious thought.

The argument that "your life is not your own to take" resonates in the Jewish moral condemnation of suicide because "every moment is sacred"[23] and in the arguments of Saint Thomas Aquinas.[24] In fact, there are actually a number of different senses within which this position is understood.

- Life is a gift from God.
- Your life is only on loan.
- You are a steward of your life.
- Only God determines when you die.

Life Is a Gift from God

This seems like a strange basis on which to argue that suicide is immoral. If I'm given a gift, do I have to keep it?[25] It's a gift after all. Admittedly, there are times when the giver's feelings would be hurt if he or she thought I had returned a gift or stashed it away in a closet. I may even drag out some odd-colored bowl or fertility statue from the Fiji Islands when the relatives who gave me the gift make a rare pilgrimage to my area of the country. I don't want to hurt their feelings, to offend. But no one finding me about to recycle such a gift through a garage sale would say I was being immoral. Even if the gift is wondrous and magnificent and people might think I'm foolish to get rid of it, it is hard to imagine that they would find my actions immoral.

As to the giver being hurt or offended, I'm not saying God transcends feelings. My God does feel, hurt, laugh. It's just that if someone rejected what I thought was a wondrous gift I'd be hurt but I'd have to get over it, let it go. God's a lot spiritually bigger than I am; God can deal with having me reject His gift. Also what hurts people's feelings about a gift is not that you returned it, gave it away, or threw it in the giveaway box in the garage. Those are just physical manifestations of your feelings about the gift. The point is that you did not like it. That's what hurts the feelings. But if you don't like a gift from God it makes no difference whether you keep it or throw it away. God knows all your thoughts and feelings.[26] God knows your heart and knows in that heart whether you value God's gift.

Some might say that the gift of life given by God is not like some birthday or housewarming present. Rather, it is like the gift of a child or some extraordinary talent. These gifts come with obligations: use them to God's glory.

I do not accept that line of argumentation. I can choose not to have a child. It may be that the only means to accomplish this is abstinence (if my religion so demands), but I can still choose not to have a child. As for some great talent—musical, intellectual, mathematical, or such—am I really obligated to use it? People certainly talk that way ("You should feel guilty wasting your talent, as it is a rare gift most people would give anything to have"). But I've often wondered if that's fair. You did not ask for the talent, and it's not as though you have the choice of giving it to someone who wants it as opposed to not using it. But even if it comes with obligations, surely as the gift diminishes so must the obligations. Must an 80-year-old man who was once a virtuoso violinist but is now arthritic be forced to play in this diminished state because of the great gift? Whatever potential was inherent in the original gift could no longer be manifested. (One could respond that, unlike the violinist, my father still possessed his gift, albeit in diminished form; he was still alive. I disagree. The great violinist still possesses the gift of music in his mind, which I could not even begin to fathom. It's just that, like my father, his body will no longer let him express it.)

Even a favorite gift at some point may get old, break down, no longer be useful. Surely, at that point, even within the etiquette of gift receiving, let alone fundamental moral law, I can dispose of the gift. For then it is no longer truly the gift; it is not what the giver bestowed. And in finally disposing of the gift I am not being ungrateful. Life is a great gift from the greatest of gift givers. Yet I do not understand why I cannot honestly stand before God and thank God for the miraculous gift of life and the life I've had but still want to end that life when, like my father's, it is old, worn, and broken—and filled with excruciating pain.

It is true that we say that each day is a gift, and it is. I saw my dearest friend fight to delay certain death from cancer, fight by resorting to nightmarish experimental treatments just so he could share more moments with his young daughter and live long enough for her to remember him. Yet saying that each day is a gift is not really so much about what we have been given as it is a figure of speech reflecting that it is a blessing, something to which we are not entitled, on which we have no claim, and which we have not earned. We are just plain lucky to see the sun rise. If we do not feel that way, so be it.

From the gift perspective, no matter how lucky we may feel to have any particular gift (even one as magnificent as life), it is a strange notion of a gift if I am *obligated* to keep and use it. We don't usually think of this as a true gift, using instead figures of speech such as "with strings attached." Not that it's unimaginable to have a true gift that comes with conditions or obligations. I'll pay for your college, but I expect you to work hard in your classes. I'll give you a skateboard, but I expect you to use it safely and always wear a helmet. In such cases, I do take on a moral type of obligation in accepting the gift. I can also refuse the gift and with it the attached obligations. But how do I refuse the gift of life? I cannot choose not to be born. So, ironically, once I enter this mortal plane of life, it seems that the only way I can refuse the gift and its obligations is suicide, which violates the conditions of this gift, which has been given without my acceptance of either the gift or its conditions. Logically, then, there should be an age at which I am considered capable of choosing whether or not to accept the gift (14, 16, 18?), at which, in some societal ritual of passage, young people can kill themselves or accept the gift and its conditions. I don't think any of us would find this "logical" system of teen suicide to be very appealing.

Your Life Is on Loan and Is Not Yours to Do with as You Wish

I can enter my own car in a demolition derby race, though my mental state may be in question. If you loaned me your car to pick up a friend at the airport, and, if, instead, I destroy it by entering it into the same race, calls to police aside, my actions would be unimaginable. You loaned me the car. It's your car, and my rights are limited to using it for the understood purposes and time to which you've agreed and to care for it during that time. Under this form of the religious argument, my life is the same. It is not my life but merely a loan from God, and, as such, it is mine only to maintain not destroy.

This, however, is a very strange sense of a loan. The normal idea of a loan is that lenders get the item back so that they can use it again as they see fit (including loaning it again). But thinking of our lives as a loan is akin to "loaning" someone a Popsicle for an hour on a hot, tropical beach. You aren't going to get it back; hence, it doesn't really fulfill the normal model of a loan. When we die, we destroy the body. We bury it in the ground to rot or cremate it. God never gets that back, although the elements composing the body are returned to the earth and sky where they can support new (plant, animal, human) life.

On the other hand, it may be some spirit, some unique human life force, that is the subject of God's loan. This is what God breathed into Adam and apparently did not breathe into the beasts of the fields, birds of the air, or fish of the sea. It is a sacred breath that is something more than the life of the ox, the mere existence of the waterfowl. If it is this life force and not the material body that is on loan, death seems to present two possibilities: (1) death destroys this life force; and (2) the life force survives death. If it's the first possibility, God never gets the spirit back, so it is not really like a loan. If it's the second possibility (which I believe), the life force is never destroyed and the loan is returned. While the notion of a mind-body dichotomy may be discredited by modern philosophers,[27] that does not refute the possibility of a mind-body versus life force (spirit) dichotomy. I believe that at death the spirit survives and it is our temporal identity that is lost.

Also, if it is really a loan, we have no right to risk damage to the item loaned. Recall the borrowed car, which was entered into a demolition derby. That means we couldn't risk our lives, even as heroes or saints. After all, it's not yours; it's on loan. No one in our society, however, would believe that the hero or saint acted immorally. (Of course, one could argue that the purpose of God's loan anticipated its use for heroism and sainthood.)

You Are a Steward of Your Life

God gave you life, and it is not so much that it is a loan as that it is entrusted to your care for safekeeping. You are the steward of that life,[28] with the responsibility to care for it and help it flourish. Here mere life is not what's important; it's the perfection of the self according to God's plan, as part of a life "mission." But what if you are dying, exhausted, continually fighting pain, and no longer have the wherewithal to carry out any perfection, any mission except to exist in a state of perpetual existential misery?

Also, as was the case with the loan and gift metaphors, this is a strange sense of stewardship. You are not maintaining something for future generations, like a beautiful park or an Earth that is unpolluted. No future generations can enjoy you (as opposed to your legacy and stories). You will be dead. If, however, you insist on adhering to this notion of stewardship, you must take seriously your own care. Like a park that must be tended, watered, and so on, you must maintain yourself. That means exercise, eat the right food, lower your stress level, avoid too much alcohol, don't smoke, and don't engage in high-risk recreation. The fact that most in any particular congregation espousing the stewardship argument likely do not follow its implications does not mean the principle is wrong. It does make one at least wonder, however, why, when having great abs, tight buns, and such seems so important in this culture, the motivation to attain these magazine-perfect bodies is never portrayed in terms of our obligation to God.

Also, if you are the steward of a park that has been destroyed by an earthquake, what further responsibilities of stewardship remain? The situation would not seem different if the life over which you are a steward has broken down, leaving you wracked in cancer-caused agony.

Only God Determines When You Die

God is sovereign over life and death. It is God who decides when you die,[29] and it is the height of human arrogance to try to make this decision for yourself. In doing so, you are literally playing God. On the other hand, if someone dies in an avalanche or from a heart attack has God made the decision that the person is to die? If you characterize these as "neutral" forces resulting in death (i.e., a nonmoral actor), then you seem to be saying that death from such causes is not God's decision. Or, if God makes any decision, it is not to intervene. Since God has no "duty" to keep us alive forever, God cannot be said to be responsible for our death from such neutral causes. God has merely chosen not to intervene as opposed to having chosen them as an instrument to kill us. But, if we can die in such a random way, then it cannot be said that God is the one who invariably makes the decision when our time is up. If, on the other hand, the avalanche or heart attack were God's chosen method for tolling our lives, it is hard to understand why God cannot use us as agents of our own deaths, ending our lives by means of suicide.

One could answer that the difference between the avalanche and suicide is the matter of man's free will. Suicide, unlike the avalanche (putting aside such nuances as the fact that the man freely chose to climb a particular mountain when the risk of an avalanche was great), was a product of free will and thus the man's choice as to the moment of his death. But that assumes that having given man free will God is incapable of or unwilling to influence those choices. Such powerlessness is inconsistent with an all-powerful being. It is also inconsistent with the record. I would say that the Flood and the destruction of Sodom and Gomorrah are two indications that God can and will try to influence the course of human choices. Repeatedly "hardening Pharaoh's heart" against letting the Jews leave Egypt so that God could demonstrate to all the world the awesome power that would support those who worshipped Him is another. So are the carnage God orders after the incident of the Golden Calf, the protection of Cain from retribution, and many other stories of God interfering in the choices of man. Also, no matter what choice a man might make as to ending his life, that choice is not final until God says it is. God can always bring the person back to life.

Looked at from a slightly different perspective, are lifesaving medicine (transplants, antibiotics, etc.), immunizations, knowledge of hygiene, and such immoral because they alter the time when a person would otherwise have died,[30] thus, intruding on God's sovereignty over the time of death? Or, as the philosopher David Hume wondered, is it immoral to leap away from a falling rock that would otherwise have killed us because by doing so we've interfered with our imminent death?[31]

One response could be that, whether developing antibiotics or avoiding a falling rock, man is aligned with cherishing God's gift of life and using the "nature" with which God endowed him to mitigate the otherwise natural world of wild animals, disease, and so on.

On the other hand, while modern medicine and ducking rocks admittedly lengthen, not shorten, life, they nevertheless alter the moment of death. As such, they intrude on the notion of absolute sovereignty over the time of death. To contend that God gave man the power to lengthen, but not shorten, the term of life cannot be logically derived from the initial stance positing God's sovereignty over death. If God gave man powers that allow him to influence death's timing, why alone among all man's techniques for influencing that timing is his conceptualization of suicide not a legitimate tool for negotiating with death?

In the end, it may be better to think of God's sovereignty as concerned with the fact that man will die as opposed to when each person's time will come. It was God, after all, who, when banishing Adam and Eve from the Garden, placed the fiery sword around the tree of life so that man, unlike angels, cherubim, and seraphim, would not be immortal.[32]

Finally, as far as I know, no one has ever said it is immoral for the suffering to pray to God for release, to beg God to let them die.[33] After all, that totally respects God's sovereignty over the moment of death. If I may make such a communication, surely God can say yes. God could, of course, just stop my heart, but God could also let me do it myself (by means of suicide). I know I have spoken to God. I can feel God's presence. I can feel God's answers to my questions. I don't get a cosmic e-mail or hear a voice in the flame of my gas barbecue. I just know. So if someone who is dying, near the end of life, existing in misery, claims that he or she spoke to God and got the go-ahead to end his or her life, who is to say it isn't true? If someone responds to this notion by arguing that this could not have happened because the person could not have really talked to God, that God doesn't tell people they can kill themselves, that this is not how God works, I'd just shake my head at such arrogance. For, in effect, that person has said, "God may work in mysterious ways, but I have a copy of God's manual, and that's not one of them."

ISSUE 3

Assuming a particular suicide or assisted suicide might be justified, condoning such a suicide or assisted suicide would/would not result in overall harm to the society

Utilitarian Arguments against Suicide

Leaving the world of moral arguments that gave no consideration to circumstances or consequences (called deontological philosophies), such as those provided by religion and cultural philosophies, I next immersed myself in moral claims against suicide specifically based on particular circumstances and consequences (called consequentialist philosophies). Suddenly, I was rummaging through my son's college philosophy books to grapple with utilitarianism.[1]

Not surprisingly, the philosophy of utilitarianism is complex and nuanced, with a number of different "schools" and literature filled with complex responses to complex criticisms.[2] That was all quite challenging and interesting, but when I finished I realized that the ideas and arguments I had acquired were far more than I needed for my purposes. It was a bit like learning calculus to decide how to divide a whole pie evenly among six people.

In fact, for my purposes, one needs only the very basics. For the utilitarian, any meaningful ethical system must yield specific answers. In other words, we must be able to use it in our daily lives.[3] As such, utilitarianism requires that: (1) of every action, one must ask if it is right or wrong; and (2) the answer to this question will always be attained by balancing consequences,[4] which in classic utilitarianism gives the nod to that which does the most good or provides the "greatest happiness."[5]

Roughly speaking, utilitarians then take one of two paths. The first considers the individual, concrete action. This is called *act utilitarianism,* under which one must perform the action that results in the most good. But there are apparent problems if act utilitarianism provides my sole moral guide.

Say I break into the home of a rich person and steal some money he was going to use to put a flat screen television into his third guest bathroom. I use the money to buy food for starving street people. Under act utilitarianism, this would seem to be a moral act when you balance and assess the overall goodness of the consequences. As you can imagine, this type of scenario presents a real problem for act utilitarianism. As a society, we do not believe stealing is a good thing. Is utilitarianism telling us that we must find this theft to be moral? Do we next have to condone the murder of a man who is physically and sexually abusing his children? If so, one might be less inclined to embrace the philosophy.

It is to address such quandaries that a second notion of utilitarianism, *rule utilitarianism,* arose.[6] While this particular act of theft may have good consequences, from our human experience we realize that the aggregate consequences of this type of act (stealing) will have bad consequences for the society if condoned. Thus, this single, perhaps sympathetic theft is wrong. The rule "Do not steal" trumps the individual case, and rule utilitarianism saves the day (although a formal philosopher might question whether a theory based on such projected aggregate consequences is more deontological than consequentialist and thus not truly a form of utilitarianism).[7]

I cannot imagine rule utilitarianism supporting suicide ("Kill yourself if the fancy strikes"); rather, rule utilitarianism would set limits, create a prohibition ("It is wrong to take your own life"). Even if a single act of suicide may achieve good results, the logic of rule utilitarianism is that if the act is one that constitutes part of what is a general practice[8] (and, given 30,000 successful suicides a year,[9] in addition to all the attempted suicides,[10] suicide would seem to qualify as a general practice), and if, at some numerical point, that practice will cross a threshold and cause harm,[11] then the act should be prohibited. So I tried to imagine all the foreseeable bad consequences that could follow from allowing the general practice of suicide. While I found all to merit some concern, they could not convince me that people like my father are committing an immoral act if they engage in suicide or assisted suicide.

COMMITTING SUICIDE WILL INFLUENCE
OTHERS TO COMMIT SUICIDE

This view claims that if there are enough suicides that suicide becomes a norm for opting out of the difficulties that invariably accompany a life, people will take this path who would not otherwise.[12] Some studies have indicated, however, that suicide does not engender such copycat responses. It is not contagious. On the other hand, studies at their best are just that, studies—random compiling, statistical assumptions, and such. And one surely can imagine someone teetering on the edge for whom hearing about another's suicide might give the last bit of validation needed to tip them over. Also we've seen that once the media show a phenomenon—such as shootings by students at schools—the concept emerges as a possibility when previously it did not even pass through the psyche. One can thus imagine, for example, a chain reaction among that emotionally volatile population we call teenagers triggered by peer suicides.

All that said, there initially is the question of how the copycat phenomenon is affected if the behavioral "image" provided is or is not labeled as immoral, as opposed to tragic, harmful, ill-advised, stupid, or the result of bad judgment. The extreme behavior to which we append the label copycat seems to be conduct in which the perpetrator intentionally stands outside the basic moral precepts of the community and flaunts his or her defiance. The moral label not only fails to deter the perpetrator; it appears to provide the incentive to act.

My focus here is not on teenagers, confused 30-somethings, or even hopeless middle-agers. My concern is with terribly ill, elderly people like my father. The image of a terminally ill, 80-year-old man ending his life presents a narrative that is totally unrelated, totally unconnected to the world of the heartbroken teen or emotionally suffering 35 year old.[13] It is not imaginable that one could affect the other. (In fact, advocates supporting legalization of voluntary termination of life as a tool for physicians dealing with end of life care take the position that this type of medical intervention does not constitute what is meant by the concept of assisting a "suicide" as that term is used in criminal statutes that prohibit helping another to end his or her life.)

From the perspective of risk and consequences, we must balance these for both our young and elderly sick populations. It seems difficult to contend that the number of young people who would kill themselves, if you do not have a *moral rule* absolutely barring suicide in addition to our society's clear and strong discouragement of suicide as an appropriate problem-solving device, would be significantly greater than the number of elderly sick people who would be deterred from ending their suffering if there were such an absolute moral rule.

SUICIDE HAS GREAT SOCIAL COSTS

Suicide can carry with it a range of costs, economic and otherwise. The person committing suicide might have had a number of economic responsibilities, which must now be assumed in some form by others. If the person has young children for whom he or she is solely responsible, the burden might fall on relatives, who may be more or less financially able to shoulder the responsibility. If no such relatives (or even very close friends) are available, the state will have to take on the responsibility for and expenses of relocating and raising the children. There will also be traumatic, emotional effects on the children (even if this were not the sole parent), which will play out in both the short and long term. And suicide generally leaves painful, unresolved, angry, and guilty feelings in those close to the people who are left behind.[14]

Suicide is a sad, awful, tragic event. But again, when considering the justification for an absolute moral prohibition under the philosophy of rule utilitarianism, we face the same dichotomy between our two disparate populations. For the young person who feels hopelessly lost, the middle-aged person suffocating under a blanket of black depression, and such, suicide may well carry serious attendant social costs in dollars, physical and emotional disruption, fragmentation of the remaining family structure, and confusion and pain caused to friends.

But the suicide of the elderly, suffering, terminally ill, like my father, does not bring with it these costs. These people are no longer caretakers, leaving behind their charges for others to watch over. They are the subjects of caretaking. Family members surely will be sad, but they will understand. The sadness is a result of the awful situation the loved one has been placed in, not the means he or she has chosen to end it. No one will think, "If only I'd called more often. . . . I should have seen the signs." Those left behind are neither responsible for nor betrayed and abandoned by the person's decision to end the suffering.

PEOPLE CONTEMPLATING SUICIDE ARE
DEPRESSED AND COULD BE HELPED

The idea here is that, if suicide is not morally condemned, people who otherwise could be helped by treatment will too easily opt for suicide rather than seeking the beneficial treatment they need to get well.[15] A moral prohibiting rule, on the other hand, will make them think twice and, in this hesitation, perhaps shift their focus to medical or psychological treatment. In favor of this position is the documented fact that a substantial percentage of people who seriously contemplate suicide are clinically depressed or suffer from some other form of mental illness.

In the first place, I have little faith that such a moral rule would provide a meaningful counterweight to a killing depression. Again, it's not like any of us were raised to think that suicide is a good idea. If this accumulated social wisdom does not take hold, how much more would the articulation of a utilitarian moral rule add? This is particularly so since those committing suicide no longer live by the same logic as you and me.[16] They, in fact, reject the logic of life that we live by, responding to an entirely different world conception.

Further, let's assume it's true that, absent this moral rule, some who would have sought treatment with the rule, and who would have been "cured," will now kill themselves. How does that counterbalance the elderly sick, who with the rule will feel compelled to suffer until the drawn-out end? The common answer is that people suffering from a terminal illness, like my father, are also depressed and with access to proper mental health treatment will no longer wish to kill themselves. After all, suffering is far more than pain. It is an emotional, psychological, spiritual, and existential mix. Also pain is not purely physical. It is inextricably bound to the psyche. So there certainly is some plausibility to this position. It is just not the trump card in the assisted suicide debate its proponents claim.

Research has shown that mental health treatment has no effect on the suicidal wishes of those with mild to moderate depression.[17] To the extent it provides some benefits to those with major depression, it is not so much that it addresses the depression per se as that it helps alleviate a sense of *hopelessness*. It is not depression but hopelessness, the feeling that there is no end to the suffering, that is most strongly associated with suicidal ideation in very sick patients.[18] In fact, in some studies it was found that, far from wishing to terminate their lives, depressed patients wanted more care than similarly ill nondepressed patients. (If the suffering is principally from the pain of clinical depression, however, the distinction between hopelessness and depression becomes less clear, as one of the features of this magnitude of depression is the sense that the crippling psychic pain will never end.)

Significantly, studies of patients with bad prognoses (e.g., terminal cancer) who had seriously expressed the wish to end their lives, through either assisted suicide or refusal of lifesaving treatment, indicate that these patients were no more likely to be depressed than not.[19]

Also it is not clear what kind of treatment the proponents of this view have in mind for people like my father. My dad died less than two and a half weeks after he asked us to kill him, and I have no basis on which to judge whether this time frame among the dying seeking release was idiosyncratic with my father. Was he to be dragged from his bed to counseling or forced to find a therapist who makes house calls? Or was he to be prescribed some form of antidepressant, even the newest of which take 10 to 12 days to have any real effect? Moreover, such drugs have significant side effects, which would have included interactions with the legion of other powerful drugs coursing through his body.

My father, of course, is only one case. There are likely other terminal patients who seek death at a far earlier stage of diagnosis and degeneration. Those patients, in turn, may be responding to controllable depression as much as any impetus from the consequences of the disease. For them, the availability of therapy is no doubt a good idea. But the fact that there are some such cases does not carry the day for an *absolute* utilitarian rule barring suicide.

THERE COULD BE A MISDIAGNOSIS

This certainly happens.[20] A close relative of mine who was first diagnosed as having surgically treatable prostate cancer was then told that further tests established that the cancer had metastasized throughout his body. Translation: he was a dead man. A subsequent test showed that the diagnosis of metastasized cancer was incorrect ("sorry"). Surgery followed, and he remains cancer free. Yes, misdiagnosis happens. I would have no problem with a rule that stipulated, "Never kill yourself within—— weeks of any medical diagnosis." But, if one is contending that the mass of people diagnosed with a terminal illness, and who are already suffering its pathology, have somehow been misdiagnosed, I'd say that's utter nonsense.

THERE COULD BE A CURE ON THE HORIZON

This book is not about people in a persistent vegetative state (PVS) since I am dealing with conscious individuals making conscious choices.[21] Nonetheless, it is worth noting that one of the implications of this argument is that no one should ever be taken off life support (i.e., pulling the plug), and, if one fully follows this implication, everyone should be cryogenically frozen prior to the moment of death to await future cure.

Moving back to reality and people like my father, this argument, while invoking our need for hope in life, seems totally unrealistic. Cures don't suddenly happen. There are years of clinical trials, protocols, and cohorts. Particularly with computer information systems, competent oncologists (and likely their patients) are aware of available and experimental treatments. Even if an experimental treatment suddenly emerged, it is extraordinarily unlikely that an elderly ill person would qualify for experimental trials. A friend of mine underwent experimental cancer treatment, early stem cell research. He was in his late thirties. He almost died during the experiment; my father never would have made it through.

As for a treatment that moves from experimental to generally available, what we're talking about is timing. The proponents of this stance imagine a scenario in which the day after you kill yourself the Food and Drug Administration (FDA) announces that a cure is available to the general patient population (or, more likely, that insurance companies will cover the treatment). But, again, it seems implausible within the modern world of medical information that this announcement would come as a bolt out of the blue. Even if we assume such a deeply improbable scenario, the treatment will not magically become instantaneously available to all who want it.[22] There will be limited supplies of the drugs and limited facilities in which to carry out the new treatment. People like my father (79 years old and already very ill) would be placed near the bottom of the list. Finally, like others in the last stages of a terminal illness, his disease was so far progressed that realistically it would have been too late for any treatment which suddenly became available to save him.

THERE COULD BE A "MIRACLE"

If, by a miracle, you mean that, after years of unconsciousness, people have come out of comas feeling fine,[23] or that our bodies are miracles and can sometimes fool science and heal themselves, I completely agree. So we're back to balancing alternative rules and consequences between the elderly terminally ill and others in the population who are physically and/or psychologically suffering. In one pan of the scale are people like my father, who an absolute moral rule would tell to continue to suffer in their dying even though they are beyond any hope of getting better. In the other pan are those individuals who, if there were not an absolute moral rule, would kill themselves when, had they just persevered, they would have "miraculously" recovered. I certainly do not have the information, knowledge, and wisdom to maintain this balance, and I sincerely doubt that anyone else does, or even would, given that I cannot see how the admittedly realistic possibility of miracle recoveries could lead to an absolute prohibition (i.e., no exceptions or excusing conditions) of suicide.

If, on the other hand, you mean a true biblical-type miracle,[24] parting the Red Sea, loaves and fishes, walking on water, and such (though this is unlikely grist for a utilitarian argument), then we should never bury or cremate anyone because God can later choose to make a miracle and raise the dead. Come to think of it, it doesn't matter whether you bury or cremate someone or even whether he or she chooses to leap from a bridge. If you are relying on miracles wrought by a deity, God can do whatever God wants, including bringing someone back to life. After all, if you're going to rely on miracles, why distinguish between whether God acts to renew the life of a person just as it's about to expire or just afterward.

THIRD-PARTY ASSISTANCE IN SUICIDE AS SEEN THROUGH THE LENS OF RULE UTILITARIANISM

I recognize that up until now I've lumped together suicide, assisted suicide, and euthanasia. And for what I've discussed to this point I do not think that matters. But I also recognize that, even if suicide is not immoral, that does not mean it is moral for a third person to help someone kill himself. The reality is that this book was not written because some abstract "third party" faced the question of the morality of helping another kill himself. It is about me; it is about my sister. My father begged, and we refused him. Yet I have no way to pursue my inquiry other than to turn back to what initially seems so cold, so academic: moral philosophy. Based in real world consequences, however, rule utilitarianism analysis quickly places flesh on its abstract philosophical bones. The rule utilitarianism argument is analogous to the one I just discussed in relationship to suicide; even if a particular assisted suicide is justified, taken as a general practice, the results are so harmful that the practice should be morally banned. Once again, I have tried to imagine all the bad consequences that could follow. Once again, while I take those consequences seriously, singly or collectively they cannot convince me that assisting someone like my father to kill himself is always immoral. In this analysis, I am not considering the assistance of doctors, leaving that for the following chapter.

Increases in the Ease of Suicide and Thereby Its Likelihood

Even if we permit suicide, that does not mean we want to encourage it. Would we want everyone to carry a lethal "poison button" on their wrists? To the extent we allow assistance, or euthanasia, we make suicide easier in several ways. First, assistance helps facilitate the act. When my father first asked us to help him die, he wanted us to put him in the car in the garage, turn on the ignition, and let the carbon monoxide do the rest. In his condition, he might not have been able to even get to the car by himself let alone locate the keys, a hose, something to cut the hose with, and duct tape and then rig this together. Without some help, most very sick people could not kill themselves (unless they use a gun, which means having a gun and not being uncomfortable with leaving a mess). Second, even if they could do it themselves, many people would not do so for fear of botching it and ending up worse off than before. The assistance of another may tend to diminish this concern. Third, the assistance provides emotional support (you are not dying alone) and social acceptance (at least one person seems to approve of what you are doing).

While in most of life's endeavors assistance makes the task easier, and thus accessible to more people, approving assistance is not likely to lead to an explosion of suicides throughout the population. We're only talking about those persons who are incapable of committing suicide without assistance. And by "incapable" I mean physically, not emotionally, incapable. If we expanded assistance to the latter group of individuals, then we would expand the reach of assisted suicide to all segments of our population, which is something most of us do not wish to do.

Also we must balance alternative consequences. If we permit assistance, some people will kill themselves who would not otherwise do so. If we do not, some will not kill themselves who would otherwise do so. So the question revolves around the utilitarian balance between two unknowables. If assisted suicide were seen as moral, would more people kill themselves, who would have been better off not having done so, on the one hand, than people who would not kill themselves (because assistance, being seen as immoral, was not forthcoming), who would then be forced to suffer, on the other?[25] My intuition tells me that there would be far more of the latter, but that is only intuition. Others might see the balance tipping in a different direction. Neither side can claim a firm moral basis for or against assisted suicide based on this single argument.

It Will Increase the Chance for Disguised Murder

The greedy relative, the rich elderly aunt who simply won't die—we've all seen the movie. To the extent you permit third parties to be legitimately involved with poisoning others, you certainly provide another way in which someone can try to get away with murder, this time under the guise of assisting a suicide. I have no question that there is a genuine risk, although the pool of potential victims is limited to those physically incapable of carrying out the act themselves. It is also a risk that seems greater with euthanasia than assisted suicide because the latter requires that the deceased take the lethal dose themselves. On the other hand, if someone committed murder he or she would lie about it. In other words, the killer could sneak the poison into some otherwise flavored drink (which is a basic method in the world of poisoning) and later lie, saying the deceased knowingly took the poison.

On the other hand, committing murder carries its own, substantial risks. Again, balancing the risk that moral approval of assisted suicide could facilitate homicide against the risk that moral disapproval could lead to needless suffering, I come to the conclusion that, while our society should generally disapprove of assisting suicide, excusing conditions that morally overcome that presumption, such as when the person being helped is suffering and dying, like my father, must be allowed. In other words, there should be no absolute moral bar.

People Will Be Coerced into Committing Suicide

This is a recurrent and real concern,[26] which appears anywhere there is a discussion of assisted suicide. Very sick people are extremely vulnerable.[27]

They are exhausted from fighting the disease and pain and often depressed by what is happening to them. In this state, they are often ambivalent about suicide,[28] changing their minds back and forth in relatively short periods of time.[29] America has such a strong culture of independence and self-reliance[30] that dependence becomes a source of shame.[31] And very sick people are extremely dependent; yet, ironically, this culture of self-reliance leads them to distance themselves from others at the very time they most need others.[32] I know it bothered my father, though he never said so. They are also extremely sensitive about being a financial and emotional burden on their loved ones. Under these circumstances, they are susceptible to pressure from those close to them conveying the message that it is time for them to die,[33] especially since they might already feel they have a "duty" to die.[34]

There is a wide range of motives for someone close to a sick person to consciously or unconsciously apply such pressure. It could be the best of reasons. Family members might think sick persons are only holding on and suffering because they, in turn, think the family would be upset if they seemed to give up or even expressed an interest in suicide. In this psychological form of rock, paper, scissors, a family member may merely be trying to give the suffering person the freedom to choose to end it all. It could also be the worst of reasons. Family members might not want to see their inheritance diminished by further health care costs or they might find the obligation of visiting and caring for the person too great an intrusion into their busy schedules. Most likely the motivations are a far more complicated mix of factors, including the pain of watching a loved one suffer, the exhaustion from being involved in caretaking, and such.

Even with the constant help of hospice, it was a 24-hour-a-day task caring for my father in the last weeks of his life. We got so tired, and it was so hard to watch him suffer, we just wanted it to end. We were good people, but we just wanted it to end, truthfully, as much for us as him. At the same time, I wanted him to live on and on. He was confused and slept most of the time at the very end. But he was still there. I could touch him, talk to him, listen to his breathing. I still had a father. It's not simple, not black and white, not even gray. It's something else that is its own world. Within that world, who can say what one's "real motives" are?

At this point, one might point out that the risk of coercion is equally great when decisions are made to refuse treatment (although many of these are not made by the patient, who often is unconscious, but by the family and/or physician). That, however, is not an answer to this concern. That we risk coercion in the realm of refusing treatment does not mean we must also risk it here. The fact that we allow the opportunity for behavior that has the risk of negative consequences (e.g., by letting people drink, knowing some will drink too much alcohol), does not mean we are committed to accepting that risk in areas where there could be even greater harm (e.g., by legalizing dangerous drugs). Withdrawing treatment takes place in an extremely circumscribed environment (in a hospital surrounded by life-support technology). In contrast, assisted suicide can take place anytime, anywhere.[35] So, again, the fact that we risk coercion in withdrawing life-saving treatment does not mean we can dismiss that concern when it is raised in the broader context of assisted suicide.

All that said, the question remains whether this very real risk justifies an absolute rule that assisted suicide is morally wrong. Like the proverbial broken record, we come back to our competing alternative consequences. Here the balance of consequences is between people who don't really wish to die but are coerced into suicide versus those who must suffer because, although they wish to die, they cannot get assistance because it is labeled immoral (and they hesitate to engage in or ask another to engage in an immoral act). Again this is simply not enough to justify an absolute prohibition. I have no way to guess what the numbers in these groups would be. Even if I knew the numbers, I have no criteria with which to compare them: how much difference has moral significance? For I have no criteria to tell me whether it is worse to have, for example, a month unnecessarily taken from my life or worse to be forced to suffer unnecessarily for an additional month.

ISSUE 4

*Permitting Physician-Assisted Suicide
would/would not result in a "slippery slope"
ending in involuntary termination of our
most vulnerable and powerless citizens*

The Slippery Slope Phenomenon

ENTER THE PHYSICIAN ACCOMPANIED BY THE
ARGUMENT THAT PHYSICIAN-ASSISTED SUICIDE
CANNOT BE CONFINED TO THE WILLING AND
COMPETENT BECAUSE OF THE "SLIPPERY SLOPE"
PHENOMENON

We never broached Dad's request for assisted suicide with his oncologist or any of the other physicians involved, although I would later give a great deal of thought to employment of the medical profession as facilitators of assisted suicide. While a deep exploration of the morality of suicide and assisted suicide without the addition of physicians was necessary before coming to this discussion, the fact is that when people discuss the issue of assisted suicide they generally are talking about the morality of physician-assisted suicide (PAS). There are a number of reasons for this. The current debate, as it focuses on assistance, almost by definition deals with those too ill or disabled to kill themselves. Those are people who fall within the province of medicine. Probably many of these very ill people could blow out their own brains with a gun, which could easily be obtained for them if they didn't have their own, but this presents a picture that likely strikes most as brutal and unfair. They are ill and suffering. Nothing could be more discordant with the narratives of finding peace, of the good death, than the violent explosion of a weapon, leaving blood and brain matter on the walls for their loved ones to find. In fact, a powerful rhetorical strategy employed by those who favor assisted suicide is to tell grisly tales of the terminally ill who are forced to end their suffering by violent means.[1] Assisted suicide needs to be clean, calm, and tidy, that is, medical.[2] Perhaps, as opponents of assisted suicide might claim, this keeps people from facing up to what they are really doing. I think, rather, that they know what they are doing. This is just an acceptable form. What they focus on is someone who has a license to obtain the type of drugs that can cause a peaceful death, who knows how to properly administer the drugs, and who can move easily in both the institutions where most people die (hospitals and nursing homes) and their private homes. That person, of course, is a doctor. And with doctors and the medical profession there comes the argument of the "slippery slope."

In this argument, something awful awaits us if we slide all the way to the bottom of the slope. The essence of the argument is that once you embark down the slippery slope you will not be able to stop until you reach the dreaded bottom.[3] In the realm of assisted suicide, involuntary killing of the most vulnerable in society (the elderly, sick, disabled, or disadvantaged minorities) lies at the bottom of the slope,[4] from which no set of guidelines or rules can prevent the inevitable fall.[5]

Philosophically, the slippery slope argument provides a method of supporting and justifying an absolute utilitarian rule. It differs, however, in the normal method of support for such a rule. Rule utilitarianism is generally based on the notion that at a certain numerical threshold an act that is part of a general practice (such as walking across a public lawn) will do harm. In contrast, the slippery slope argument is not concerned with numerical thresholds as such but with the idea that the initial practice will inevitably lead to a different and far more morally abhorrent practice.[6] As such, I find the analysis as much or more akin to the type of social policy analysis one associates with law than with moral philosophy.[7] Although I am aware that this distinction between "social policy" and "morality" can be deconstructed, I believe the general contexts in which the two are applied in our common experience are sufficiently distinct so as to be useful for this portion of the analysis. (Perhaps the policy argument differs from the moral one we are considering here in that the former can be a nuanced position of comparative risk while the latter requires a much greater sense of certainty.) Regardless of how one classifies the slippery slope argument, however, it is a pivotal one in the debate over assisted suicide.

Central to any consideration of this form of argument is the issue of burdens of proof. Who has the burden here and what is the nature of that burden? Must those proposing physician assisted suicide (or voluntary euthanasia) prove to some standard of certainty that this doomsday result will *not* happen or does the duty of proof rest with the opposition? On either side, how does one prove this?

In order to sift through this crucial notion of burdens, I found that the following hypothetical helped to shape and clarify my thoughts. You are on a hike with a companion when your friend comes upon a patch of mushrooms. He starts to pick some, saying that they will taste great with the sandwich he brought for lunch. When you say that you think they may be deadly, he asks if you are sure. When you answer no, he responds, "If you can't prove to me they're poisonous, I'll eat them." I think most of us would find that the friend's attitude crosses the threshold of idiocy. If instead you had the same dialogue about a package of mushrooms from a grocery store, or even an apple plucked from an apple tree (assuming you wash off the pesticides), the friend's decision to eat the mushrooms or the apple would seem reasonable. In fact, your opposition would seem extremely odd. It is true that literally every food on the planet will cause a life-threatening allergic response in some small percentage of the population, but unless someone provides us with specific information that convinces us otherwise, we happily gorge on our food. So why is the mushroom example different and what does it tell us about burdens?

It tells us that there is no single burden of proof, such as the prosecution's burden in a criminal case, but a sequence of shifting burdens. First, the party objecting to the practice must show that there is such risk and that it is of a sufficient magnitude to be of concern. Magnitude, in turn, will be a function of two interacting concepts, frequency and seriousness. Eight out of 10 should get our attention if that's the established frequency of a particular risk. If we engage in the conduct, we know the chances are pretty good that the risk will come to fruition. One out of a 100 seems like a fairly low frequency. But if the one out of a 100 risk is that we'll accidentally set off a nuclear explosion then the risk grows in magnitude. This is what the mushroom scenario is all about. We know that many mushrooms are poisonous. If the friend guesses wrong, he may die. That's serious magnitude. In light of this, his claim that I must prove to him that this mushroom is unsafe appears deeply stupid.

Having established a real risk of significant magnitude, the burden now shifts to the person proposing the practice to bring forth evidence either that in this particular case the risk will not come to fruition (he knows that the mushroom is safe or he knows it's poisonous but he has an immunity to that poison) or that he can create safeguards that avoid the risk (he has a test kit that will tell him if the mushroom is safe).

I would, however, place the ultimate burden of proof on the person who relies on this particular slippery slope analysis.[8] Recall that the starting point of this moral argument against assisted suicide is that the initial action of participating in it might be seen in isolation as not immoral. The immorality comes from the consequences of permitting this action: an inevitable and inexorable slide to the horrific narratives of unconstrained, involuntary euthanasia of vulnerable populations, which will be the equivalent of geriatric genocide, mass murder. It would seem that if people are to be labeled as immoral under this slippery slope scenario, those providing this theory must put forth a convincing position that people like my father are (or at least should be) aware that their actions carry a realistic risk that this scenario will come to be. After all, it is in the willingness to take that risk that any claim of immorality must find its source.

How heavy should this burden be? That depends on the particular society's view of risk aversion and thus on what level of risk taking could be considered "acceptable" or "unacceptable" in that culture. While there may well be risk-averse societies, America would seem to be quite the opposite. Risk taking lies at the core of our cultural mythology—a small group of Puritans in search of religious freedom crossing the Atlantic in a small wooden craft named the *Mayflower;* English subjects risking certain execution for treason in fomenting a revolution to gain independence; pioneer families making the dangerous trek west on the Oregon Trail to build a new life, thereby becoming the embodiment of our "pioneer spirit"; and, of course, the American entrepreneur, risk taker par excellence. In fact, the very structure of our society under the Constitution bespeaks of our willingness to accept great risk as a necessary cost of providing each citizen the space for full human realization free of government interference. Thus, we accept the risks accompanying almost limitlessly unconstrained freedom of speech and expression, the risks of a politics based on majority rule, and the risks of criminality due to constraints on police that make detection and prosecution of crime more difficult.

Under this ethos of extreme risk taking, it would seem that we would not label someone as "bad" (and in fact partially responsible for the killing of countless innocents) for performing an otherwise moral act unless it is demonstrated that the otherwise moral action carried a clear and likely risk of the substantial harm envisioned at the bottom of the slippery slope. Of course, a legislature could prove to be extremely risk averse in the PAS arena and ban the initial conduct based on the fear that it could conceivably lead to the slippery slope scenario, but that would be a statement of pragmatic policy, the result of balancing risks, consequences, futures studies, conflicts among constituencies, costs and realities of effective supervision and regulation, and such. It would not turn on the sources of moral labeling we are investigating.

In the domain of the slippery slope and assisted suicide I do not doubt that the risk is real in the sense that if you condone physician-assisted suicide (and euthanasia) at some point there will be a case of killing without the patient's consent. Nor could anyone dispute the seriousness of such a consequence. Rather, the debate is over frequency. Will this happen so frequently as to become an all but routine aspect of future medical practice?

In attempting to meet their burden, the opponents of physician-assisted suicide rely on two sources for their proof: assumptions about likely human behavior within the social, cultural, and economic world of medicine and illness;[9] and empirical analyses of actual programs that permit physician-assisted suicide (the Netherlands and the state of Oregon).

A CLOSER LOOK AT THE SLIPPERY SLOPE

The Paradigm Case: The Nazi Eugenics Program

We have already touched on the Nazi eugenics (selective breeding) program,[10] which was ostensibly pursued in the quest for a master race. A fuller exploration of the progressive steps through which the program devolved will give a sense of an apparent slippery slope in action and provide a vivid image of what those opposed to physician-assisted suicide most fear. As I said before, I am not neutral when it comes to the Nazis. Most of my relatives from my father's family were among the six million murdered. Six million. That's mind-boggling. Kill 100,000 people in a giant football stadium. Then do it again and again and again, 60 times. That is more people than the entire population of the state of Maryland. And this wasn't done by dropping some horrific bomb. In effect, it was done one person at a time, face-to-face, six million times. My father had a cousin who lived in Lithuania. In the late 1930s, she wrote to him asking for money so she could come to America. He was young and full of himself and thought that if she wanted to come to America she could earn her own passage. He never wrote back and never heard from her again. She died in the camps. Dad lived with the guilt until the day he died, knowing that he could have saved her.

The eugenics program began with the forced sterilization of 350,000 people with "genetically determined" diseases (feeblemindedness, insanity, etc.).[11] Next followed the Nuremberg Laws, which forbade sex or marriage between Jews and gentiles. In 1939, a mercy-killing panel was established. Beginning with so-called disabled children at birth, the panel expanded its scope to the mentally ill, retarded, and epileptics.[12] By 1941, 70,000 had been killed under the program. It has been documented that half of all the doctors were members of the Nazi party prior to Hitler's rise to power.[13] It is still discomforting to know that regular doctors who were committed healers could so easily shift their focus from the good of the patient to the "good of the state." This shift was so dramatic, in fact, that killing "useless eaters"[14] to free up hospital beds for wounded soldiers became a routine part of medical practice.[15] World-renowned humanist psychiatrists willingly took on the task of killing mental patients,[16] their eagerness going beyond even what the government requested of them. One of the doctors on the mercy-killing panel for disabled children was the inventor of the ultimate lifesaver of the newborn, the incubator.[17] The extermination of the Jews then followed through a rhetorical play on medical terminology. The Jews carried "dangerous genes" and "racial poison."[18] They had to be eliminated.

With this history of doctors so readily switching from their role as healers to that of killers, it is hardly surprising that opponents of physician-assisted suicide would see the risk of a similar tragedy if we begin to let doctors in America participate in killing their patients.

But this analogy can only be taken so far, supporters of physician-assisted suicide will say. It is, to be sure, a cautionary tale of which we must never lose sight. Rather than providing a glimpse into the future, however, it will serve as a brake on slipping down the slope, just as the shameful image of the interment of Japanese Americans in World War II likely constrained the actions of the government against persons of Middle Eastern descent after 9/11. Anyway, Nazi Germany was totally different. That was a society in which all allegiances were to the state. It was the fatherland, not the individual, that counted.[19] In such a society, sacrificing the individual for whatever the government perceives is the greater good was inevitable (particularly in an all-out war). America could not be more different. It is a government of the people, by the people, and for the people.

The state exists to serve the people. The individual is guaranteed civil rights against the state, which are enshrined in the Constitution. We believe in patriotism, but its purpose is to defend the "Land of the Free." The slide down the German Alps simply is not replicable on the freedom-bathed American Rockies.

I, too, believe that it can't happen here, at least not anything that monstrous. But, on the other hand, I know that when our nation is under stress bad enough things can happen (e.g., the suspension of habeas corpus and the ban on criticizing the government during the Civil War, the criminalization of dissent during World War I, the interment of Japanese during World War II, McCarthyism, the illegal conduct of the FBI in attempting to undermine the antiwar movement during the Vietnam War, and the government's attempt to broaden police powers at the expense of civil liberties after 9/11). Also the Nazi eugenics program did not function in an intellectual vacuum. The Nazis had a theory, which was subsequently mirrored in a 1927 opinion of the U.S. Supreme Court. In 1920, the preeminent legal expert Karl Binding and noted humanitarian Alfred Hoche published an article entitled "Permitting the Destruction of a Life Not Worthy of Life."[20] Seven years later, in the case of *Buck v. Bell,* the Supreme Court approved an involuntary sterilization law. In that case, Justice Holmes declared what could have been the slogan for the first stages of the German eugenics program when he wrote, "Three generations of imbeciles is enough!"[21]

The Physician-Assisted Suicide Slippery Slope

The slippery slope that leads from physician-assisted suicide to involuntary killing of the vulnerable goes approximately like this.

- The psychology of doctors will begin to subtly change as they become comfortable with the idea that they can kill as well as heal within their concept of being a medical professional.
- Initially, their historical focus on healing, with an accompanying sense of failure if they cannot heal, combined with the new possibility of killing, will lead some doctors to hide their failures through assisted suicide.
- Next they will avoid failure all together by using assisted suicide to solve the problem of tough cases.

- Doctors are not well trained in, and thus not very good at, palliative care (comfort care focusing on pain control and support for the spiritual, psychological, and emotional needs of the dying). Yet, most desires for suicide in the terminally ill can be attributed to suffering that could be alleviated by means of palliative care. The availability of assisted suicide, however, will take away incentives to increase physicians' knowledge of and patients' access to palliative care. Thus, a vicious cycle will take place in which the less palliative care is available to treat the common causes of suicide requests the more people will seek assisted suicide. The more patients resort to assisted suicide the less will be the incentive to develop a quality system of palliative care, and so on.

- At the same time, the psychology of the dying will begin to change. Not only will they be subject to coercion from family members to whom they have become an emotional and financial burden, but incrementally they will begin to believe that because they can die (have a right to die) they should die (have a duty to die).

- Run by huge bureaucracies focused on the bottom line, medicine will increasingly have an incentive to cut costs by terminating persons nearing the end of life (especially given that the final month of care is by far the most expensive). The easiest targets will be the most vulnerable (the isolated, elderly, poor, sick, and mentally diminished).

- Finally, the medical bureaucracy will receive the tacit support of the wider society. As medical resources become scarcer and scarcer, society will have to find methods of allocation (i.e., triage). Euthanizing old, very ill people near the end of their lives will be condoned as a partial solution to this resource crisis both because it will be perceived that, as a group, these old people have already had their fair share of health and life and because, as a practical matter, old sick people are incapable of acting collectively as a countervailing political force.

All in all, this is a pretty scary scenario.

Is this scenario of institutionalized, involuntary euthanasia a realistic one? Will acceptance of physician-assisted suicide lead us to insulate ourselves from moral realities to the extent that everything is so cloaked in sterile medical technology that we are no longer capable of distinguishing between medicine and murder? Those terrifying questions led me to carefully examine each premise in the preceding behavioral scenario.

The Psychology of Doctors

The first major slide down the slippery slope is based on an implicit argument that goes something like this.[22] Doctors are trained to be healers.[23] When they no longer can heal, they are at a loss. They face the limitations and failures of their craft and their exercise of that craft. In the past, they dealt with the inability to treat by throwing up their hands and saying, "There's no more I can do for this patient," leaving what remained to family members and nurses. If you add the notion that they can kill their patients as well as treat them, this additional dimension of their role will gradually be used to fill the uncomfortable void left when their medical arts no longer can perform medical miracles.[24] They do not have to be confronted with their failures. They do not have to agonize over cases so close to hopeless that failure is all but certain. They can employ their medical knowledge to make that failure disappear; they can utilize their authority to convince the patient that he or she should die.[25]

I, too, think of doctors as healers. Incredible advances in medical technology (bypass surgery, transplants, chemotherapy, CAT scans, MRIs, laser surgery) have expanded the doctor's healing arts toward the miraculous. Of course, doctors know that they cannot conquer death, that death defines us as human. Yet it is not so simple. While doctors know this, they also know that the immediate cause of death is always some disease or system failure (heart failure, kidney failure). Since they believe that they can combat any disease or system failure on some level, doctors do believe that they can cheat death.[26]

No doubt it is painful personally and professionally not to be able to save a patient in spite of all your knowledge, skill, and access to technological resources. Yet to move from that to the conclusion that "once they taste blood" in assisting a suicide doctors will so lose feelings for the human value of their dying patients that, in order to not face their failure, they will kill them (like someone would throw away a clay bowl they made because it did not turn out right) is quite a leap. When we imagine that doctors would conduct nonvoluntary (though not involuntary) euthanasia by killing people who are not even dying but are demented or semiconscious, that leap is greater still.

To make that leap, one must make a number of assumptions. First, we must assume that doctors are problem-solving virtuosos who only see the medical problem (heart murmur, flu, facial burn, sprained ankle, pregnancy, cancer) as unconnected to the human being whose problem it is.

Second, doctors have no respect for the value of human life in general, only valuing life to the extent they personally can save or improve it. Third, the current consciousness, perspective, and training of doctors at this date will continue unchanged even if the medical profession accepts physician-assisted suicide as a tool (albeit an extreme tool) in end of life care. Fourth, the role of the doctor has always been limited to mechanical healing without concern for patient suffering or the need for compassion.

As to the first two assumptions, I have certainly encountered a few doctors in my life about whom these assumptions would hold. They are not encounters one easily forgets, and they were not individuals I thought were good doctors or would ever wish to see again. In my experience, the vast majority of doctors do see their patients as people and value their lives individually and as part of a network of family and friends. They do their best to fight for the patient in tough cases but know that they can only do their best. I cannot imagine these doctors killing patients to avoid failing or facing failure. Admittedly, my perspective was formed as an educated, upper-middle-class, Caucasian male patient who has the support of a broad, similarly situated group. I am not a sick person in his nineties lying alone in a bed in an understaffed state nursing facility.

As to the third assumption about training and perspective, I will address it next when I discuss palliative care. At this point, I can say that with the significant focus on end of life care over the past decade, and as the baby boomers care for their aging parents and face their own mortality, recognition of end of life care as a part of medical practice is an evolving reality.

As to the fourth assumption, the idea that, for doctors, it is either heal or nothing, this seems vastly overstated. Relief of suffering and compassion have always been part of the doctor's role.[27] It was at the center of the school of Hippocrates. I recognize that opponents of PAS point to the Hippocratic oath as an argument against a physician ever aiding a patient in committing suicide.[28] And it is correct that the oath specifically bars giving a patient poison and thus bars assisted suicide.[29] The oath, however, also forbids surgery, abortion, and fees for teaching.[30] Thus, no one particular portion of the oath can be taken as more than a function of the particular historical context. The broader sweep of the oath, however, transcends its particulars. The oath provides a vision of medicine as nonintrusively aligned with nature as the real healer.[31] The medical philosophy is one of restraint. It also offers a school of healing that pledges to act with less self-interest than competing schools of healing and other trades in general.[32] The hope, then, was that patients would avoid seeking extreme self-remedies and, when they chose healers, would choose the school of Hippocrates. In fact, Hippocrates believed in trying to do away with suffering, lessening the violation of the disease, and refusing to treat those who were "over mastered by the disease."[33] In other words, he believed in compassionate care.

Patient Mistrust of Doctors

A related argument against physician-assisted suicide focuses on the projected effect on the psyche of patients. As doctors become willing to assist in suicides, and perhaps euthanasia, more vulnerable patients will gradually become less trustful of doctors and may in fact even grow to fear that the doctor will kill them.[34] With this loss of trust, doctors will become less able to care for patients. After all, patients must have confidence in both doctors' competence *and* motives if they are to make the wholehearted commitment to their treatment that is often required. Patients who, as a result, become sicker and more vulnerable will fear involuntary euthanasia even more and will trust doctors even less, and so the downward cycle will spiral. Surveys conducted on this issue come to contradictory conclusions.[35]

Now, if I were old, sick, and alone, I certainly would not want to think that my doctor might creep through the hospital or nursing home at night and inject me with some lethal drug. But it is difficult for me to see how I might come to this conclusion merely from the fact that I am aware that my doctor was willing to assist in the suicide of a suffering, terminally ill patient or even carry out voluntary euthanasia under the same circumstances. It seems as likely that my trust will actually be greater knowing that my doctor will do everything possible to relieve my suffering, including (as a last resort) assisted suicide. (In fact, many patients, once they know assisted suicide is available, relax and never use it.)[36]

To the extent that I perceive my doctor not as *my* doctor but as a foot soldier in a profit-obsessed medical bureaucracy, however, my feelings may well be otherwise.[37] But the problem then is not so much that there is a lack of trust because of some issue with the appropriate parameters of the physician's role (saving versus taking life). It is a lack of trust based on what I perceive as a conflict in loyalties. This, not the doctor in the role of killer, is the real issue. The fear accompanying the sanctioning of assisted suicide and euthanasia, then, is that we are placing a lethal weapon in the hands of someone we cannot trust. I will discuss this later when we consider bureaucratic medicine and the slippery slope.

The Vicious Cycle of Palliative Care

Palliative care[38] is concerned with bringing comfort not a cure.[39] As such, it provides all the technologies available to alleviate, or at least control, pain. Since suffering is composed of more than raw, physical pain, palliative care attends to the emotional, psychological, and spiritual aspects of suffering as well.[40] The angels from hospice obtained whatever pain medication my father required at whatever hour it was needed. They also offered to arrange for massages, spiritual or psychological counseling for my father and our family, special mattress pads, storytellers, and more. They dealt with the whole man as situated within his full world.

Most people who seek assisted suicide do not do so because of uncontrollable pain.[41] They may fear such pain, but in fact most pain (though not all,[42] as appeared to be the case with my father) can be brought under control.[43] They wish to die for other reasons such as not wanting to be a burden on others or having difficulty accepting their increasing dependence, which they associate with a lack of worth.

On the other hand, most doctors historically have not been well trained in pain control[44] and certainly not in dealing with what appears to be the less scientific (emotional, spiritual, psychological) aspects of suffering.[45] Doctors, after all, are there to diagnose and heal. Medicine is a heroic enterprise, not one that provides comfort once the battle is lost. And there surely is something to this position. Traditionally, little of medical school training dealt with pain relief and almost none with end of life cases. Further, the fear of addiction led doctors to ration the most powerful painkilling drugs (such as opiates) until absolutely necessary,[46] that is, when the pain is rampaging out of control. Also doctors do not want to bring themselves up against state licensing boards or Drug Enforcement Administration investigations.[47] Thus, even as late as 1994, studies found the quality of palliative care, including pain control, to be deplorably poor in American hospitals.[48]

Admittedly, from my own experience I know that there is a generation of doctors that holds onto old notions of pain control and drugs ("Let's see if aspirin works before we give you aspirin with codeine for that abdominal surgery"). But, also from my experience, I've seen modern ideas about pain control becoming more the norm. Act before it begins to get out of hand. And forget this fear of addiction.[49] You're dealing with very sick and dying people. My father did not get high on the drugs; they just got him to the place where he was not writhing in pain, where he could interact on some normal, human level.[50] Also there appears to be an expanding awareness of the role of palliative medicine and end of life care in the medical practice.[51] After all, for well over a decade the American medical profession has been bombarded with book after book, article after article, and talk show after talk show about their deficiencies in these areas. At some point, some of that seeps through.

Enter the slippery slope. Whatever admirable progress we might be making in palliative care will come to a halt. With assisted suicide and voluntary euthanasia as options, there will be no incentive to invest in learning about and expanding facilities for palliative care. After all, people who are dead do not suffer.[52] Since palliative care addresses many of the motives patients have for seeking to end their lives, however, lessening availability of palliative care will lead to more patient requests for death, which, in turn, will further reduce incentives for palliative care, and so on,[53] a vicious cycle in which more and more patients are driven to death by what increasingly is unrelieved suffering.[54]

I can see that this could happen, but I do not see why these consequences are any more likely than their opposites. Imagine widespread acceptance of physician-assisted suicide. In that world, I would know that as a physician I could be called on to assist in, or even carry out, a patient's death. I would also be aware of the relationship between good palliative and end of life care and requests for death. Rather than a disincentive for learning more about pain control and general palliative care, it would seem to be quite the opposite. Physician-assisted suicide would only be part of a continuum of care. Ending the life of a patient is a professionally and emotionally difficult thing, as narratives of doctors who have participated in such a death (other than Doctor Kevorkian) reveal.[55] I would not want to carry that burden if there was another reasonable alternative. I certainly could not imagine having to face the fact that because I did not apply principles of palliative care a patient needlessly committed suicide with my assistance (or that I actually killed him or her).

Enter Bureaucratic Medicine

In truth, the bureaucratic nature of current medical practice is the most frightening aspect of the slippery slope argument because all baby boomers know that the practice of medicine has completely changed since we were young.[56] We grew up in a time when our family doctor would come to our homes when we had the measles or mumps. There were no bypasses, MRIs, or sophisticated antibiotics. Science has plainly moved far forward. But there were people we considered *our* doctors. For most of us, that is no longer the world in which we live. We have someone called a primary care physician who we see, often as a prerequisite to being sent to a fragmented array of specialists and subspecialists. If and when some loved one must go to a hospital for surgery or some serious illness, in my experience, the lack of a sense of being watched over by an identifiable, responsible physician is even greater. You cannot leave a friend or family member alone in a medical facility.[57] Information does not always pass accurately from person to person or shift to shift. Let me tell a short story, one that ten years later is still vivid.

🐦   🐦   🐦

We were increasingly having problems with controlling Dad's pain, and controlling his pain was literally the number one focus of all of our lives. After weeks of trips back and forth to the hospital and changes and additions to medications and dosages, we all agreed that the best solution would be to hook Dad up to a morphine pump at home. That way my father could push a button whenever he wanted more pain medication. The hospice nurses, of course, were responsible for calibrating the machine for the appropriate time (which increasingly was set at shorter intervals) and dosage (which was increasingly set higher).

To hook up the pump, however, first required a short and simple surgical procedure in which a shunt was inserted into Dad's chest.

When we went in for the procedure, the surgeon approached us with an additional surgery that could be done at the same time—a sort of two for one. Tumors were obstructing the passage into Dad's stomach, blocking what little food he ate. Why not remove these as long as Dad would already be in surgery?

We were, if anything, a proactive group. What will this accomplish? A bit more comfort and a bit more nutrition, which might lead to the patient living longer. How much longer? Hard to tell. Days, maybe a week or more. This sounds like major surgery. Won't he be in pain and have a significant period of recuperation? That's possible. But he's dying. Won't this diminish his quality of life during the little time he has left? I guess so. Forget it! Just put in the shunt. (In fact, within a week, Dad decided to stop eating and drinking any-

way in order to move things along as quickly as his body was willing to cooperate.) Later that afternoon Dad was back from surgery with a brand new shunt and feeling all right. We left later that evening, planning to bring him home the next day.

We were home the next morning arranging for something the exact nature of which now escapes me, regarding Dad's final stay. The phone rang, and I answered. "John, you know this is wrong. This is so very wrong. How can a son do this to his father? You will have to live the rest of your life with this on your conscience." What?! Dad sounded calm and clear. He also sounded totally delusional. I told him I loved him and that we were coming right over, and we all jumped into the car and rushed to the hospital.

When we got there, Dad was strapped to the bed with the type of restraints they use in mental hospitals. My dad, strapped down. It was unimaginable. It took a while to piece it all together.

The night before, Dad had become restless. He wanted to walk around and yak with the nurses. That was Dad; he talked everywhere to everyone. But they had work to do. They couldn't watch Dad in order to ensure he wouldn't fall while he walked around, and they thought he needed rest before what they mistakenly believed was "upcoming surgery." So, they gave him a sedative, and he had what is termed an adverse reaction. More specifically, the pills triggered a temporary psychotic break—Dad was just nuts when we arrived that morning and had apparently been even crazier the night before. So they had strapped him down "for everybody's safety." "Fine, we're here now. Unstrap him!" But here the insanity was not Dad's alone.

Early in the morning, hospital attendants had come to prep him for the major surgery we had rejected the day before. Somehow it had been written on his chart, and, though crazy, Dad had maintained enough awareness to tell them that the surgery had been rejected. Why believe him? He was insane, in restraints, and "the chart had no notation other than the surgery was a go." Somehow, Dad convinced them to call us. "Sorry, your conversation with the surgeon rejecting the procedure was not put on your dad's chart." Okay. Again, do you want to discuss insanity? We all immediately agreed that if Dad ever had to go back to the hospital one of us would be there with him around the clock.

🙿   🙿   🙿

For most geriatric residents of nursing homes, state hospital wards, and even state mental institutions (where, as in a facility near me, they warehouse elderly dementia patients who cannot afford a nursing facility), no one is watching. The residents comprise some combination of the sick, weak, confused, and demented. Many of these individuals are poor, and many are people of color. All are powerless. From what I saw during Mom's odyssey through a series of assisted living and nursing facilities following Dad's death, even the vast majority of somewhat affluent residents are alone, totally vulnerable. For many, family members live far away. For others, the family took heart that the patient was receiving expensive care but took little time to visit.

Back to the slippery slope. High-priced private assisted living facilities and nursing homes have little economic incentive to shorten the lives of their clients. That would be killing the goose that laid the golden egg. Stays of geriatric patients in hospital and nursing home facilities that are funded by insurance or state funds or are part of a health management organization (HMO) may well be a different story. In 2000, the average life expectancy for Americans was 76.1 years old, and those over 85 were the fastest-growing segment of the population.[58] With this increase in longevity, however, has come a parallel increase in people suffering from chronic illnesses. By 2030, one in five people will be over 65[59] (i.e., 64 million people),[60] placing great strain on the health care system. By far the greatest cost in caring for an individual suffering from such a chronic illness is during the last month of his or her life.[61] Thus, when you add in the increasing Medicare enrollment in HMOs, and the fact that 40 percent of total Medicare expenses come in the last few months of life,[62] the economic pressures to shorten those last few months only increase.

The slide down the slippery slope thus becomes clear. Permitting assisted suicide has two interrelated effects. Regularizing the taking of life of the suffering begins to instill in the physician the notion that, for some, death is a "blessing." Once doctors begin to accept their role as one of delivering this blessing, it will be natural to gradually analogize from the terminal cancer patient begging for more morphine to the shriveled, perhaps a bit confused or even demented, all but helpless hospital or nursing home resident. What could their life mean? Wouldn't death be a blessing? At the same time, when this perspective is melded with physicians' increasing loyalty to a medical bureaucracy that is centered on the bottom line and profits for shareholders,[63] the physician has an incentive to try to encourage these powerless, vulnerable, yet expensive individuals to agree to kill themselves.[64] We've already discussed coercion from family members. Think of the power of doctors.[65] They are the primary, and authoritative, source on the patient's health. They can provide information in ways that encourage or discourage patients to continue their lives. They are the ones who will decide whether a request for PAS is "reasonable," and their judgment will ultimately be powerfully influenced by their own subjective views of the "quality" of the life of the patient. To an extent, they can encourage hope or despair. They can look for possible depression-laden underpinnings of requests to die or take the request at face value. Again, this likely will be influenced by their sense as to whether "if it was me, I'd rather be dead" or not.

In nursing homes, doctors may visit, but generally nurses provide day-to-day treatment for the patient. In this domain, from what I've seen, the nurse has a professional and moral authority comparable to that which the doctor carries in the hospital.

Add euthanasia to the equation and you only make it easier to kill and increase the bottom line by providing a mechanism through which doctors can claim consent but which does not require any substantiation (as would be the case if patients must take the lethal pills themselves) outside of the doctor's word.

How realistic is this scenario? Some of the elements certainly are. Hospitals and nursing homes are filled with extremely vulnerable geriatric patients and residents. Managed care companies, and health insurance firms in general, care about profits. They are, after all, businesses. State budgets, on the other hand, are almost always strained. The expense of providing decent health care for our population is increasing, costing more than we as a society are willing to allocate. It is likely we will eventually confront making resource allocation decisions, whether those are done by categories of treatment options (routine procedures, such as physical exams and flu shots, versus more costly procedures such as heart transplants), treatment populations, and such.[66] Finally, physicians working in managed care are constrained somewhat by the economic interests of the HMO. But is that enough?

Already 80 percent of us die in hospitals and nursing homes, and 70 percent of those will have their lives ended by withdrawal of some form of lifesaving support.[67] All of one's concerns about coercion and preemptive medical decision making resulting in death are surely present here (remember, in order to pull the plug, the doctor does not even need consent if he finds the care to be medically "futile"). The question is what assisted suicide, and even voluntary euthanasia, adds to the mix. It seems to add two things. First, there will be patients who are not on life-sustaining machines, so there will be no plug to pull. Most patients in nursing homes, for example, are not on respirators and such. In fact, many resident facilities for the elderly will not even accept people who require medical care beyond dispensing prescribed pills. Therefore, assisted suicide could potentially reach a far larger population. Second, withdrawal of treatment generally takes place during the last days of the patient's life. Assisted suicide could shorten the life of a geriatric patient in a hospital by weeks and one in a nursing home by months or even years. Could it happen here? Possibly it could, but I don't think so.

Admittedly, extreme scarcity could change that, not by making doctors secret killers but through a cultural understanding that, under some circumstances, one has an altruistic "duty to die." This was, after all, part of Eskimo, Norse, Samoan, and Crow Indian culture. From my current perspective, putting my grandmother or mother on some ice floe to perish is incomprehensible. And I believe that it is not a place we can arrive at incrementally, small step by small step, without noticing along the way. I believe it would take something far beyond inconvenience and scarcity of medical resources.

The behavioral underpinnings of a slippery slope rationale for an absolute utilitarian rule banning physician-assisted suicide paint a troubling picture, which I think must be taken very seriously. On the other hand, we are not considering the wisdom of assisted suicide as a social policy, though the means of inquiry may appear similar to such an analysis. We are deciding whether the slippery slope argument justifies a position in which it is always *morally* wrong for a doctor to assist in a suicide. The arguments resting on assumptions about the behavior and psychology of doctors and those in the medical field do not persuade me. While the projected ride down the slope would be a frightening abnegation of the most basic values of our society, there are far too many speculations and contingencies to conclude that, if we permit doctors to help people like my father end their suffering, the end of the ride to the bottom is "a clear and likely risk." At the same time, the decision to protect the vulnerable from a coerced or involuntary death by deterring assisted suicide through labeling it as immoral impedes the choice of people like my father (rational and supported by a strong family network) to end their extreme suffering in the face of an imminent and certain death.

Interestingly, some have made a slippery slope argument in favor of assisted suicide: if we do not legalize and regulate assisted suicide, then it will happen anyway, Kevorkian style, with the type of abuses accompanying any such underground practice.[68] I do not find what is in effect a lesser of two evils argument to be a very compelling one from a moral perspective. After all, those who believe assisted suicide is otherwise morally supportable do not need this argument. Such a stance is only needed if one is implicitly saying that assisted suicide is wrong but it's going to happen whether we like it or not, and, given that, we're far better off if it's out in the open and regulated. Again, this might be acceptable as real politics, but it is hardly inspiring morally. Plus I disagree with the factual premise. While I believe that there are instances when doctors or nurses surreptitiously assist in patient suicides, or even perform euthanasia, these happen in medical facilities or private homes, not in a Kevorkian van or any other setting comparable to the image of the back alley abortionist that added so much moral force to the pro-abortion movement. Many such incidents, in fact, happen under the medically sterile guise of PDE. Also most of those seeking to end their lives with medical assistance are very sick, often in hospitals, under home care, or in nursing homes. They are not likely to jump into their cars and go into the night searching for some dark angel of death.

THE NETHERLANDS AND THE DUTCH STANCE

Sooner or later anyone discussing assisted suicide and euthanasia will focus on the Netherlands. Generally, it will be those opposing assisted suicide and euthanasia who will cite the Dutch experience. They will treat it as a laboratory experiment that has produced data verifying the slippery slope hypothesis. To place these claims in context, it is best to first appreciate the legal structure within which physician-conducted euthanasia was first tolerated and subsequently legalized in the Netherlands.

The Legal Evolution

In 1973, a Dutch court convened over the murder prosecution of a physician who had intentionally injected a lethal narcotic dose into her seriously ill and suffering mother.[69] What happened in this case would not be comprehensible in a similar trial in the United States. We have a strong commitment to a true adversary system, and, at least in a case involving such a serious charge, the prosecutor's only concern would be to ethically obtain a conviction that is legally sustainable on appeal. In the Netherlands, however, adversariness takes a backseat to the "principle of expediency and advisability."[70] Under this principle, good "public policy" is more significant than individual guilt. To this end, the court trying the physician listened to expert testimony about the prevailing ethical standards of Dutch medical practice and found that euthanasia is acceptable to the medical community, assuming a given set of circumstances.[71] Although legislation declared the physician's admitted conduct to be homicide, the court created something hovering between law and social policy that was intended to rationalize the discrepancy between legal norms, on one hand, and societal morality on the other. The judge thus found the defendant guilty of murder and then, finding that she had followed the protocol for euthanasia in the Dutch medical profession, sentenced her to *one week* of incarceration (suspended) and a year's probation.[72]

Subsequently, cases in 1984 and 1986 created an actual defense to a homicide charge in the context of physician-conducted euthanasia.[73] The law had long recognized a defense of *necessity* (force majeure)[74] wherein one can violate a law to avoid a far greater evil (e.g., tearing down someone's house as a firebreak to save an entire neighborhood or speeding to rush a child who has swallowed poison to the hospital).[75] The Dutch courts applied this concept of necessity to what they found was an irreconcilable "conflict" between two duties incumbent upon the physician: the duty to preserve life and the duty to avoid suffering.[76] Euthanasia was found to be an acceptable choice under this necessity theory. That defense, of course, required adherence to the type of criteria for carrying out euthanasia followed in the general medical community.

In 1993, this medical protocol was enacted into law, though not through amendment of the penal code.[77] Rather, the protocol was appended to an act dealing with coroners, death certificates, and burial.[78] If physicians followed the protocol, reporting their compliance to the prosecutor, they would not be prosecuted, though their act of intentionally taking a life was still considered murder under the law.[79] In theory, of course, the prosecutor could determine that the guidelines had not been met and file murder charges. The specific guidelines were:

- The request must be made entirely of the patient's own free will and not under pressure from others.
- The patient must have a lasting longing for death: the request must be made repeatedly over a period of time.
- The patient must be experiencing unbearable suffering.

- The patient must be given alternatives to euthanasia and time to consider these alternatives.
- There must be no reasonable alternatives to relieve suffering other than euthanasia.
- Doctors must consult with at least one colleague who has faced the question of euthanasia before.
- The patient's death cannot inflict unnecessary suffering on others.
- Only a doctor can euthanize a patient.
- The euthanasia must be reported to a coroner, who is to be supplied with a case history and an affidavit stating that the guidelines have been followed.

THE DUTCH NOTION OF "PRAGMATIC TOLERANCE"

The Dutch approach to euthanasia is a product of the social upheavals of the 1960s, of the rise of a "secular morality" focused on individual choice,[80] and of the uniquely Dutch form of compromise between existing legal norms and the realities of the prevailing morality in the society known as "pragmatic tolerance."[81] The treatment of possession of a recreational amount of hashish or marijuana is a well-known example of this concept. The Dutch maintain the prohibition against possession of those drugs under their penal law, but they tolerate open violation of the law if a particular protocol is followed (e.g., smoke in designated "coffee shops" or private residences and only possess that amount determined by the government to be appropriate for personal consumption).

The point of these compromises is to avoid serious social fragmentation and dissent, while maintaining an open public dialogue on important social issues.[82] This tradition of pragmatic tolerance is deeply embedded in Dutch culture.[83] From the nation's inception, the Dutch needed cooperation across a range of different constituencies without the possibility of a strong central framework to coerce it. In a nation comprised of a confederation of culturally different provinces, the Dutch had to live and let live if they were to work together in national self-defense, carry out the extraordinary task of reclaiming and protecting their land from the sea, and create a commercial empire from which this tiny nation once (incredibly) dominated the globe.[84]

Admittedly, American law enforcement has its own variant of pragmatic tolerance, which we term "discretion."[85] It is said that our society would be intolerable if the police enforced every law on the books in every situation (e.g., when I pass a police car parked on the shoulder of a freeway and I'm going 58 miles per hour in a 55 zone, I'd be both shocked and incensed if I were stopped and given a ticket, though I'd clearly violated the literal letter of the law). Also police must ration resources. They simply cannot enforce all the laws on the books. Therefore, they may decide to concentrate on heroin, cocaine, or PCP, leaving enforcement of marijuana possession to informal warnings and confiscation should they happen to come across an offender in the course of their other priorities. As such, the motivation in America for actions akin to pragmatic tolerance are not based on fears of cultural fragmentation but concerns about freedom in the sense of having some "breathing space" and the constraints of limited resources.

Problems with Self-Reporting Euthanasia in the Netherlands

Initially, one can imagine a number of reasons why a physician in the Dutch system might choose not to self-report a death by euthanasia instead violating the protocol by listing the cause of death as "natural causes" on the death certificate.[86] First, the entire process, leading up to and including the actual death, would tend to be a private matter between family, patient, and physician.[87] Reporting risks bringing government officials into the center of this intensely personal world at the very time when the family is likely to be emotionally spent and seeking acceptance and closure for what has happened. Understandably, a physician may hesitate to put a family through this. Second, reporting involves forms, interviews, and time spent away from the physician's practice.[88] The tendency to avoid all this time, effort, and unpleasantness by simply not reporting, thus, also would seem to be a motivation.

But reporting is a requirement of a protocol that assures the Dutch physician he or she will not be charged with murder. This would seem to offer a powerful incentive to follow the protocol. Perhaps it does, but there is a third, powerful, countervailing force. Reporting *guarantees* that the physician's action will draw the attention of a prosecutor. The doctor will then be at risk that the prosecutor will find, under his or her interpretation of the statutory guidelines, that the physician has not met the requirements of the protocol and therefore could be subject to a murder charge.[89]

In fact, in the United States this entire process would likely violate the Fifth Amendment protection against self-incrimination (and possibly the roughly analogous international law principle of nemo tenetur).

In the Netherlands, the real risk if one does not report is that someone in the family will say something and this will be communicated to the police. Family members, however, generally understand that they should not say anything (especially knowing that this will bring the government into their lives and get the doctor in trouble). Even if something inadvertently drops, unless the person receiving the information is a police officer, that person, too, will be unlikely to breach the circle of privacy and secrecy. Even if word does leak out, moreover, the physician is not in a much worse position than if he or she had reported. As long as physicians can establish that they followed the guidelines (and it will generally be their word and characterization of the events backed up by supportive family members), all they'll get is a slap on the wrist for not reporting.[90]

Under these circumstances, one would predict that only a minority of physicians performing euthanasia would self-report. In the Netherlands, this prediction proved correct, with 18 percent reporting in 1990[91] and 41 percent in 1995[92] (as established by surveys that guaranteed anonymity). In 1998, the reporting system was altered to lessen the disincentive for self-reporting. Under this system, the physician now reports to the medical examiner.[93] The medical examiner then sends his or her report to the prosecutor, not for a charging decision but only to decide if the body may be released for burial or cremation. The medical examiner then sends the report and that of the physician to an interdisciplinary regional committee composed of a physician, a lawyer, and an ethicist who will make the decision whether the case should even be referred to a prosecutor. Available statistics to date vary on the percentage of cases referred for prosecutorial inquiry by these regional committees: 2, 6, and 2 to 4 percent.[94] In any event, the numbers are low, which is what one would expect given that euthanasia by doctors has widespread cultural support and the treating physician basically controls the evidence.[95] Under this regime, reporting by 1999 had jumped to 60 percent.[96] That still means that 40 percent are not taking the initial step of reporting, which leaves a rather large hole in the system. On the other hand, we are seeing a tremendous increase in reporting over less than a decade (from 18 to 60 percent), which, in the life of a nation involved in somewhat radical experimentation, is not very long. There is no reason to believe that this upswing will not continue.

In 2001, the Dutch moved from pragmatic tolerance to legality.[97] The legislature amended the penal code to exempt intentional killing by means of physician-conducted euthanasia, called voluntary assisted euthanasia (VAE), from the definition of murder as long as the physician followed criteria roughly paralleling the previous legislative guidelines.

> VAE must be performed in accordance with "careful medical practice." Requests must be voluntary, well considered, persistent, and emanate from patients who are experiencing unbearable suffering without hope of improvement, and the doctor and the patient must agree that VAE is the only reasonable option. At least one independent physician must be consulted, who must see the patient and give a written opinion on the case.

Under this new law, the process using the regional committee as the screen for determining whether a case would be referred for prosecution was retained.[98] Individuals were also given the ability to include the desire for VAE in their living wills (e.g., "If I live past 80 and am demented, please euthanize me").[99]

Problems with the Guidelines

It is fair to contend that, in supporting the guidelines, the Dutch medical community sought sufficient clarity to protect it from criminal prosecution. After all, physicians didn't want to live in fear that, although they were attempting to follow the rules in good faith, they nonetheless were constantly at risk of inadvertently violating some interpretively unclear boundary and facing murder charges. On the other hand, they sought sufficient flexibility to give fair play to their professional judgment.[100] Arguably, the guidelines meet both goals but only if seen in the context of actual practice.

Phrases such as "reasonable options," "intolerable suffering," "well-considered request," and "without hope of improvement" surely offer flexibility for the exercise of professional judgment. The lack of clarity in those terms, on the other hand, initially might seem to put even the most well-meaning physician at risk of misinterpretation by officials and, with that, possible prosecution.

In fact, this is not a problem. Since the doctor writes the report, and thus has the opportunity to rhetorically fill and shape the narrative of each case as fulfilling each of these *subjective* terms (although the physician's statements still must conform to and reflect some form of material reality), he or she should generally feel safe, having made a good faith attempt to follow the guidelines. I would also anticipate that, over time, the regional committees will act like our administrative regulatory agencies and promulgate (formally or informally) some concrete consensus about the permissible interpretive range available to the physician when trying to follow the rules. The greater problem is the extent to which the guidelines protect the basic interests of the patient in not being wrongly and/or unnecessarily killed and the interests of the broader society that VAE not become a routine tool for interpersonal problem solving.[101]

Opponents of VAE argue that the Dutch guidelines are so vague,[102] flexible, and incomplete that, though championed under the flag of personal autonomy of the patient, they actually position the physician as the ultimate arbiter of the worth of the patient's life and the desirability of his or her death.[103] Let's look at a few examples. To begin with, the guidelines mandate that the patient be enduring intolerable suffering.[104] If this means physical pain beyond the human capacity to endure that no medical technique can bring under control, *intolerable* has a medical context. When you go beyond that to recognize the complex, individual nature of suffering as a brew of physical, psychological, emotional, existential, and spiritual ingredients, the word *intolerable* becomes contextual, with the context ultimately likely being the doctor's evaluation of the quality and worth of the patient's current existence.

In fact, the Dutch have even cut the moorings of physical pain from suffering and have interpreted suffering to include extreme psychological pain. That obviously greatly expands the pool for VAE. Now it's not just extremely ill (generally elderly and dying) patients who can be euthanized. The net can pull in far younger, physically healthy individuals who are suffering in mental anguish. Further, in addition to this multiplication of potential numbers, there are other problems as well.

The suffering must be "without hope of improvement." What can this mean when considering a mentally suffering 52 year old? Perhaps there are literally untreatable mental illnesses, although I am not aware of that being the case. In any event, such cases would seem to be relatively rare and not something that a family practitioner would have the expertise to determine in a case in which a life is literally at stake. Yet the act does not require the involvement of a psychiatrist.[105]

Also the request must be voluntary. But what does this mean, and how is it to be determined? There are no criteria in the guidelines for what constitutes voluntariness and no requirement of any kind of investigation or, again, expertise in the form of a consulting psychiatrist.[106] The patient in mental agony raises additional problems. The question of how someone could be competent to agree to VAE when he or she is so mentally damaged that the only apparently viable choice is death is a challenging one to say the least.[107] Surely, the guidelines do not envision VAE for persons whose mental illness makes them suicidal. After all, in most cases suicide is connected to some form of severe mental suffering (i.e., clinical depression).

Also what would it mean in this context to say that there are no other "reasonable" options for this person? Can the fact that the patient refuses to take antipsychotic medication, for example, make this option any less reasonable? It wouldn't seem so under Dutch law, which stipulates that VAE is not appropriate when there is a reasonable treatment option even if the patient refuses to accept the treatment (although there is some indication that Dutch physicians do not always follow this rule). So, again, what is the basis of a conclusion that this psychiatric patient has no reasonable options other than suicide? When all is said and done, it would appear that the physician's determination that the person who is living in mental anguish qualifies for euthanasia entails a subjective judgment that this terribly depressed person is doomed to a miserable life and it isn't worth the effort to try to change things. Again, over time, the regional committee may clarify these ambiguities.

Problems in Application

Research in the Netherlands from 1990 and 1995 indicates that,[108] under any reasonable interpretation, the protections afforded patients by the guidelines have been significantly circumvented.[109] No major studies have appeared since the formation of the regional committees in 1998 and legalization in 2001. We therefore need to remember that we are dealing with a small window of time in an evolving practice played out on a national scale. Nonetheless, the data merit very serious consideration.

The finality of VAE requires the type of caution reflected in the requirements of consultation with a second physician and exploration of alternative, less drastic methodologies to curb suffering. Available data indicate that physicians have not regularly followed this requirement of consultation (only 50 percent of the time)[110] and that those who did consult tended to choose a close colleague for a brief discussion in which the decision of the treating physician effectively was "rubber stamped" in almost all (93 percent) of such consultations.[111] Matters, however, are changing rapidly. The guidelines were revised in 1995, making clear that the consultation must be both "formal" and "independent."[112] Recently, a commission of 10 experts created a protocol for consultation in the VAE setting, including the requirement that the consulting physician be truly "independent" of the treating physician and have knowledge of and expertise in palliative care.[113] This likely will elevate the quality and effectiveness of these consultations as a safeguard for the patient. In fact, panels of trained, independent consultants are now available.[114]

Requiring the presentation and evaluation of alternatives presupposes both that the physician be aware of pain control and other palliative care possibilities and that there exist facilities, expertise, and resources to deliver these alternatives to VAE.[115] In the mid-1990s, knowledge of palliative care in the Netherlands was in its infancy, with little expertise and few facilities. It was predicted that the acceptance of euthanasia would stunt the emergence of quality palliative care in the country[116] and that the vicious cycle we've discussed between lack of palliative care and requests for suicide would gain momentum.

In fact, that does not appear to have happened. Policymakers gradually are becoming convinced that the Netherlands can only have a well-considered euthanasia policy if it has a well-developed system of palliative care.[117] Accordingly, in 2000, centers of national health care policy announced that it would be national policy that palliative care be used to prevent euthanasia in order to rule out the possibility that future requests for euthanasia could be the result of inadequate palliative care. To that end, significant funds were provided to establish six centers for academic study and physician education on palliative care and to integrate hospices into the formal health care system.[118] At the same time, grassroots movements for palliative care education have sprung up and are being eagerly sought out by practicing physicians.[119] Thus, the situation on the palliative care front appears to be improving and rapidly so. Even critics of the Dutch system acknowledge that palliative care in the Netherlands has improved.[120]

A Specific Request by the Patient

The source of greatest concern based on the data, however, comes from what is a breach of the cornerstone of medical euthanasia: you do not kill people without their request. The source of these disturbing data is two government surveys (in which anonymity from the prosecutor's office was assured)—a 1990 survey (the so-called Remmelink Report) and a 1995 follow-up study.

The 1990 survey established that *1,000 patients* had been euthanized without any request on their part.[121] The response to this violation of the basic tenet of the guidelines was that most had previously indicated their wish for euthanasia, or had at least discussed euthanasia with the physician,[122] but had subsequently become unconscious or incompetent.[123] Saying that "most" had had such a conversation with the physician, however, is not the same as saying "all." As to those who had asked for euthanasia, moreover, there is no indication that this was a persistent request over time. It is not uncommon for very sick patients to say they want to die one day and feel very different a week later. Finally, as for the group that had "discussed" euthanasia, a discussion is a long way from a specific request.

Some of my concern would be assuaged by the claim that in 94 percent of these cases the family was consulted and in 84 percent the counsel of a colleague was sought (one can't tell from these data if there were cases in which no one was consulted)[124] if it were not for one other piece of data. Fourteen percent of those euthanized were fully competent and 11 percent partially competent.[125] Those who conducted the survey, perhaps wishing to foster an atmosphere of harmony, never asked these physicians the tough question: why did you kill a competent patient without his or her explicit request?[126]

The answer may be that they were close to dying anyway and in agony. Some statistics indicate that 87 percent of the "Remmelink 1,000"(as they have become known)[127] would have died within a week.[128] Yet that still leaves 13 percent, 130 human beings. Other data indicate that the percentage predicted to die within a week was 70 percent, with 21 percent (210 people) predicted to die in one to four weeks[129] and 7 percent (70 people) in one to six weeks.[130]

In 1995, the number of patients euthanized without a specific request dropped to 900.[131] I found no data indicating whether any of these patients were competent or what their projected life expectancy was.

Another category of data in these reports covers the use of pain medication administered with *the specific intent* or *partial intent* to cause death.[132] On its surface, this would also seem to constitute some form of euthanasia as opposed to PDE. In 1990, physicians employed painkillers to intentionally kill 1,350 patients, 450 without a request.[133] In that same year, physicians administered painkillers when it was "partially" their intent to kill the patient, resulting in 6,750 patients killed, 5,050 without a specific request. The numbers in 1995 were (approximately) 2,000 as the result of the physician's specific intention, 1,600 of those without a specific request and 2,850 the result of partial intent (there are no data on the percentage of specific requests in this category).[134]

What does this mean? The partial intent data are not very compelling to me. This seems like an exploration of the physician's psych rather than a clear indication of what he or she was really doing. The complexity of human motivations is such that the responses may reflect no more, for example, than "He was in such agony that I guess deep down, somewhere in my soul, I was hoping he would die, hoping this was the end." I just don't know.

The explicit intent to kill is far more troubling. Yet even there ambiguities exist. The physicians were not asked if the dosage of pain medication they administered was any more than what was necessary for pain control. If it was no more than the dose needed for pain control, their intent may have been no more than an honest expression of hope within an otherwise legitimate regime of PDE. One has to wonder: do most cases in America involving PDE, DNR (do not resuscitate) codes, and such really reflect an intent to kill and the Dutch are simply more honest about it? Again I do not know. It may be important to note, however, that the Dutch consider PDE, pulling the plug, and so on to be forms of "involuntary euthanasia."[135]

For those attempting to use any of these Dutch data to carry the burden of establishing the slippery slope (as opposed to giving some support to the position), a simple fact stands in the way: There are no pre-1990 data on the practices of the Dutch medical profession with regard to VAE.[136] So one has no hilltop from which to judge whether there has been a slide or if matters have even improved.[137] The Dutch experience does confirm what one would expect in the implementation of any policy permitting VAE: there will be a tendency to broaden the meaning of the term *suffering,*[138] some physicians will intentionally violate the guidelines and/or hold onto unreasonable interpretations,[139] and sometimes euthanasia will be practiced without a request. That is not sufficient to carry the burden of the slippery slope as the basis for an absolute moral prohibition of assisted suicide.

Yet the Dutch experience hardly provides one with a basis for contending that the slippery slope argument is all unrealistic speculation. Doctors killed 1,000 people without their consent, a quarter of which were competent or partially competent. It is also difficult to ignore a survey of senior citizens in the Netherlands in which 66 percent of those living independently and 95 percent of those living in nursing homes said they opposed the legalization of euthanasia. Similarly, in a survey of senior citizens on general health care issues (in which euthanasia was not mentioned in any form), 10 percent expressed the fear that they would be killed against their will.[140] Seeing as they live there, maybe these Dutch senior citizens know something.

THE UNITED STATES AND THE NETHERLANDS: A CULTURAL DIVIDE

In assessing the Dutch experience with VAE for purposes of making decisions about the implications (if any) of that experience for America, we have to recognize differences in our respective cultures that are relevant to the likely impact of legalizing VAE. Initially, there are differences that might lead one to think that any problems in the Netherlands will be magnified in the United States.[141] The Dutch have family doctors who they know and who know them.[142] Few Americans have any such relationship with a physician.[143] Many of us have no doctor, relying on the emergency rooms of county hospitals in times of medical necessity. Others, like me, have a new "primary care" physician every few years whose principle role seems to be to serve as a procedural prerequisite under my insurance policy for referrals to specialists. The Dutch doctor, thus, may be in a far better position to assess a suicide request since he or she will have a much fuller appreciation of the patient's history, personality, family, and social network.

All Dutch citizens have free and full medical coverage.[144] Forty-two million Americans have no form of health insurance.[145] Financial costs, therefore, will not play a part in the decision of a Dutch patient regarding treatment options. For Americans, the specter of using up life savings and family resources (sometimes encompassed by the concern characterized as "being a burden") can influence such choices given that VAE ensures that no more money will be expended.

The Dutch are basically nonviolent and tolerant.[146] They do not carry handguns or have a death penalty. Killing as a response to a problem is not in their consciousness, nor is racism. In America, well . . .

There are some forces in the two cultures, however, that push in the opposite direction. The Dutch trust their doctors.[147] We are far more wary and can be very proactive in questioning a physician when a loved one is under his or her care. The Dutch unwillingness to cause conflict and fragmentation by means of criticism, which underlies the notion of pragmatic tolerance, also leads them to try to ignore or make excuses for doctors who violate the euthanasia guidelines.[148] Americans do not have this fear of division and dissent; in fact, we encourage it in our culture and Constitution. As such, we would not be shy about criticizing a professional who had plainly stepped over the line.

OREGON

In 1994, the citizens of Oregon passed the Death with Dignity Act by a margin of 51[149] to 49 percent.[150] The act legalized physician-assisted suicide but prohibited voluntary euthanasia. Implementation was delayed by a federal court injunction until 1997 when the injunction was lifted by the Federal Court of Appeals for the Ninth Circuit.[151] In November 1997, voters rejected a proposal to repeal the Act by a margin of 60 to 40 percent,[152] although this may have been a mandate reflecting sensitivity to their state's rights as much as PAS.[153]

The Terms of the Act

The act is described in a 2001 Oregon Health Department (OHD) report as follows.

> The Death with Dignity Act allows terminally-ill Oregon residents to obtain and use prescriptions from their physicians for self-administered, lethal medications. Under the Act, ending one's life in accordance with the law does not constitute suicide. However, we use the term "physician-assisted suicide" because it is used in the medical literature to describe ending life through the voluntary self-administration of lethal medications prescribed by a physician for that purpose. The Death with Dignity Act legalizes PAS, but specifically prohibits euthanasia, where a physician or other person directly administers a medication to end another's life.
>
> To request a prescription for lethal medications, the Death with Dignity Act requires that a patient must be:

- an adult (18 years of age or older)
- a resident of Oregon
- capable (defined as able to make and communicate health care decisions)
- diagnosed with a terminal illness that will lead to death within 6 months

Patients meeting these requirements are eligible to request a prescription for lethal medication from a licensed Oregon physician. To receive a prescription for lethal medications, the following steps must be fulfilled.

- The patient must make two oral requests to his or her physician separated by at least 15 days.
- The patient must provide a written, witnessed request to his or her physician (two witnesses).
- The prescribing physician and a consulting physician must confirm the diagnosis and prognosis.
- The prescribing physician and a consulting physician must determine whether the patient is capable.
- If either physician believes the patient's judgment is impaired by a psychiatric or psychological disorder, the patient must be referred for a psychological examination.
- The prescribing physician must inform the patient of feasible alternatives to assisted suicide, including comfort care, hospice care, and pain control.
- The prescribing physician must request, but may not require, the patient to notify his or her next of kin of the prescription request.

Implementation of the Act

The implementation of the act is very recent, with the primary data on it coming from the 1999, 2000, and 2001 reports of the OHD, which assessed the practice of PAS in Oregon from 1998 to 2000, respectively.[154] (Subsequent yearly reports have been consistent with these initial reports in all relevant respects.) Reviewing the reports, one is left with the impression that, unlike in the Netherlands, there is no real problem in Oregon.

The number of instances of PAS, while rising, are still relatively small:

23 requests for lethal pills granted in 1998 with 15 acts of suicide as a result, 33 requests granted in 1999 with 26 suicides as a result, and 39 requests granted in 2000 with 26 suicides as a result.[155] The 2002 statistics reveal 38 suicides,[156] a number that has basically remained stable to date.[157] Throughout the operation of the act to date, most of the patients who requested suicide were suffering from cancer or ALS (amyotrophic lateral sclerosis, commonly known as Lou Gehrig's disease);[158] they had a median age of 69 in 1998 and 71 in 2000.[159] Physicians in Oregon, moreover, do not appear to be indiscriminately dispensing lethal medication, granting only one in six requests, out of which one in 10 patients actually took the pills.[160]

Concerns that good palliative care will not develop if PAS is an option, and, in fact, will lead to the vicious cycle created by poor palliative care coupled with PAS, also appear to be overstated.[161] Seventy to 80 percent of patients choosing PAS were already in a hospice,[162] the epitome of palliative care. Moreover, Oregon physicians appear to be eager to learn about palliative care,[163] with the result that palliative care in Oregon has improved since passage of the act.[164] In fact, doctors commonly respond to requests for PAS by referring the patient for palliative care.[165] Recently, nurses from the Oregon Hospice Association, an organization that strongly opposed the act, stated that they were relieved that their fears about PAS had not been realized.[166] The patients these hospice nurses saw who chose PAS (and these nurses attended to 70 to 80 percent of this group) did not do so because of finances, depression, or lack of social support.

In addition, the patients requesting PAS were not poor, uneducated, or vulnerable. They were 12 times more likely to have a college or graduate degree than to have failed to finish high school. They generally were white, middle class, and increasingly married.[167] They were not in physical agony. Their decision to seek PAS was instead a product of multiple factors: loss of autonomy, inability to control bodily functions, inability to participate in pursuits from which they had once gained enjoyment, and the desire not to be a burden on others.[168]

Critics of PAS in Oregon counsel caution and skepticism.

The Perspective of Critics of the Act

Critics raise a number of thoughtful points that draw into question the capacity of the act to provide clear boundaries that will protect patients over time. Does the standard "terminal" mean that the patient will die within six months even with treatment?[169] If not, serious diabetics would qualify since six months without insulin would lead to their demise. Also predicting the life expectancy of a terminal patient is far from an exact science. Fifty percent of doctors in Oregon indicated that they were incapable of accurately predicting whether a particular patient with an illness such as cancer, AIDS, or ALS would or would not die within six months.[170]

Of equal concern is what the act does *not* require. Unlike the Netherlands, patients in Oregon do not need to be "suffering."[171] Further, even if they are suffering, and that suffering is at the root of their requests for death, while the physician must consider and inform the patient of "feasible alternatives" to ameliorate the suffering, he or she is not required to have any knowledge of or training in pain control and palliative care.[172] So what protection for the patient does this requirement *meaningfully* add? It becomes no more than a perfunctory step along a mechanical checklist of statutory requirements for conducting PAS without risk of liability to the physician.

The same can be said of the requirements of consultation[173] and referral to a mental health professional if either the physician or consulting physician "believes the patient's judgment is impaired by a psychiatric or psychological disorder."[174] Not only does the consultant not need to be "independent" (i.e., not a colleague, member of the Hemlock Society, etc.),[175] but neither of the doctors need have any expertise or training in palliative care, psychiatry, or psychology.[176] So how can the consultant serve as a check on the crucial determination of the physician that there is no "feasible" alternative other than death?

And how can either physician determine if the patient should be referred to a mental health professional? Even trained psychiatrists have difficulty assessing a patient's competence. In fact, only 6 percent of Oregon psychiatrists surveyed felt that they could reliably determine in a single session a particular patient's competence to choose PAS,[177] while 57 percent doubted that they could make the assessment at all.[178] This leads to two additional problematic possibilities under the act. If experts have difficulty determining in a short amount of time whether a patient's "judgment is impaired" by mental problems, one might question how general physicians can effectively determine when to refer a patient to a psychiatrist or psychologist. Granted, having the ability to sense that there *may* be a problem so as to justify a referral is different than having to determine that in fact there is one. Yet even the first judgment would seem to require some amount of training and a degree of expertise. Assuming that such a referral takes place, even the mental health expert will have difficulty assessing competence in what will almost assuredly be a single appointment.

Further concern as to overall safeguards under the act regarding this central issue of patient competence comes from data, which show that, although national studies indicate that two-thirds of patients requesting PAS are depressed,[179] referrals from physicians to psychiatrists and psychologists under the act *dropped* from 31 percent in 1998 to 19 percent in 2000.[180] We are, of course, dealing with very small numbers, so this may have little statistical significance. But it does lead one to pause before giving the act unqualified praise. Additionally, critics have provided a few anecdotal reports of cases of PAS in which the physician's conduct seemed questionable under the terms of the act. Proponents, on the other hand, cite other anecdotal reports that show how well the act functions, as well as the tragedy of individuals and their families who, having no access to PAS, were forced to kill themselves by some violent means.

Problems with the OHD Reports

Critics allege that, far from acting as a watchdog, the OHD has become an advocate and apologist for PAS in Oregon. In fact, they contend there is pressure throughout the entire Oregon medical community not to question the efficacy of the act or speak out about troubling individual cases.

As for data collection, the physician merely fills out a short form, which is basically in a check-the-boxes format. Only a line or two is left to discuss the basis of the diagnosis, the patient's reasons for desiring PAS, the grounds for determining patient competency, and such. While the OHD then conducts a telephone interview with each physician, in which these and other topics can be explored in more depth, the results of those conversations, as well as the forms themselves, are maintained as confidential by the OHD. Thus, there can be no real study of the data or the process. Also the OHD has no idea as to the number of physicians who did not send in a report (although this is likely to be a relatively small number, if any, given that nothing will happen to physicians if they turn in the form while they risk attracting the attention of the police and prosecutors if they fail to report).

The OHD report, moreover, is based almost entirely on the postevent reports of the interested physicians. The OHD never seeks information from patients prior to PAS (by having them fill out a questionnaire or filling one out for them), never talks to hospice nurses or social workers, never contacts the doctors who refused to grant the patient's request for PAS in order to find out why, and obtains information from families only on limited topics (e.g., in gathering information for one of the annual reports, interviewers were instructed that the family was not to be asked about the patient's symptoms).[181]

Some other data are worth considering. Forty percent of the patients were rejected by at least one doctor before finding a physician who would provide PAS.[182] This may have been a function of the first physician's religious beliefs, a consequence of the fact that the patient was not yet "terminal," or perhaps due to the fact that the physician thought there were less drastic options that the patient had not yet tried (and subsequently tried without success). It may speak to the persistence and determination of these patients, evidence that this was truly their committed choice, and of the stability of their choice over time. On the other hand, it may mean that the standards are hopelessly subjective and subject to manipulation. In this case, one only has to "shop around" for a pro-PAS doctor, who will be able to justify the decision as long as the patient has a life-threatening disease.

The data included in the three OHD reports concerning patients' motives for desiring PAS indicate that concern that the patient would become a "burden to others" influenced 12 percent of all decisions in 1998, 26 percent in 1999, and 63 percent in 2000.[183] What does this mean? Again we are dealing with very small numbers. Also becoming a burden is stated as only one among multiple factors. There is no ranking of its importance in the mix. Taking all this with a further grain of salt is merited since these are not the direct reports of patients but rather the physicians' impressions or recollections after the fact. For all we know, most patients never said this but the doctors "heard" it because of their own projections into the patient's situation. "Becoming a burden" also could have just been another expression of patients' increasing dependence on others. Nevertheless, there is a concern. As we've discussed, some have feared that the "right to die" will quickly be transformed into a "duty to die." Is that what is happening here?

Standing back and looking at Oregon's brief experience with PAS, one must be candid that, at least at this point, it does not conjure the specter of the Netherlands. There is no evidence, and no one has even hinted, that a single competent (or incompetent) person has been killed without his or her request. The Oregon experience gives no real support to those attempting to carry the burden that the risk of the slippery slope justifies an absolute moral ban on PAS.

The experiment, though now with eight years of experience, still carries too many areas of concern about both the act and the data compilation practices of OHD, however, to be able to cite the Oregon act and experience as absolute *proof* that there is no significant risk in legalizing PAS. On the other hand, the number of assisted suicides has remained relatively small and stable over the past few years, and a number of credible observers have concluded that the Oregon data of the past eight years demonstrate that the act has not had the negative impact on end of life care that those opposed to it predicted.[184]

BACK TO BURDENS AND SAFEGUARDS

The Proponent's Burden

While I believe the opponents of assisted suicide make a troubling claim in their slippery slope argument and provide both human behavioral reasoning and empirical support, again I question whether it is sufficient to carry their initial burden for establishing an absolute utilitarian moral rule. Yet it is a serious enough claim that, if only out of respect for its proponents (who I recognize are not acting out of self-interest but trying to protect us all), it merits a response from those supporting PAS either as to why in a particular case the risk will not come to fruition or to the effect that they can provide safeguards to avoid the risk. In the first part of this section, I will expand on a concept I've developed, which I call "resilient lines," to explain why I believe the feared risk will not come to fruition. The second part is far more traditional, focusing on safeguards. These safeguards would come in a three-part package: consciousness, watchdogs, and guidelines and standards. In assessing these safeguards, it is appropriate to look not just at the individual parts but at the entire three-part package as providing the safeguard.

Resilient Lines

As I stand back and look at the assisted suicide debate as it will likely unfold in the future, I see what will ultimately be a struggle over lines. Virtually every moral theory I encountered valued life. They also accepted suicide and intentional killing under some circumstances. All allowed self-defense, employing deadly force to repel an unprovoked, lethal assault; all condemned murder. All would condone a soldier who swallows a death capsule rather than reveal under torture the site of a planned counterattack against an evil enemy; all would disapprove of helping a clinically depressed teenager end his or her life. The real question becomes where each theory draws the line.[185]

In the area of suicide, assisted suicide, and euthanasia, the lines have been moving. Doctors at one time were not permitted to pull the plug.[186] Later they were permitted to terminate "futile" medical treatment. From futile, the line moved to "excessive" or "extraordinary." Then artificial feeding and hydration were added to those practices defined as "medical treatment."[187] Again the line moved. Concurrently, the right of patients to refuse even lifesaving treatment was clarified and publicized. Now it appears that someone could refuse treatment even if death were a certain result. The patient could even incorporate these desires into living wills and give third parties the authority to substitute their judgment in these matters when the patient is no longer capable of doing so. My interest at this point is not whether any of these particular lines make sense or not.[188] It is whether they can hold, whether they are what I term *resilient lines.*

I envision a resilient line as a large barrier made of elastic material. People can push against it and move it a bit, but basically it holds. While in some historical sense all lines are temporary, there are boundaries that seem to hold for a particular society over a substantial period of time. Most people respect and maintain the line, though there will always be a minority that will challenge the line, defying the boundary by pushing against it. Yet the line will not move. There will be an occasional bulge here and there. It nevertheless will maintain its stability overall.

In thinking about this phenomenon, I find that resilient lines are those that meet four conditions. As these conditions are eliminated, or even weakened, the line can no longer hold its position and must move. The conditions are as follows.

1. Acceptable authority. The line must be the product of some socially acceptable authority—school, church, courts, traditions, and such.

2. No empirical slide. As factual reality begins to conflict with assumptions underlying maintenance of the line, the line weakens (e.g., DNA evidence that innocent people have been sentenced to death weakens

the notion that the line between those who do and those who do not merit capital punishment is a coherent one).

3. Narrative coherence. The underlying "story" maintaining and justifying the line must make "sense." (Of course, this will tend to be weakened to the extent empirical slide becomes a factor.)

4. Functional clarity. The line must be clear yet posses sufficient flexibility to be capable of absorbing complexity.

Let me take as an example the traditional moral line that existed when I was growing up in the 1950s about young women and sex. The line could have been, for example, that sex was acceptable only if you were in love, in a stable relationship, or living with someone in a committed relationship. But it was none of these. The line was you must be married. No premarital sex was permitted. The line was very clear, had strong social support, and brought general negative labeling and condemnation to any woman who did not respect it. Of course, there were those who did not. Some were feminist pioneers, some were just rebels by nature, and some were confused and disturbed. Some openly flaunted their defiance of the line and pushed against it. Others violated the line in secret, hiding their conduct from all the world but their lovers. Still the line stayed in place. What changed?

To begin with, the power of the defining authority—religious, medical, and cultural pronouncements regarding the rules and consequences of pregnancy—diminished. The sway of religion, along with all centers of authority, lost its hold as we marched through the 1960s. At the same time, there was an empirical slide as the widespread availability of the birth control pill greatly reduced the fear of unwanted pregnancy.

When all this happened, the "good girl/bad girl" narrative no longer made sense. Young, unmarried women throughout America's colleges and universities (and other locales) were having sex. These were the daughters of my parents' generation, and no one could say that they were anything but normal young women. (In fact, a counternarrative arose. A conception of feminist theory, this counternarrative told the story of men attempting to control women's natural sexuality by maintaining the good girl/bad girl narrative, which kept the good girls in check but allowed for a supply of bad girls whom men were free to exploit in satisfying their sexual desires.)

Finally, the line could not absorb the complexity of such phenomena as women choosing to be single mothers, lesbian couples having children through insemination, and such. The line moved and moved dramatically. When it came to rest, mainstream society set a line that merely insisted that sex be "safe." Unprotected sex was wrong; safe sex was generally condoned (though there certainly remain significant segments of the culture that adhere to the old "no premarital sex" line, principally on religious grounds).

Let me offer another illustration of how the concept of resilient lines describes the necessary conditions for maintaining a publicly held moral belief: witchcraft.[189] This may seem an odd example at first, but I think that beliefs about witchcraft provide fertile ground for the analysis. To be clear, I am not talking about beliefs in the existence or plausibility of witches, sorcerers, magic, and witchcraft. Rather, I wish to delve into the belief that those people identified as witches posed some ultimate threat to the very existence of society and thus appropriately were first tortured with hot pokers and sharp instruments and then thrown in pots of boiling water or burned at the stake.[190]

In fact, estimates of the number of people killed as witches in Europe by the church, state, or mobs in the fifteenth, sixteenth, and seventeenth centuries range from 500,000 to over nine million (making America's Salem witch trials a kindergarten exercise by comparison).[191]

Every society on earth has some witchcraft concept.[192] In the ancient world, witchcraft and magicians were a normal part of daily life.[193] Today witchcraft is practiced in West Africa, and voodoo is alive and well in the Caribbean and the Creole culture in New Orleans.[194] Many of us have met people who were reputed to be white witches and others we feared were of the darker variety. The occult is part of our culture. Along the roadways are signs advertising palm and tarot reading. Some people attend séances to communicate with the dead, while others contact the "psychic hotlines" advertised on television. Carlos Castaneda's apprenticeship with the Yaqui sorcerer Don Juan made for best-selling literature.[195] There is even a branch of scientific study—parapsychology—that investigates psychic and extrasensory phenomena. And yet, as inundated with the occult as we may be, we never for a moment think that our government, our religious institutions, or any group of private citizens should grab these people or their patrons, tie them to a stake, and burn them to death.

How witch-hunting and the witch craze came to be is a matter of history and historical theory. Why the belief system underlying witch-hunting lost its hold and collapsed, on the other hand, is an illustration of the concept of resilient lines in action.

Initially, as the Middle Ages receded the power of the defining authority (the church and the nobles) diminished. While religion continued to play a significant role in the day-to-day lives of the people of Europe, the church lost its position as the primary political institution guiding the state. Also many more people rejected the idea of religion itself, and with the decline in belief in a God came a corresponding decline in belief in the devil (and his allies, the witches).[196] Similarly, increasingly democratic movements in Europe throughout the eighteenth and nineteenth centuries sapped the power of the aristocracy to legitimate witch hunts, particularly when some among the ruling nobility began to pronounce the witch craze "delusional."[197]

Accompanying this dilution of the authority that legitimated the belief system underlying the witch craze was a substantial empirical slide. The arbitrary nature of the accusations,[198] as well as the inadequate evidence used to support the execution of thousands of innocents,[199] gradually led to growing opposition by the educated. As the accusations began to be directed at higher-ranked men (earlier 82 percent of the victims had been women, generally poor, and older),[200] the judges lost confidence in the confessions.[201] The herbs and potions used by peasants for healing and curing illness, which had been associated with witchcraft, started to become incorporated (as in our current culture) into mainstream medicine,[202] while alchemy gradually metamorphosed into chemistry.

Likewise, the notion that people's neighbors and their families were the cause of hunger, illness, crop failures, hailstorms, animal deaths, stillborn children, and on and on ceased making sense. Society was learning about medical diagnosis and the causes of disease and overall began taking a scientific approach to understanding natural phenomena.[203] Magical explanations, and evil ones at that, were antithetical to a mind-set in which power was in the reasoning ability of humans and their corresponding ability to dominate nature. Witchcraft, therefore, began to fall not into explanatory narratives but into narratives embedded in folk superstition[204] and stock characters in Shakespearean plays.[205]

Finally, the belief system that supported the witch craze did not possess functional clarity; it was an either-or belief with no capacity for flexibility and adaptation. One had to believe that witchcraft was responsible for the major problems in society and daily life. When this belief could no longer be sustained, witchcraft could no longer be perceived as a danger to the state. Even if there did exist a few bad people practicing witchcraft here and there, casting an evil spell or two, that could not begin to fuel a witch craze.

What, then, are the resilient lines in the suicide, assisted suicide, and euthanasia discussion? The resilience of the line separating PDE, refusing treatment, and withdrawing treatment from physician-assisted suicide first will be a function of the magnitude of any empirical slide. To the extent that social experiments, such as the one Oregon has embarked on, indicate that fears of PAS underlying the line are unfounded, or at least vastly overstated, the line will tend to move. If narratives routinely arise of elderly, suffering patients driven to violent, horrible suicides or of those who seek death failing to obtain the assistance they require under law (even though similarly suffering patients who are able to refuse treatment can end their suffering), the line will also tend to move. The question then will be whether it will move from PAS to voluntary euthanasia.

Those who propose legislation permitting PAS generally draw the line between it and voluntary euthanasia. It is a line, however, that I do not believe can hold.[206] The legislature is certainly a legitimate source of authority, but legislators are elected. Their votes can change to match the public will and pressure from lobbyists.

Courts can surely provide legitimate authority, particularly since their pronouncements ultimately are backed by the legally sanctioned use of force by the police, who enforce the law. In an area of moral controversy, such as that swirling about PAS and euthanasia, the legitimacy of any such authority will demand the type of judicial unanimity evidenced by the nine-to-nothing vote of the Supreme Court in *Brown v. Board of Education*. In contrast, five-to-four votes, such as in the court's abortion decision, may momentarily set laws but cannot set clearly accepted moral lines. For reasons I will make clear in chapter 8, where I discuss law, it is hard to imagine a unanimous Supreme Court vote holding PAS to be constitutionally protected. In fact, as I will discuss later, the Supreme Court recently held nine to nothing in the opposite direction. But, even if some future court held that PAS, though not euthanasia, was constitutionally protected, the line between assisted suicide and euthanasia would not hold.

The real assault on the PAS/voluntary euthanasia line will come from empirical slide and narrative incongruence. Helpless, suffering, elderly people on machines can find release with the pull of a plug. Suffering elderly people who can hold pills in their hands, put them in their mouths, and swallow them also can find release. Then we'll have a television special about people so sick and/or disabled that they cannot take and swallow the pills. They are not being kept alive by a machine that can be disconnected.

And they are in agony. At some point, the immediacy of such real life narratives will overshadow the hypothetical stories that voluntary euthanasia will turn into involuntary euthanasia. It simply will not make sense, and will in fact appear arbitrary, to make certain sick elderly people suffer because of their inability to swallow pills. The line will not hold.

Predicting the trajectory of the current line that we must not let people end their lives by means such as PAS unless they are informed and competent is a more complex task. Law, cultural tradition, and logic all provide authority for this line. The complexity will come from the juxtaposition of our narrative of competence from everyday life with the reality of the world of the elderly sick and dying. I predict that we will adjust our story of competence so that we will find people competent to end their lives even though we would not find them competent to sign a contract to purchase a car. In doing so, inevitably we will factor in our perceptions of the quality of their lives in the process of interpreting whether the request to die is "reasonable" and then from that assessment of reasonableness infer whether the requester is competent.

One line that I believe is resilient and will not move is the one that states that we do not intentionally participate in killing an innocent person who does not wish to be killed. There would be no involuntary euthanasia. This does not mean that no one would do it. Even the most resilient lines are violated. Yet our culture would have to change beyond recognition to publicly condone this as an accepted value.

But what about causing the death of a clearly incompetent elderly person who is just as clearly suffering (so-called nonvoluntary euthanasia)?[207] Perhaps a mitigation on punishment for homicide or a separate crime of mercy killing might be our culture's response. I do not believe, however, that we will ever find this permissible. On the other hand, I cannot say that we wouldn't finesse the issue by the sleight of hand of using some form of living will or substituted judgment permitting it. Such a living will then might become such a strong cultural expectation in the face of scarce resources that elderly people will feel compelled to concur in signing what may eventually be nothing but a routine form on the Internet. "Substituted judgment" will not add much more as a protection. It will just mean that the person given the medical power of attorney, or an ethics board or court, will assign someone to say it's alright to euthanize the person. If killing off unconscious or even incompetent elderly people becomes an accepted norm, the substitute will merely follow the norm. This would not require as drastic a cultural change as condoning involuntary euthanasia, yet it would still require a significant change in our medical narratives and accompanying empirical realities.

SAFEGUARDS

Consciousness

Things do not happen in isolation. Always there is context. Within this context, action begets reaction, revision, reformulation, and response. This is, in fact, an underlying assumption of the slippery slope argument. One action will lead to another while diminishing the likelihood of a second action and redefining the meaning of a third. There seems no reason to believe that inevitably, in the course of this process, some of the resulting actions and reactions won't run counter to the momentum of the slide. What I'm writing is an example, another pebble in the pond, a warning against the slide. The risk of the slide, therefore, is not sneaking up on people. It is the subject of a large and growing volume of literature and discussion. It raises a topic increasingly on the minds of that bulge in the population we call the baby boomers. Would-be patients and their families (for those who have that support) inevitably will bring with them an awareness of these risks.

On the other hand, this may not fully enter our public consciousness until after some story about a hospital or nursing home "death camp" comes to light and becomes the topic of television exposés and talk shows. That is in part because, while the poorest and most vulnerable may have perceived this risk all along (as demonstrated by the general disfavoring of assisted suicide by racial minorities in opinion polls), the more affluent and educated (those likely least at risk), who tend to be advocates for physician-assisted suicide, have focused much more on its benefits. Their concern, thus, has focused on nightmare visions of suffering, loss of control, and degeneration rather than on the risk that they will be killed against their will. When this last possibility becomes a reality to them, we can expect them to respond accordingly.

Watchdogs

At some point, the argument goes, watchdogs will emerge if the risk of involuntary or coerced euthanasia becomes palpable. While the business of medicine is organized, focused in its goal, and capable of applying political pressure through lobbying, so are organizations such as the American Association of Retired Persons (AARP). Additionally, investigative journalists are always looking for an appalling scandal. Killing old people is a good one. While the state may have economic interests that coincide with coercion and euthanizing of the elderly infirm in its care, I do not think it could conduct such a program for long without attracting public scrutiny. More likely, to the contrary, state agencies would be authorized to conduct special inspections,[208] demand paperwork as a condition of supposedly consensual suicides and euthanasia, and begin investigations (potentially leading to criminal charges) where appropriate.

Rules and Guidelines

Finally, any proposed program of assisted suicide is always accompanied by guidelines and standards, which purport to ensure competency, consent, and justification (e.g., terminal illness). The response by opponents, as we've seen when discussing the Netherlands and Oregon, is that these guidelines cannot provide a realistic safeguard against the slippery slope.[209]

I both agree and disagree with this stance. There will be cases of abuse, and there will be pressure at times to interpret a particular term in a broader way than before.[210] That is inevitable. Yet it does not lead one to conclude that permitting assisted suicide inevitably leads to the slippery slope, unless by that you mean that we've hit bottom if even one person is wrongfully killed. But if that's the case you have to measure the harm that results from this one wrongful death against the harm that results from keeping another person alive and suffering. I don't know how you can do that.

To say that because rules, standards, and guidelines can be abused, pushed at the edges to interpretations beyond the intent of the original drafters, is a long way from labeling them as worthless. Far from it. People who decide to deal with rules by intentionally deviating or relying on some expanded interpretation on the margins generally know that they are doing so at their own peril. The centerpiece of all assisted suicide guidelines is that the choice must be a voluntary one (with full information) made by a competent person. While I'll discuss the difficulties with both coercion and the cognitive capacity of very sick people in chapter 6, such a guideline makes one line abundantly clear: you don't kill people who haven't asked to be killed.[211] And that is the precise line that divides voluntary from involuntary euthanasia and an American hospital or nursing home from a Nazi death camp.

Certainly there will be foreseeable issues in policing and enforcement, including the risk that if there is overregulation and too much autocracy any PAS regime will fail.[212] Further, policing requires government intrusion into the physician-patient relationship, giving assisted suicide a public aspect. Assisting suicide, however, is a very private, intimate matter. Somehow a balance must be created between public and private.[213] Also, within a closed institution such as a hospital or nursing home, unless there's a whistle-blower (and, as in any field, we can expect the medical profession to protect its own within reason), deaths of those who were dying anyway are hardly likely to lead to inquests in which the cause of death on the certificate is questioned. On the other hand, doctors who euthanize patients and then write, for example, "cardiac failure" on the death certificate take real risks with their careers. Why would they do that (except in the rarest of circumstances)? They can already kill most dying patients in their care by means of legally approved methods: withdrawal of treatment, DNR codes, failure to treat flu or pneumonia, and double effect.

In short, all of the concerns underlying the slippery slope, though certainly considerations in the halls of policy-making, again cannot for me support an absolute *moral* prohibition. In fact, no concept or theory ultimately justifies morally labeling assisted suicide as wrong under all circumstances.

My beliefs had changed. But for me the journey was far from over. Throughout my inquiry into moral theories holding assisted suicide to be always wrong under all circumstances, I came across claims in the opposite direction, that is, that one has a right to assisted suicide. It was to those claims that my path then turned.

ISSUE 5

Assisted suicide is/is not morally
supported by the principle of "autonomy"

My Path Turns: Looking at Autonomy and Moral Claims to the Right to Assisted Suicide

The concept of autonomy provides the principal moral foundation for the current assisted suicide movement,[1] although, interestingly, some opposed to assisted suicide have attempted to hijack the concept for their own uses.[2] This concept of autonomy has many faces in both literature and everyday discussions. For some, autonomy takes the form of the inherent right to define oneself through one's own choices. Others characterize it as controlling one's own narrative (i.e., creating the story of who one is). Still others have characterized autonomy as one's right to make significant choices since only in that way does one's life truly become one's own[3].

However garbed and ornamented, at the core of each of these variations of the autonomy theme remains the same notion: It is my life, I have ownership of that life, and the freedom to make choices about who I am is what it means for me to have a full human life. Children say, "You can't tell me what to do." The answer to this predictable exercise in self-definition and limit testing is, "Yes I can because I'm your parent" (i.e., "You aren't completely your own person; I have legitimate and likely physical authority over you"). An adult says, "Whose life is this if not mine over which to make choices that do not directly injure others?" That is autonomy honed to its basics.

Of course, no theory of autonomy supports the notion that I can make any choice I wish (e.g., ritual human sacrifice). Those espousing the primary importance of autonomy have always made it clear that I may not do things that hurt others (in the Ten Commandments sense) or violate explicit, enforceable obligations. The religious arguments just add to this limitation. In addition, I must not choose to do things that hurt or offend God. Nevertheless, even persons in this culture who ascribe to these religious arguments believe that they are entitled to make a wide range of choices as to how they will live their lives.[4]

Yet, though I value my own ability to make choices about how I will live my life, I simply cannot conclude that the concept of autonomy provides the moral power to carry the field for those who use it as a blanket endorsement of assisted suicide. My reservations about wholehearted reliance on autonomy follow.

THE LIMITATIONS OF THE PRINCIPLE OF AUTONOMY AS A MORAL BASIS FOR ASSISTED SUICIDE

In my reading, I found that people use *autonomy* like a magic talisman. You just say the word, and that puts an end to all argument. When used this way, autonomy feels like the invocation of some secular "religion." It has to be accepted on faith and is not open to debate. But it was not clear to me that autonomy, standing alone, was even a *moral* principle. What is the basis for saying that my ability to freely choose who I will be has some kind of moral imprimatur? Admittedly, the idea of perfecting myself, making my life my own, surely resonates well with me. But just saying that doesn't get me to the point where my choices, solely by virtue of being mine, have moral validity. I think I should be able to choose who I will be, what I'll wear, where I'll work, who I'll wed, where I'll live, and on and on. I shudder to imagine what it would be like to live in a society in which I did not have this freedom, in which my role was to be an interchangeable cog in the machinery of the state. But I'm an American. I was raised to think that the denial of my autonomy, in the sense that I cannot choose my own path, is "bad." Countries like that are "evil." But are they, or am I just an inevitable product of my culture?

Maoist China was repressive in our terms, but the system provided food, education, and health care for hundreds of millions of people who had previously lacked them. Of course, you may respond by asking, "At what price?" That's a good question, but your notion of price incorporates and reinserts all *our* values back into the equation. From where we stand, it might not have been worth it. On the other hand, we weren't among half a billion starving Chinese.

You might respond that there must be something in our "nature" as humans that makes autonomy so valued that we will die for the freedom to choose, to speak freely, to vote. When, after all, was the last popular uprising (as opposed to military coup) in a liberal, Western-style democracy complete with a free market? I certainly agree with all that, but, again, I'm an American. Of course, I agree; it's hard to get beyond my lifelong cognitive framework. Yet everything we're now facing in confronting Islamic fundamentalism (i.e., those who wish to return to strict Koranic beliefs and laws) says that there are those who find this notion of unrestricted autonomy anything but a moral principle. Rather, autonomy in the fundamentalist framework would seem to be a handmaiden to immoral behavior. I've thought about this, and I just don't know.

SOCIAL INTERRELATION AND AUTONOMY

I have a problem with the current moral emphasis on the autonomous person because I believe it inaccurately portrays the nature of existence as a human being. It is true that I carry a confirmed sense that I am a unique, separate individual. I walk along "creating" the world around me. There I sally forth, my cartoon bubble over my head encapsulating my thoughts. Beside me walk crowds of others who, like me, are experiencing the same existence: fully autonomous beings with their own cartoon bubbles floating overhead, masters of their own private universes. Each of these others, like me, has a complete world. It is a world composed of things that are passions for the others that never even cross my mind (needlepoint, fly-fishing, restoring antique cars, curling, collecting fountain pens, and so on) and intimates I've never even heard of let alone met. Everyone's close friends likely have close friends whom you do not know. It's funny how we are shocked to find that people we know well are complete strangers to others we know well. It is as if our sense of our individual existence is so strong, the pictures we have of the components of our lives so powerful, that we believe we can bind together in reality what exists only in the perceptions, clutter, and chatter that fill our cartoon bubble.

Yet, in the most basic, simple sense, we are all connected to others.[5] I drink a soda from a glass. That glass was made by others, is filled with liquid from a product conceived and manufactured by others, was purchased in a store in which the can was stacked and sold to me by others, and from which I now drink employing conceptions of how to use a glass that I learned from my parents and others. If I were a hermit who had consciously fled to the wilds to avoid the company of fellow humans, I would have gone there, nevertheless, with clothes and tools made by others or made by me with knowledge passed down from others.[6] In fact, the whole notion of being a hermit depends on the existence of those from whom you separate yourself. Even in the mythical "state of nature," man was never alone but lived in small family groupings or tribes.

THE BRAIN AND AUTONOMY

Most significantly, it is not just that we are socially and culturally connected to others. We are *cognitively* connected to them as well. My mind was necessarily formed in interaction with the human culture, whether with individuals, groups, media, music, art, literature, cultural artifacts, newspapers, or schools. The combination of all this information and these experiences is the grist from which I built the cognitive structures I use to facilitate understanding and give meaning to my interactions with the world.[7]

Contrary to prior beliefs that thought processes function in direct stimulus-response chains (i.e., you see a chair in the external world and think "chair" in your brain), current theories and research posit that thinking is both active and creative. So, if I'm walking through an art museum and come across an exhibit in which the artist has created fantastic but supposedly functional furniture, I will look at the pieces and compare them to my concept of a chair, a table, and such. Then, when I look at this elaborate, abstract, swanlike construction that matches my cognitive construct (which contemporary theorists term a schema) for a chair, I immediately "see" the possibility of moving it about, know that if I sat in it it would support me, and perhaps even imagine how funny it would look in my living room. If, in fact, it would not support an average person, I was mistaken. I chose the wrong schema. The object should have been interpreted by my schema of an artistic sculpture and not of a chair.

We have schemas, ranging from simple "patterns" to complex models, that cover the endless aspects of life—car (driver), car (passenger), car (fill-up at the gas station), car (taking it to the car wash), car (buying), car (selling), and on and on. And, again, these schemas are created from our interactions in society (what we're told, our culture, experiences, stories, myths, and so on). Therefore, our brains are really an accumulation of mental constructs of the external world through which we filter and interpret the data of day-to-day experience. Our "autonomous selves" are necessarily creations of a history with a community, a history that began long before we existed.

THE NOTION OF MAINTAINING A LIFE STORY

Some have found a moral foundation for suicide at the end of life (when the person is facing total physical degeneration and dependence) based on the notion of maintaining the coherence and integrity of a person's "life story."[8] The dying person has always been strong, in control, relied on by others. This failing person is not the character he or she has been or wants to be in the last act. So assisted suicide is an appropriate way to avoid an end that would violate the character and integrity of this person's life story.

Yet, as was the case with the general notion of autonomy, I find the notion of maintaining a coherent life story to be something of an illusion. What I perceive as "my" story is totally constructed in my mind, in which I impose a plausible interpretive theory over what really is a series of often fragmented pieces. It is a story determined by interpretive choices, which themselves are a function of my culturally constructed schemas. Am I a success or a failure? Look at Jimmy Stewart in that ultimate holiday classic *It's a Wonderful Life*. The answer depends on how I choose to tell the story, which pieces I leave in, which I take out; what I choose to emphasize and deemphasize, and what theory of success or failure I rely on to make these artistic decisions. In a movie role, you might have a coherent story because there's a script, editing, and 90 minutes to take you from early youth to heroic death. In real life, there is no single story; it's all selection, spin, and construction.

The story of who I am, moreover, can completely change at different times and stages of my life. Some stages can be under my control, a product of conscious choice involving clothing, hairstyle, and pastimes to match. Other plot changes are not within my control. The nation goes to war, I win the lottery, or I'm diagnosed with pancreatic cancer.

Let me refocus on the idea of tying the moral entitlement to assisted suicide to maintaining the integrity and coherence of one's life story. Those espousing this notion must not be referring to how people *really* are but to how they want to have others see them and how they wish ultimately to perceive themselves. Even if control is central to how they identify themselves, the point is that much of life is beyond their control. My father no doubt wanted us to remember him as capable and in control, not helpless, confused, and in agony (although, admittedly, he may not have cared what anyone thought, only what he thought of himself or maybe just getting the pain under control). But no matter what he wanted or did not want, he had no power to control how we would see his story. For, like all humans, we interpreted his life through our own constructed cognitions (schemas). I do remember him dying and confused. I do remember him not having the strength to walk a few feet to the bathroom by himself. I do remember what his breathing sounded like when he was dying and what he looked like moments after his death. I also remember him at dozens and dozens of other moments throughout my life, some fondly, some not. He was a very good man, who, like us all, was flawed. I think of him as a man who tried to do his best; who was sweet with a bad temper; and who, when all was said and done, was so very brave. At the end, he became my hero.

Maintaining your fictional persona, holding on to the created story of who you are, even if you have to kill yourself to do it, is something with which I can empathize, but what's the point? You're going to be dead. You don't get to sit and watch the movie portraying you in your lifetime role. Perhaps you want to be remembered as the person you perceive you are. But this is illusion upon illusion. It is illusion to think that anything as complex and chaotic as a human life can have a single, coherent story. It is further illusion to think that, even if you've achieved the creation of such a story, those left behind will perceive the same one. What, after all, did Melville intend when he chose to color the great whale white?

Maybe I'm being too inflexible. We all try to create life stories, and they seem important to us, even if, at their base, they are illusion. Perhaps, then, rather than dismissing the notion of such stories out of hand, we should cling to our storytelling but recognize the need to develop more flexible self-tales, tales that can adapt to the inevitable cycle of life in which (like flowers) most of us will progressively degenerate until we die.[9]

ISSUE 6

Individuals can/cannot be mentally competent and/or rational if they choose suicide (and a fortiori assisted suicide or euthanasia) as the best choice for themselves

Act Utilitarianism as a Moral Basis
for Justifying Assisted Suicide

Although I did not find that autonomy alone could serve as a moral basis for the decision to commit suicide, that was not the end of it. For as I read more deeply I came to realize that autonomy could be understood as something other than a freestanding moral system based on the unchallenged value of humans defining themselves by means of their choices. In this new understanding, autonomy is a conception that is necessary to the broader philosophy of utilitarianism. As I explained, the philosophy of utilitarianism requires that the moral actor make constant choices among alternative actions (or inactions). Autonomy provides the individual with the "space" in which to make these choices. Thus, one does not exercise autonomy for its own sake within this utilitarian framework. Just as the purpose of using a saw, computer, or blender is not to validate the importance of saws, computers or blenders, autonomy's significance within the world of utilitarianism is as a means, a tool, to achieve a task.

I've already discussed—and rejected—utilitarianism as a moral basis for condemning suicide and assisted suicide. But this portion of my journey was going in the opposite direction, and that led me back to utilitarianism, this time to act utilitarianism.

It seems plain that, under act utilitarianism, a particular suicide under particular circumstances could be found to be a right action. My father was such an example. He was suffering, in severe physical pain that could only marginally be controlled, and was losing his mental and physical capacities. He had done all he could to ensure that my mother would be taken care of when he was gone, and our whole family prayed that it would end for him. Put all that in the act utilitarian calculus, and the balance of consequences is clear: suicide is good.

This is not surprising. Utilitarianism can serve as a strong philosophical support for the prosuicide (assisted suicide) movement. Yet one can quickly grasp the irony. Utilitarian philosophy, with its focus on actual consequences in the world and the necessity that the individual be given the accompanying space to choose among alternative actions (or inactions) in the face of these perceived consequences, can also lead to the conclusion that a particular suicide is wrong. No other religious or nonreligious philosophy I studied convinced me that suicide, in whatever form, is always immoral. Act utilitarianism, in contrast, is not bound to such all-encompassing absolutes. As such, it is capable of labeling some suicides as bad.[1]

Imagine that a certain surgeon has perfected a lifesaving operation that only he can perform successfully. His wife leaves him, and with conscious thoughts of punishing her and "all those who've never appreciated me" he plans to commit suicide. If he carries out his plan, 100 people who would otherwise have lived productive, happy lives as the result of his remarkable surgical procedure will die. Put in the utilitarian calculus, the outcome is just as clear: suicide is bad.

When dealing with the very sick, and particularly the terminally ill, like my father, there is, however, a serious problem in applying a utilitarian system driven by autonomy. The entire system presupposes that two conditions exist as to the choosers: (1) they have full information,[2] so, for example, I can stop an uninformed person from jumping off a bridge;[3] and (2) they are competent.[4] Here act utilitarianism looks beyond the particular action to the integrity of its entire ethical system. Somebody totally misinformed and completely delusional could nevertheless make a choice that in balance results in a maximum good. Over time, the odds of this repeating itself on a routine basis, however, are probably not that great. Utilitarianism depends on people using their self-knowledge, reason, and access to rules of thumb (i.e., the cultural lessons about the predictable consequences of certain types of actions) to make the best choices. Adequate information and mental competence are, thus, necessary preconditions for the human decisions that will drive the utilitarian system.

The first precondition seems to me to be the lesser of the problems, at least from a moral perspective. None of us is likely to have full and accurate information about much. The type and magnitude of information we're talking about here, however, are not like that regarding the conflict in the Middle East. Answers to such questions as "Is the diagnosis accurate and can this pain be brought under control?" would appear to suffice.

The precondition of mental competence, on the other hand, raises very difficult issues, particularly when you're talking about suicide and the terminally ill.[5] One school of thought holds that no one who seriously attempts suicide is mentally competent. By definition, if you try to take your life you have a severe mental problem.[6] And, in truth, most people who attempt suicide do have some associated mental problem. But we're not talking about some heartbroken teenager or misfit 30-something. My concern is with the elderly, terminally ill person like my father. The question, then, is whether the idea of a rational suicide is a logical impossibility. Those adhering to the position that an attempt at suicide is a clear indication of mental illness would say yes. I disagree.

However, even if suicide is associated with mental problems,[7] that does not lead to the conclusion that the individual is incompetent. A significant percentage of people in the American workplace suffer from clinical depression, a variety of character disorders, and even (medicated) psychosis. Many of these people function successfully in high-level jobs. They may lead troubled or even tormented lives, but no one would say that they were not mentally competent. No doubt there are those who commit suicide who, at the time of their final act, we would consider incompetent. But the mere existence of a mental disease, by itself, does not lead to this conclusion. Depression is not the same as incompetence.[8] And, in fact, empirical research has not found a clear correlation between depression and decision-making competence.[9]

Nevertheless, I think this is the toughest question I faced in thinking about suicide and the terminally ill. Did you ever have the flu—the four- or five-day, sick as a dog flu? Lying in bed, aching, half sleeping and half waking, drifting in and out of dreams, too weak to move, snatches of conversations and faces of caretakers briefly moving through your consciousness and then forgotten, and always a pervasive sense of being miserable. For the worst of those four or five days, you did not live in the same world as other people. The sick do not. And that's the flu.

Now imagine dying from pancreatic cancer. You've taken all kinds of extremely strong medications, at extremely high doses, many of them painkilling narcotics. As your blood chemistry begins to get out of balance, you tend to become confused. At times, you experience such excruciating, wracking pain that there is no longer a you. The self is obliterated; there is only pain.[10] When the pain is under control again, you feel relief, but at the same time you are apprehending that it will return. You become depressed, as life is just lingering, waiting, with time marked by the space between times of crisis when you have to be rushed to the hospital. You are also exhausted. Everything is so difficult, so unpleasant, and there is no hope. So you suffer in this misery. And even if you fully comprehend the treatment choices and options, all of this can lead to "affective" mood disorders, which skew how you weigh and value these options.[11]

So how could my father move from his world (with its logic of pain, suffering, routine, endurance, and just maintaining)[12] and cross the bridge into ours—a world demanding detached reason and review of options, a world demanding its notion of competent decision making?

Near the end, as his organs began to fail and his blood chemistry went awry, Dad was very, very confused. When he asked me and my sister to kill him, however, it was weeks earlier, and he was totally calm and rational. At the moment, his pain was under control, though he was generally uncomfortable and very worried about what would happen to Mom. He was probably also very depressed. Why shouldn't he have been? His life had been great, and in a snap of a finger it was all being taken away. And it was being taken away by a horrible disease that was relentlessly breaking down his body and driving him nearer and nearer to the imminent death for which he had to patiently sit and wait. Depression under these circumstances seems as rational a response to his condition as was his desire to accelerate the end via suicide. This seems very different from the kind of clinical depression (responsive to drugs such as Prozac and Zoloft) during which a person might say, "I have a wonderful wife and kids, a great job and friends—I know—but it never seems to be enough. I'm always disappointed in myself and others, sad and miserable, but why?"

Also I think competence must be understood as a relative, contextualized concept, not an absolute, all-or-nothing one. Look at our notion of task competence. A ten-year-old child is competent to care for a pet, make breakfast, and operate much commercially available technology. He or she is unlikely to be competent to drive an 18-wheeler or be an airplane mechanic. I believe mental competence is the same. A person in the final stages of a terminal illness may or may not be competent to make decisions about the wisdom of committing to a complex real estate transaction. The capacity to make the decision that it is time to end it all is quite different.

On the most basic of basic levels, such persons understand who they are, whose life it is, and whether they want it to go on. That, I believe, is enough for being competent to make that particular decision.[13] I believe that, but, again, this is the area regarding suicide (and assisted suicide) that I find most problematic. I am not alone in my uncertainty. Those in the mental health community recognize that the notion of competence is not really a scientific concept. It is a creature of social policy formed in the negotiation between patient autonomy and medical paternalism.[14]

ISSUE 7

Physician-assisted suicide is/is not morally supported by the combined concepts of "medical autonomy" and "mercy"

The Moral Claim Justifying Physician-Assisted
Suicide with the Combination of
Autonomy and Mercy

In the specific arena of physician-assisted suicide, some have sought to go from rebutting the arguments labeling such a practice as immoral to presenting a position establishing its morality under certain circumstances. This position combines patient autonomy in making medical decisions (perhaps the dominant theme in current medical ethics)[1] and the element of mercy.[2]

I have discussed the notion of individual autonomy at some length. To this point, I have described two possible contexts. In one, autonomy is meant to encompass the notion that it is only by exercising choices (or, from a sectarian perspective, exercising our God-given "free will") that we can truly define ourselves as individual beings. The second posits autonomy as a prerequisite for putting the philosophy of utilitarianism into practice. In medical autonomy, we now encounter a third context for the concept, one that intersects with my own world of law.

MEDICAL AUTONOMY

Medical autonomy is the product of two other concepts—my right not to be harmfully touched without my consent and what we call "informed consent."[3] The right not to be harmfully touched without my consent exists in all aspects of my life. I have a right to expect that people will not push, punch, or slap me; am entitled to insist on the support of the informal and formal (governmental) portions of my community to maintain and protect that right; and am also entitled to seek redress if that right is violated. In the world of medicine, this means that I cannot, for example, be drugged, dragged from my hospital bed, and taken to surgery to remove my leg even if, in the doctor's opinion, that is the medically best decision. It is my body, my choice.

Informed consent means that (unless I am unconscious, bleeding to death in the emergency room, or such) I must be provided with sufficient information (benefits, alternatives, risks) to make the choice as to what will be done to my body. This means, as all of us are now aware, that I will often be told about some pretty scary, remote risks. Doctors do not want to be sued on the basis that my consent was not informed when that remote risk comes to fruition.[4]

It also means that doctors will not use us as guinea pigs in experiments without our knowledge. This actually happened in the past, when young black men with syphilis were left untreated and discouraged from seeking treatment elsewhere in order to study the progression of the disease.[5] This notable example and others provided specific historical motivation for requiring informed consent. Thus, while the broader notion of autonomy may have been a philosophy born out of the reaction to abuses by governments (e.g., monarchies) and the majority in society (e.g., rejection of the unique, the eccentric, or the rebel), medical autonomy arose in reaction to abuses by the medical profession.

Put these two concepts together (i.e., the right not to be touched and informed consent) and you have patient autonomy. Underlying this concept is the notion that only I can really know what is going on with me. I am a black box, a mystery to those outside me.[6] And it is therapeutic for me to participate in and make these choices about the course of my medical treatment. Some would even say that, as an autonomous being, I have a moral duty to so choose.

On the other hand, while acknowledging these past abuses by the medical profession, there are those who nonetheless dispute what they term the black box premise of medical autonomy.[7] They dispute that I am self-contained, separate from the world, and unknowable from the outside and that no doctor can know me like I know myself.

I can see value in both sides of this debate. As a general proposition, I do know myself and what's best for me. I also know my own body. I know that better than others because I live every instant of my life with myself, am my primary interest, and have continually studied myself. Yet that is also the problem. I am often too close. My idea of myself, mixed with hope and fear, leads me to construct the world I perceive in ways that may skew what others would consider the "reality" of my situation.[8] Surely, at some time in our lives, all of us have been confronted by friends or family members who force us to face some self-destructive or self-defeating behavior we have chosen not to see. They could "see" us better than we could. Or maybe "we" do understand at some level, but we also have mechanisms with which to delude ourselves, to hide what we do not wish to face. Our health seems to be one of those things. People smoke—a lot of people smoke. What does that say about our capacity to control the effect of outside knowledge on our behavior?

Even when we know best, we don't do best. Maybe that's our choice under the broad philosophy of autonomy as defining ourselves through our choices, but it's different from medical autonomy wherein my supposed superior expertise in my own health is one of the cornerstones of the concept. One could respond that when I say "I know best" I don't mean that I know what's medically better for me than does a doctor. I mean that I know what's best for my life, and medical decisions are only one piece of that puzzle (such as the decision whether or not to amputate a limb). The doctor can tell me that smoking may kill me over time, and I may believe he or she is correct on a purely medical basis, but I may nevertheless feel that, in the specific context of my life, it's worth the risk. That's a plausible position, but I don't think it's what people mean in this debate.

Moreover, under this view of the rationale for medical autonomy, even if I generally think I know what's best for my life that is not always true. And it seems that the more stressful the situation the more difficult it is for most of us to make good decisions.[9] When we are not only under stress but the cause of that stress also affects our physical and cognitive capacities (such as being in the throes of a life-threatening illness), the difficulties with good decision making only increase.

Also, while it may be therapeutic for some to participate in their treatment,[10] in fact that is not what many people want to do.[11] There are a number of reasons for this. Medical autonomy is not limited to "important" choices; it covers all choices.[12] This may be far more than people wish to deal with, especially when they are weak, exhausted, and ill. Many, though far from all, people in these situations just want to be cared for without having the strain of making more decisions. Medical diagnosis and treatment decisions are extremely difficult even for doctors.[13] Is it any wonder that untrained, desperately ill people would not want to take the lead in the direction of their treatment? Even a very proactive patient like my father generally was more interested in having information and the illusion of control such knowledge imparts than in actually making the decision.[14]

When my father became too ill, he ceded his decision-making power to the family. We did as he did. We wanted information, to know what was happening, but we generally approved the course of medicine (or the option among alternative courses) suggested by the doctors. They were the medical experts. There were exceptions, one of which I discussed in the story of the "shunt and the phantom surgery." But it was an exception, though surely a vivid one.

There also is an irony when using the concept of medical autonomy as a platform on which to build a moral basis for assisted suicide. Medical or patient autonomy represents more than individual patient rights and protections. It is a metaphor for a dramatic alteration in the physician-patient power relationship. In years past, all the power was with the physician, as was all the trust. Patient autonomy represents a universe in which the doctor works for the patient; it is the patient who has the power, and trust is no greater than when dealing with any other professional.

Yet one could contend that in placing physician-assisted suicide under the banner of patient autonomy one has in effect returned to doctors far more power than they previously possessed.[15] Now they literally have the power of life and death; they will, in effect, decide whether or not PAS is "reasonable" for a particular patient.[16] Ironically, now a concept that was intended to shift the power balance from the traditional doctor-patient relationship, in which all power was in the hands of doctors, to one in which the power is somewhat more evenly distributed is being invoked by patients as the rationale for ceding to doctors a power they never before had—the ultimate power, the power to intentionally kill the patient.

Although, in theory, it is the patient's choice, as we've discussed, with their ability to control information (both the selection of content and how that content is presented) and their professional authority, doctors can manipulate patient choices to a great extent.[17] I understand this from my experience as a criminal defense attorney. It's the day of trial, and the prosecution offers a plea bargain if my client will forgo trial. Whether or not to accept that offer is legally and ethically my client's decision. My obligation is to convey the offer. Yet I am aware that how I choose to characterize and emphasize such factors as the strength of the case, the risks at trial, the likely jurors, personal aspects (such as having to call family members to the stand), and the likely sentence if we go to trial and lose can completely skew the client's decision in one direction or the other. Doctors can use this same power to push patients toward or away from death by assisted suicide.

THE ADDITION OF MERCY

Those finding a moral basis for a physician participating in a patient's death do not rely solely on the patient's autonomy.[18] Assisted killing is not solely a matter of consumer preference to be honored upon request. It requires the addition of the further concept of mercy, mercy in the face of suffering.[19] For me, *mercy* is an interesting choice of words. I generally think of mercy as an act motivated by human compassion, an identification with the other person as someone who but for fortune could be us. That act, however, takes place under circumstances in which one has the power and legitimacy to inflict a form of extreme suffering (striking a fallen enemy on the battlefield, sentencing a convicted criminal) but relents. Religious orders such as the Sisters of Mercy metaphorically can be said to be agents of God's mercy.

But that is a funny way to think about a doctor and a patient such as my father. My father's actions did not justify his suffering, as would a combatant on the battlefield or a criminal at sentencing. Nor can a doctor be placed in the position of the victorious warrior or sentencing judge who can legitimately inflict some extreme consequence. Rather, doctors see people suffer all the time and generally are committed to easing that suffering.

What this position seems to be saying is that at some point, when that suffering is heartrendingly great, nothing in the conventional doctor's arsenal can stop it, and the patient begs for death in place of continual agony, then, as a compassionate human (who, due to his or her professional knowledge, is able to help the patient), the doctor may accede to this request. I am completely sympathetic with this view and would fully understand an individual doctor who chose to act under these circumstances, but I have trouble relying on the conjunction of autonomy and mercy (compassion) as a reliable moral beacon.

In the first place, this conjunction of autonomy and mercy would equally appear to be a justification for any (requested) mercy killing whether carried out by a doctor or a layperson. And, again, the moral basis would be that, if people are suffering enough and request it, we may kill them. Perhaps, however, this is implicitly based on some interpretation of the duty of doctors to alleviate suffering. Fine. If you believe this, you believe this. It hardly offers a clear moral path given that many doctors who embrace the notion that the duty to relieve suffering is part of the doctor's role would, nevertheless, take the position that killing a patient is antithetical to that role. (In fact, some argue that, as a deontological proposition, the very notion of relieving suffering is premised on a surviving former sufferer.)[20]

There are, I believe, even more serious concerns with this concept. Eventually one will face difficulty trying to limit "suffering" to physical pain.[21] Physical pain is, as we've discussed, not an objective, physically perceptible phenomenon. It is only known by its outward symptoms (grimacing, moaning, groaning, screaming). It is a construction created from the physical, psychological, experiential, and imaginative. A child will stub a toe and cry hysterically at the pain. An adult will grimace, swear, and hop around. What accounts for the difference? I don't think the magnitude of the physical impact on tissue and nerves is different (though it may be). I think, rather, that two things explain the difference. We know from experience that the pain will soon subside. The child likely does not. We know that we cannot seek the comfort of others to ease us in our pain from a stubbed toe. Socially, a child is permitted to seek the arms and comforting words of its parents to ease the pain. Pain, thus, is complex, hardly providing a clear line for when or when not to kill another person.

If the notion of suffering is extended beyond physical pain, the limits of physician-assisted suicide become quite broad indeed. Psychological pain can be nearly as excruciating as physical torment. Do we want doctors to give lethal pills to a patient judged to be in mental agony who the doctor somehow determines has no reasonable prognosis of recovery (analogous to a terminal cancer patient)? Once we focus on terms such as *mercy* or *suffering,* we have to recognize that the content of these emotively powerful concepts will be filled in by a process of constructing persuasive analogous narratives. In other words, particularly because they are founded on the depth of compassion and fellow feeling in the human heart, they are far more likely to expand than contract.

Finally, one needs to take into consideration the risk that, given the individual power of the conjoined concepts—autonomy and mercy—in individual cases an extreme version of one concept may, in practice, suffice.[22] Thus, an articulate, charming person whose suffering may not seem extreme may be so persuasive in his or her request for assistance in dying that autonomy will carry the day. The other possibility is even more troubling, that patients may be in such extreme, uncontrollable agony that, without a clear request, doctors will euthanize them. None of what I've said leads to the conclusion that assisted suicide is wrong in all instances. I have not seen a moral argument that convinces me that this is so. I just do not think that this concept of joining autonomy and mercy adds to my understanding of the circumstances under which assisted suicide is morally justified.

ISSUE 8

One does/does not have a constitutional

right to suicide, assisted suicide,

or euthanasia

Law and Assisted Suicide

COMING AT LAST TO LAW

I've often thought of the ways in which the scenario with my father might have been different if assisted suicide had been legal at the time. I guess that my sister and I would not have been afraid of committing a crime and being charged with some form of homicide (although my sister was probably far less afraid of any legal consequences than me; when she is doing something she believes in, she tends to be fearless). I think we both would have still been frightened about bumbling and making Dad's suffering even worse while, at the same time, being judged by our father as incompetents. On the other hand, had there been PAS, and Dad requested it, I can't imagine going very far in attempting to talk him out of it. I would have even helped him find a doctor because by then he was far too ill to navigate medical channels alone. At that time, I would still have felt it was wrong but that, ultimately, it was not my right to impose my moral beliefs on a suffering, dying, 79-year-old man.

Even now the thought of helping Dad die makes me very uncomfortable. That I no longer believe such an action to be immoral does not diminish the awfulness of having to make such a choice. It is disturbing to imagine helping him, knowing that I would conduct what was in effect a death ceremony through which I would converse with him and then stick him into the running car, shut the door, and watch and wait knowing that I was literally seeing my own father die before my eyes; in fact, waiting for him to die, because that was the whole point. Of course, with PAS it might have been less traumatic. Instead of a garage complete with storage boxes, gardening tools, and oil-stained concrete, it would have been a medical bed. Instead of me and my sister, duct tape, and rubber hoses, it would have been a doctor providing medicine. Clean. Sterile. Medical.

While obviously this discussion is filled with strong emotions for me, as we at last come to the question of legality, the literature and concepts fall within the center of my expertise. I am a guilty, confused, hopeful, sad, grieving son. I am also an attorney and law professor. So, if I appear to slip into that role, it is not to use the academic role to shield me from my feelings. Rather, it is because I believe that readers cannot really appreciate what they read and hear about legal decisions concerning assisted suicide without some basic understanding of the various policies involved and the decisional methodology courts have employed to assess constitutional claims of a right to assisted suicide.

Our completed moral analysis will not have a direct bearing on these questions. Law is not bound to trace the path of morality.[1] Law may include prudential considerations: practical ends, social needs, ease or difficulty of enforcement, and such. In other words, law is a pragmatic tool of social policy, although as part of that policy it can set aspirational norms. While criminal law does often coincide with the immoral (theft, murder), not everything that we might consider immoral is illegal (e.g., cheating at the game of monopoly). On the other hand, not everything we make illegal has moral content. Traffic signs merely reflect some planner's idea of how best to coordinate the flow of traffic. If you run a stop sign under circumstances that endanger others, under those circumstances the stop sign law does seem to bear a certain moral quality. We all know our reaction when we see someone who violates the rules at an intersection and almost causes a serious collision. But you violate that same stop sign law if you run a stop sign at 3:00 am on a country road with a full moon and no cars in sight. The law is indifferent to the magnitude of the risk taken (from which any moral content would emanate) in favor of uniform deterrence and bright line enforcement. If you run a stop sign, you've violated the law.

One could, of course, question any attempt to make a sharp distinction between social policy, on the one hand, and morality on the other. After all, social policy may be motivated by morality, may be directed at achieving moral values, and may even use moral labels to achieve instrumental ends. Morality, on the other hand, does not label for the sake of labeling.

The labeling is instrumental, intended to channel individual behavioral choices. Yet even recognizing such deconstructive possibilities, I find the distinction between morality and social policy a useful one for a discussion about assisted-suicide. Whether a particular debate has a more moral or pragmatic tone very much alters the nature of how the debaters' message is given and received and the possible paths down which the discussion is reasonably likely to proceed.

TWO MISCONCEPTIONS BASED ON THE FACT THAT THE LAWS CRIMINALIZING SUICIDE HAVE BEEN REPEALED

Early in our history, suicide was illegal. Today suicide is not a crime, although assisted suicide is illegal in most states. Our decision to decriminalize suicide in America certainly takes us a long way from the days in European history when the corpses of suicides were buried at crossroads[2] with stakes in their hearts,[3] desecrated,[4] hung[5] (so that, in some bizarre logic, they could not escape the "punishment" of hanging), or floated down a river in barrels[6] (so they wouldn't return). They were denied burial in consecrated ground[7] and had all their goods and land forfeited[8] (something that would violate the Bill of Attainder clause of the Constitution).[9] Such a forfeiture would not take place if a jury found the deceased mentally incompetent, however, and by the end of the nineteenth century juries routinely found such persons to be non compos mentis, thereby mitigating somewhat the harshness of the law toward the survivors of the deceased.[10]

Some may argue that the decision of every legislature in this country to withdraw the criminal sanction from suicide represents approval of the individual's decision to kill himself or herself and even a tacit acknowledgment that the private decision to commit suicide is beyond the interest of society and the law. I do not believe that either of these inferences is correct.

Decriminalization Does Not Indicate Societal Approval of Suicide

As to the first inference,[11] there are a number of reasons to conclude that, while suicide is an undesirable action, it is bad social policy to try to deal with that action within the criminal justice system.[12] Most people who attempt suicide suffer from some type of mental disorder. Since they rarely threaten others, it demonstrates our sensitivity and compassion that we take them out of a system whose primary purpose is to label individuals as blameworthy and then to punish them. Those who attempt (but fail) to commit suicide have suffered enough, and further punishment would border on the sadistic ("Your suicide failed, and you lived, so you're under arrest"). Also the threat of arrest, trial, and punishment would hardly be a deterrent to those contemplating suicide. Such persons plan to kill themselves, and among all the consequences they fear if they botch it the criminal sanction likely would be far down the list. Admittedly, the threat of criminal punishment theoretically might deter those who don't really intend to die in their attempt (the so-called cry for help), but among whose ranks a certain number do inadvertently die. But even with these, I think our first reaction would be that they need treatment not a jail cell. After all, if they were depressed before, a stay in jail is not likely to be just what the doctor ordered.

In fact, criminalization in this particular context will have the tendency to be counterproductive with regard to channeling those attempting suicide into the mental health system. It is true that a criminal court judge can put a defendant on probation and order mental health treatment. But to get to that point, the individual must be prosecuted and made a defendant in the criminal justice system. Under these circumstances, particularly when there is no guarantee that a particular judge will order treatment, it is likely that people close to the person attempting suicide will not even report the attempt (or will characterize it as an accident). As a result, those who need treatment and those close to them will be deterred from even acknowledging that they have gotten to the point where they have tried to take their own lives. Therefore, although taking suicide off the criminal books was good social policy, it does not mean that the society lacked good reasons for wishing to discourage suicide.

Decriminalization Does Not Mean That Suicide is beyond the Interests of Society and Its Laws

Withdrawing suicide from the criminal books likewise does not support the inference that suicide is a totally private matter beyond all interests of the law. In formulating laws against suicide, the legislatures were relying on their so-called police powers. The sweep of these powers, in spite of the law enforcement ring to the name, covers all matters of public health and safety (and, to an extent, morals), including housing codes, restaurant hygiene, regulation of access to pornography by children, and such. In employing this power to legislate against suicide, the state has traditionally arrayed a list of very plausible, though hardly undebatable, state interests to justify an absolute legal ban on suicide. This same list appears in almost every court opinion that involves a discussion of withdrawing lifesaving medical treatment and assisted suicide, including PAS. Each of these interests plainly has general merit,[13] which refutes any claim that suicide, assisted suicide, and euthanasia are beyond the interests of society and law.

The Highest Obligation of Society Is to Protect Life

One finds oneself at a loss to quibble with this notion regarding the obligation of society to protect life. Even if you think a society has higher obligations, this one has to rank near the top.[14] We look to and count on the state to protect us from being murdered or run over by a drunken driver.

Also, even though the practice reeks with paternalism, in matters affecting our health we do let the state protect us from ourselves. Young people may not legally buy cigarettes, and none of us may legally buy heroin. Bartenders may not serve intoxicated patrons. The FDA may deny us access to medicines not yet proven safe and effective. Surely suicide is a health-affecting decision that is far more determinative of our well-being than any of these. Also, by making suicide illegal, the state sets a societal norm that killing yourself is "wrong" (i.e., the state expresses moral disapproval), and the image created by this norm may be just enough to deter some people from killing themselves on a momentary impulse.[15]

Letting People Kill Themselves Symbolically Devalues Life throughout the Society

The idea here is that if we condone people killing themselves we may risk more than the loss of such individuals from our society. We risk sending a ripple through our society in which, beginning with our acceptance of suicide, we begin to devalue life, cheapen it, and make it less significant.[16]

When I hear about someone committing suicide, I feel a little hollow and sad. I do not have the sense of life being devalued. In fact, I feel quite the contrary. I think how tragic it is that life, which can be so wondrous, was so painful for that person. On the other hand, one could argue that the deceased, by committing suicide, provides an "image" of possibilities (particularly when broadcast through pervasive media), possibilities that now will be seen by some as falling within a range of heretofore unimagined choices. The result might then be a few more suicides. This is plausible: Witness the copycat phenomenon of shootings in public schools.

Social Costs and Dislocation

Having considered these consequences (e.g., support for dependents, the emotional shock and long-term effects on survivors, and so on) in the discussion of formal utilitarianism and suicide and assisted suicide, I have concluded that they are legitimate given the appropriate context (chapter 3).

Loss of Productive Citizens

Suicide deprives society of citizens, people who could have served in its armed forces, produced products and offered services, paid taxes, and participated in its social and political life. As such, suicide harms society by diminishing its resources, and society accordingly has an interest in stopping it. This makes sense except unless you consider that we don't outlaw smoking, dangerous recreational pursuits, and such. Why choose to focus on the statistically small group of would-be suicides? There are a number of possible answers. The point of these other activities is not death, nor is death a certain outcome. They do not deprive the society of *all* the citizen's potential. Also, unlike suicide, those other activities have some perceived social utility.

A Matter of Public Concern: Assisted Suicide

When you add assisted suicide to the mix, things change a bit. Now, from the state's perspective, you are no longer concerned with an individual who is acting privately. You must add all the concerns that accompany the participation of a third party discussed in chapter 3.[17] When you add physicians to the mix, you have left the notion of an individual acting privately far behind. You now have the medical profession, a governmentally regulated calling, and with it all the concerns about the slippery slope discussed in chapter 7. Only this time these concerns appear through the lens of law and social policy rather than just individual morality.

CONSTITUTIONAL CLAIMS TO ASSISTED SUICIDE

U.S. Supreme Court Law and Analysis

While academics have proposed that a right to assisted suicide can be founded on the First Amendment right to religious freedom,[18] the two grounds that commonly have been raised in support of a claim of a constitutional right are *fundamental rights* (specifically, the protection of our right to "liberty" found in the due process clause of the federal Constitution) and *equal protection*. In *Washington v. Glucksberg*[19] and *Vacco v. Quill*,[20] the U.S. Supreme Court rejected both the fundamental rights and the equal protection claims.

Rather, the Supreme Court left it to the various state legislatures to determine whether to permit or forbid such practices. My point in examining the legal arguments that support a right to suicide, assisted suicide, and euthanasia is not to demonstrate how they are correct or incorrect or to critique the opinions of the court. Rather, I want to show that, given the legal standards and techniques of interpretation available to the court, combined with the intense moral debate in this country concerning assisted suicide, one can expect the court to provide answers consistent with the individual justice's sincere moral beliefs. I am not saying that individual judges will intentionally manipulate the law to produce results they know are wrong. Rather, it is my belief after over 30 years of working in the law that, in a morally charged arena such as assisted suicide, in which reasonable people differ in their moral views, the law of fundamental rights and equal protection provides a language in which the expression of one's own moral predilections will seem natural and correct.

In this arena, the language to which I am referring is expressed within the "standard of review." Appellate courts, of which the U.S. Supreme Court is one, do not review legal decisions in a vacuum but rather assess the cases in front of them through the frame of text-based guides, which are termed standards of review. These guidelines reflect the nature of the subject matter being reviewed and the hierarchy of legal relations among levels of courts and between courts and other branches of government. The standards of review federal courts employ when assessing the constitutionality of particular pieces of legislation are characterized in terms of levels of scrutiny.

The key to case outcomes under either fundamental rights or equal protection analysis is what level of scrutiny the court applies when reviewing a particular statute. This concept of "scrutiny" refers to how carefully the court will question the rationale underlying a piece of legislation. Generally, the courts show great deference to the work of this elected branch of government and require only "minimal rationality" or "rational basis" for the legislation.[21] Under this standard, if the judge can imagine any justification, even if it seems completely misguided, the law will not be found unconstitutional. There is, however, a much higher level of scrutiny known as "strict scrutiny." If this level of scrutiny is applied, the judge will really dig into the statute and its purported rationale and will only find the statute constitutional if the piece of legislation is "narrowly tailored" to serve a "compelling state interest."[22]

If the rational basis standard is applied, the party challenging a state statute (e.g., one forbidding PAS) will lose; if the standard of strict scrutiny is applied, there's a real shot at winning. As I'll now discuss, the rules for deciding which level of scrutiny should apply are sufficiently malleable that the outcome is unpredictable (save knowing the moral predisposition of the judge).

ARGUMENTS THAT ASSISTED SUICIDE IS A "FUNDAMENTAL" CONSTITUTIONAL RIGHT

If a right is fundamental, the court will review any law that unduly burdens that right under a strict scrutiny analysis.[23] If a right is not fundamental, the court will review the law through a minimum rationality lens. Simple. The only real question is whether the particular right in question is or is not a fundamental constitutional right.

The Nature of the Right

When you really look at the argument, no one claims that there is an identifiable right to assisted suicide literally written into the Constitution akin to the right to counsel or to be free from unreasonable searches and seizures. Rather, assisted suicide is seen as a concrete manifestation of some broader right of which assisted suicide is an expression. The right has often been termed a right to *privacy*. Yet, while suicide is surely an intimate decision that is often carried out in private, assisted suicide is not. Nor is the concern really one of privacy in the sense of a media personality being stalked by a tabloid photographer with a telephoto lens. If it is privacy, it is privacy in the sense of being left alone by the government to lead our lives as we choose as long as we are not hurting anyone. In other words, we're really talking about autonomy and the correlative right to make choices about how we wish to live our lives.[24] And, whether or not one finds autonomy to be a viable concept for purposes of moral analysis (chapter 6), it most assuredly is a legitimate political and legal construct within a system of liberal democracy.

For me, though, positing that the right to assisted suicide is underlain by our right to make autonomous choices is not a final answer as to the precise right being sought to protect. Suicide, assisted suicide, and euthanasia are actions chosen as a means to terminate life; they are the product of choice. But what is the precise nature of the *choice* that people are seeking the freedom to make? I have found various expressions of this choice characterized as a right: (1) to waive the right to live, (2) to die, (3) to die in the time and manner we choose, and (4) to die with dignity. I will look closely at each of these before I go on to discuss the legal methodology employed by the courts in determining whether a claimed right qualifies as a fundamental right.

The Right to Waive the Right to Live

That there is a "right to waive the right to live" is an interesting argument because its first premise is the same as the first premise of the legal version of the position against assisted suicide, that is, that the primary function of society is to protect life.[25] I have a "right to live." If I have a right to live, that right is for my protection and is *my* right. As such, I can waive that right, just like I can waive my right against self-incrimination and confess or waive my right against illegal search and seizure and consent to police looking through my house. To be sure, we sometimes require a waiver ceremony or ritual in which persons waiving must appear before some formal body or tribunal to make sure they fully understand the right(s) they are giving up and that this is their unfettered choice.[26] And maybe that would be a good idea in this case, given the irreparable nature of the decision, the concern about coercion, and even the risk of disguised homicide. But in the end I should be able to give up my right to live and end my life however I choose. This argument has a nice rhetorical ring to it, but ultimately it is unconvincing.

What can it mean to say you have a "right to live" when people *always* die and die all around us from a variety of causes? I do not think that the idea would resonate well with most if I refused to serve my country in a war because I think the particular action is too dangerous and thereby unduly burdens my right to live. In fact, we do not really possess anything that can be characterized as a true right to live. I do have a fundamental right that my life not be taken without due process, that is, that I "not be killed unjustly." But that is not the same as a right to live.

Moreover, even if I have a right to live, the state may have sufficient interests in my well-being and its effect on others as to deny me the right to waive it.[27] This is hardly without precedent. I have a right to be free from "harmful and offensive touching" (i.e., battery). I'm glad that people can't legally hit me whenever I go out shopping. But even if I wanted to consent to being hit (other than in, e.g., a sanctioned boxing match), I could not. The law will not let me waive my protection against battery. As another example, I have the right to a direct appeal in a death penalty conviction. The state has such significant interests in a fair and accurate determination in such a case, however, that in many state jurisdictions I cannot waive this right to appeal. Finally, while I am protected by the Thirteenth Amendment against being sold into slavery, that institution is so offensive to a modern society that in many state jurisdictions I cannot waive the protection of the Thirteenth Amendment and voluntarily sell myself into slavery.[28] So, even if I have a right to live (which is questionable), the state does not necessarily have to let me waive that right.

The Right to Die

At first blush, this seems a bit silly. We will all certainly obtain the benefits of this right since we will all eventually die. That, however, does not give fair breath to this phrase. What seems to be implied is that at some point, when life is unremittingly intolerable and there is no hope for the future, one has as much right to end one's life as to continue living it. It is not a claim for at-will suicide and death on demand. The question, however, is how broad a narrative this phrase envisions. If the concept envisions a 32-year-old depressed paraplegic, those espousing such a concept would be relatively isolated from even the mainstream of those who support assisted suicide. To the extent the envisioned narrative moves toward those suffering from AIDS and ALS and then toward people like my father, the concept moves into the political mainstream. As such, it might lead to success in the legislative arena, but for reasons which will be discussed in the section on legal analysis, claiming this right as fundamental and meriting the resulting legally mandated deference is unlikely to be successful in court.[29]

The Right to Die in the Time and Manner We Choose

I think we all have a vision of our Thanatos, our "good death."[30] We have had a good life, are not suffering, and are at peace with the world and those we love. Some might wish to go to sleep one night and just not awake, while others may wish to be more aware of the approaching moment of death so that they can consciously say good-bye. Yet there is only so much in life that one can control. Anyone who has children learns that rather quickly. Needing to control all things makes us incomplete, separated from the rich experiences that come when we do not control. The idea of a "right" to control the time and manner of our death is a strange one, as if we could control death. Death defines us; we do not define death. That we are even in a position to control the time or manner of our death is a matter of random chance. Unless we propose that everyone carry "death buttons" on their wrists, moreover, this opportunity for control is unlikely to be available to the majority of us. Again, it will just be random chance. But perhaps I am not being fair. This right, like the others, is not free floating but is moored to a discrete set of narratives of the sick and suffering. As such, it is in substance a rhetorical alternative to the right to die.

The Right to Death with Dignity

This "right to death with dignity" has constituted a rallying cry for assisted suicide proponents,[31] not because of the logical import of this right but because of the emotionally powerful narrative image it triggers. The image is of persons near the end of life. Their lives are kept in suspension by a complex of tubes and machines. Weak moans are the only evidence of their suffering. They soil themselves like newborns, as day by day their mental faculties further degenerate. What is lying there on the hospital bed is a cruel parody even of them in old age and less than a shadow of them as they were when strong and productive. They cannot bear to look or have those close to them watch. Please let them end it and die with dignity.

If you see it this way, then you see it this way, and my thoughts probably do not matter. There are other ways, however, to look at the issue of dignity. Initially, we are not really talking about *death* with dignity. Death is just death. I suppose that, if we were to attempt to place such a label on death, some would argue that it is the final indignity as it takes *everything* and there is no way to make it otherwise. Others might disagree and say that death cannot take away the parts of us that exist in those we've touched during our lives. For me, death is neither dignified nor undignified; it just is. Whatever we may conclude about whether death is dignified or undignified by definition, the right we are considering is more accurately portrayed as dying with dignity.

What is dignity? One view is that it's innate in being human.[32] If that's so, you can't help but die with dignity. Another view is that it is a function of human reason.[33] If that's so, it would seem that killing yourself because you are losing your reason would maintain your dignity. Still another view is that people "earn" their dignity by the way they conduct themselves.[34] If so, whether or not you die with dignity has nothing to do with how many tubes are protruding from you. Perhaps, as to this latter notion, we should not confuse the notion of basic human dignity (which can be offended by harsh prisoner of war camps or segregation laws) with that of a dignified person, the latter being a socially inscribed quality few of us possess.

For me, dignity has less to do with our environment than how we react to it. In fact, it would seem to be at its apex when it is maintained in the face of extreme indignity. I will never forget the quiet dignity of the black defendant in the movie *To Kill a Mockingbird* as he took the stand facing the full force of a racist social system.

This image of the horrifyingly undignified death that underlies the concept of death with dignity, while understandable in this culture, is just that—a construction of this culture. We are, after all, animals, albeit very clever ones. We devote entire aisles of our drugstores to diapers for adults. Incontinence happens. So what is our obsession with this very rigid notion of dignity?

I felt bad for my folks when they were suffering physical or emotional pain. My father was often confused and pissed all over himself when I helped him to the bathroom. I thought he was extraordinarily brave, my hero. My mother often spoke nonsense and would suddenly swear a blue streak that would make a sailor blush. I loved that she had made a life, even a crazy one. My parents were not undignified; they were sick.[35]

But now let's take a huge step back from this human reality to a more distanced, abstracted realm. I want to look at how courts actually decide cases using the concept of fundamental rights under the Constitution. What does losing the ability to control your bladder or the gradual dissipation of your mental acumen have to do with any protected right under our Constitution?

THE CURRENT INTERPRETIVE TECHNIQUE FOR DETERMINING IF CLAIMED CONSTITUTIONAL RIGHTS ARE FUNDAMENTAL

The current analysis employed by the courts to determine whether a claimed right, although it doesn't appear in the literal text of the Constitution, nonetheless merits protection as "fundamental" has several parts.[36] First, the right claimed to be fundamental to liberty must be "carefully described." Second, it must be "deeply rooted" in the traditions of our nation so as to be "implicit in our view of ordered liberty." Without going any further, it should be clear to you that with indeterminate, subjective modifying terms such as *deeply* and *implicit* at the center of the analysis there is not going to be very much predictive dependability to it. You and I can apply this analysis to the same claim, come to opposite conclusions, and both sound reasonable. Deeper analysis only confirms this initial impression.

Let's begin with what seems to be the easiest portion of the interpretive technique, the careful description of the claimed fundamental right. After the 1965 *Griswold* case, which struck down a state law denying married couples access to contraceptives and information about them, I'd have said that the right involved could be carefully described as "marital privacy,"[37] a right protecting the essential features of that special and intimate relationship. I would have been wrong. It turns out that seven years later, in striking down laws denying contraceptives to unmarried couples, the court characterized the right as "protecting individual decisions in matters of childbearing from unjustified intrusions by the state."[38] I sometimes tell my students, only half jokingly, that you don't know what a Supreme Court case means until the next case, when they discuss it. Court members, times, and cultural attitudes change. It is not uncommon for the Supreme Court to reinterpret the meaning of its own prior language without acknowledging that it is doing so. After all, the court likes to give the sense that there is some stability to its precedents.

The second requirement, that of being deeply rooted in "tradition," is even more problematic. What counts as a deeply rooted tradition in our national ethos? If it's the particular practice, then miscegenation laws forbidding blacks and whites to marry, segregated schools, and abortion bans would still be on the books. Those, more than the opposite practices, were national traditions when the cases were decided.

The malleable nature of this aspect of the analysis is illustrated by the case of *Bowers v. Hardwick* (1986), wherein the court upheld a state law banning gay sex between consenting adult men in their own home. The analysis looked at history and found that sodomy was not a big part of the American tradition.[39] But what about the right to be left alone in our homes if we are not hurting anyone? What about the deeply rooted tradition that the state will not impose particular religious views on its citizens? The court's choice of the "tradition" as sodomy, thus characterizing the conduct in question in its most concrete, literal form, predetermined the outcome of the analysis.[40]

"Implicit in ordered liberty" presents the same uncontrollable interpretive flexibility because it depends on how broad or narrow a frame you use to interpret the right. Let's go back to *Bowers*. If in *Bowers* the right was interpreted to run from *Griswold* and *Roe v. Wade* as that of making fundamental decisions about our personal, intimate relationships, then the right to have sex in the privacy of one's own home fairly could have been found to be implicit in our concept of liberty. If, on the other hand, you define it as "having gay sex," then it is likely not implicit. The *Bowers'* court, in fact, did neither. The justices constructed an interpretive frame so that the line of cases spawned by *Griswold* and *Roe* were not about making intimate relational decisions in our lives but about "procreation." That pretty much leaves gay men out. This is a game you can never count on winning.

Seventeen years later a somewhat different mix of Supreme Court justices considered a state law banning male sodomy. Reading the law as if restricted to gay persons, the court defined the right involved not as the right to engage in gay sex but as that of mature, consenting adults to be free to engage in private sexual conduct in the privacy of their homes. Not surprisingly, with that definition of the right, the court easily reversed *Bowers v. Hardwick*. The interpretative methodology made this flip-flop as easy as had been reaching the initial *Bowers* decision.[41]

INTERPRETIVE TECHNIQUES FOR FINDING FUNDAMENTAL RIGHTS AND THE ASSISTED SUICIDE CASE

Deeply Rooted

As I've noted, the Supreme Court considered (and rejected by a vote of nine to nothing) a claim that assisted suicide was a fundamental constitutional right (*Washington v. Glucksberg*, 1997). As in *Bowers*, the court characterized the tradition involved in its most concrete terms, that is, as helping someone commit suicide.[42] From there, the analysis was predictable. Far from being "deeply rooted," for over 700 years the common-law tradition has punished or otherwise disapproved of suicide and assisted suicide.[43] The justices, of course, could have chosen as their tradition one that goes back at least to that society on which most of Western civilization, including democracy, is founded: the ancient Greeks and the tradition of "relieving suffering at the end of life." And the advent of life-prolonging medical technology that was not available for most of the past 700 years (during which time people with diseases generally died quickly) could have played a role in the court's story of tradition. These were just not rhetorical moves the court wished to make.

Implicit in Ordered Liberty

The proponents of assisted suicide were hoping to clear the "implicit liberty" hurdle of the analysis by citing the following language from the last case at that time upholding the constitutional right to abortion, *Planned Parenthood v. Casey* (1992).

> "[There is] a realm of personal liberty the government may not enter . . . [and at the heart of this liberty is the right to] define our own concept of existence, of meaning . . ."

That argument had carried the day for PAS supporters in the federal appellate courts. The *Glucksberg* court, however, refused to employ this frame.[44] As discussed, the court instead relied on the literal, concrete characterization of the proposed action as "suicide with assistance." As was true with the "deeply rooted" analysis, once the court chose this concrete framing of the issue, the result was a foregone conclusion.

ARGUMENTS THAT BANNING SUICIDE AND ASSISTED SUICIDE VIOLATES EQUAL PROTECTION: EQUAL PROTECTION BASICS

Legislation frequently makes distinctions among classes of people, placing benefits on some, burdens on others. The principle of equal protection in its most basic application ensures that legislation will not make arbitrary distinctions. Thus, doubling the license fee for cars with red as opposed to blue floor mats would be constitutionally troubling. Proponents using this equal protection argument as a constitutional basis for opposing the legality of any legislation barring assisted suicide would claim that the distinction between forbidden assisted suicide and permitted double effect, refusing treatment, pulling the plug, and terminal sedation is as "arbitrary and capricious" as the line between the red and blue floor mats.

In most cases, the court will apply the most minimal review of the legislature's justification for any distinction in a statute (e.g., persons over 18 and under 18, those who own dogs and those who don't, property owners and renters). As we have already discussed, this "level of scrutiny" is called "minimum rationality" or "rational basis." But imagine that you went to put money in a parking meter and it said, "50 cents an hour, except one dollar an hour for Asian Americans." Would a court approve this law by accepting or making up some rational basis (e.g., Asian Americans make more use of the public school system per capita than other racial groups and should therefore contribute more to the public coffers) or does this demand a different legal approach?

As you have likely sensed from this example, laws making distinctions based on race are a different matter. It is not that such distinctions can never be made; they can. Rather, before a statute can pass constitutional muster when it treats, for example, Hispanics differently than Asians or African Americans differently than Caucasians, the court will apply an intense level of scrutiny looking at the legislature's actual justifications and in effect deciding whether these distinctions along racial lines are really necessary ("narrowly tailored to serve a compelling state interest"). Similarly, when the distinction is grounded in gender, in order to pass constitutional muster, the law must not reflect a gender stereotype, the law must serve an important government objective, the chosen mean must be "substantially related to the objectives," and the objectives must be genuine.

But are state statutes barring assisted suicide properly subject to these higher levels of scrutiny or just rational basis?

THE EQUAL PROTECTION CLAUSE AND SUICIDE

With that background, we can now return to equal protection and suicide. The argument is that those who have lifesaving treatments that can be refused, plugs that can be pulled, a need for pain medications that can kill, or the wish to be terminally sedated can end their lives. Those equally sick and suffering who don't happen to need a respirator, pain medication, or such are forbidden to end their lives.[45] That distinction in the law violates equal protection. Let's look at this very appealing argument that the Supreme Court unequivocally rejected a bit more closely.[46]

People Like My Father and the Appropriate Standard of Scrutiny

I do not think that even if we define the class to contour with my father's circumstances this results in a class that necessarily is entitled to the higher levels of scrutiny; rather, minimum rationality will provide the standard for review.

The elderly dying were neither the subject of the Fourteenth Amendment nor, as far as I know, historical objects of discrimination.[47] In fact, before the medicalization of death, they were taken care of by family members in their homes. While they cannot participate in the political process in their current condition, they hardly represent anything akin to an "insular racial minority" that has been systematically cut out of meaningful participation in the political process.[48] They cover the full spectrum of race, gender, and wealth. When young and healthy, they had the opportunity to influence the democratic, political process—in fact, they may have been congresspersons or even the president. In their current state, many have influential family networks and the support of organizations such as AARP. And their interests, which coincide with a broad and powerful spectrum of the society, are likely to be protected by the active middle aged, who (unlike youths) know that their time with old age and likely illness is on the horizon. So I don't think strict scrutiny is likely.

Nor can I see anything about the class comparable to gender. With gender, one had harmful stereotypes.[49] There are certainly such stereotypes about older people. My grandmother used to tell me how furious she would get because "people either talk to you like you're some kind of little child . . . or they think you can't hear and they have to scream at you." I do not know of comparable stereotypes, however, concerning the elderly dying that would require courts to carefully screen legislation that may affect them.

All of the Accepted Methods That Can Result in Terminating a Life Can Be "Rationally" Distinguished from Assisted Suicide for Purposes of an Equal Protection Analysis

Let me use terminating life-sustaining treatment (pulling the plug) as an example of why the equal protection argument fails under a minimum scrutiny or rational basis analysis. A similar result would follow such an analysis of PDE, refusing treatment, and terminal sedation.

The argument here is that we should permit people to die this way and in fact most people who die in hospitals and nursing homes will die this way (or through related methods such as withdrawing artificially provided food and hydration, do not resuscitate orders, intentional decisions not to treat flu or pneumonia, and such).[50] Yet this is indistinguishable from intentional killing. Hence the equal protection claims. And when you review basic principles of the criminal law this position surely has some merit.

Legal Principles Regarding Shortening of Life

If I come upon my worst enemy lying on the ground in his death throes resulting from a mortal wound administered by another and I put a bullet in his head, I'm guilty of murder.[51] Every moment of life has equal value in the eyes of the criminal law. As a consequence, if I intentionally shorten that life for even one of those moments I am a murderer. Besides the philosophical basis for this rule, there are pragmatic aspects. Law requires some clarity in application. If intentionally shortening a life by one minute did not count as homicide, what about three minutes? Seventeen minutes? Four hours and 32 minutes? The law avoids such imponderables by setting a clear line—a single moment.

Shortening Life in the Medical Context

From this it should follow that if I withdraw artificially provided food and hydration from a dying patient (who is not in the final phase of dying where withdrawal will not accelerate death), and this shortens his or her life, I have committed an intentional killing.

However, the fact that analytically there may be no difference under criminal law principles between delivering the coup de grâce to my enemy and pulling the plug, and, therefore, a fortiori between intentional killing and pulling the plug, does not mean that these different situations cannot rationally justify different treatment. Again, those delineating the boundaries must consider policy as well as neat, analytic lines. The narrative of the deathbed, resting within the co-narrative of the neutral, nonemotional world of medical science, comfortably separates pulling the plug from intentional killings on the streets. In other words, we can treat the two situations differently without concern that how we deal with one will affect the other. They are not of the same world in any of our eyes; one is criminal, one is medical.

But, what about treating pulling the plug differently from assisted self-killing? That, after all, is the focus of the equal protection argument. In the first place, most people do not talk about pulling the plug as the equivalent of administering a lethal injection. And how we talk and think about things is important in social policy settings.[52] It informs what people will comfortably support and what are the current cultural norms, the currently accepted boundaries. That does not make dominant majority perceptions right. We only have to look at discrimination against women and racial minorities to know that. In fact, the Constitution is in part constructed to protect the minority against the potential tyranny of the majority (e.g., through the Bill of Rights). Yet, when in legitimate doubt, following an existing line that also happens to be the one of least resistance is not a bad maxim for policymakers. We accept pulling the plug, and even likely depend on it (as we do the related means such as DNR), as an unarticulated means of rationing scarce medical resources at the end of life. Through these means (and PDE) we already have a powerful method for terminating the lives of most suffering, terminally ill people. So why open the whole suicide/assisted suicide can of worms? In fact, some have argued that it is only through holding the line between pulling the plug, on one hand, and assisted suicide, on the other, that medicine has managed to keep the courts out of the former.[53]

In the second place, pulling the plug is naturally self-limiting and circumscribed. It is narrowly limited as to time, place, and circumstances: a hospital, a dying patient (I'm not concerned for our purposes with those in persistent vegetative states) who is dependent on a machine with a few days or hours to live. Suicide, even for the terminally ill, can cover a far broader scenario of time, place, and circumstances.

Of course, you do not have to accept this analysis, and you may be very persuasive in voicing your disagreement. Saying something is incorrect in your view, however, is leaps and bounds away from labeling the position as irrational. And I do not think that you can credibly take the position that distinguishing pulling the plug from assisted suicide lacks even a rational basis.

Again the same would hold true for PDE, refusing lifesaving treatment, and terminal sedation.

ISSUE 9

Legislation permitting physician-assisted
suicide would/would not be
sound social policy

The Question of Whether Legislatures
Should or Should Not Legalize
Physician-Assisted Suicide

The U.S. Supreme Court has made it clear that it is leaving it to the legislatures of the individual states to decide whether or not to legalize assisted suicide. So at this point in my journey it is my turn to take a position on the question of public policy: what do I believe should be our stance toward assisted suicide at this moment in history?

In trying to think through any suggested policy, I've decided to borrow a device from the philosopher John Rawls. Rawls, who is a deontological philosopher in the tradition of the great German philosopher Immanuel Kant,[1] sought to develop a philosophical basis for preferring the types of institutions and institutional arrangements that ideally constitute a liberal democracy.[2] To this end, he reenacted the social contract,[3] with the contractors deliberating under a "veil of ignorance."[4] Specifically, they did not know their place in the natural and social lotteries (rich or poor, brilliant or mentally disturbed, man or woman, black or white, and so on). So, for all they knew when creating the contract, once the veil was lifted they could wind up on society's bottom rung. As such, they tended to be somewhat risk averse. Within my veil of ignorance, I imagined that I did not know my age, health, gender, race, or religion if any (although I agreed that if after the veil was lifted I found out that I possessed deep religious beliefs regarding suicide, assisted suicide, and euthanasia opposed to what I've decided under the veil those religious beliefs would trump). I also knew that most people in modern society die in hospitals and nursing homes after long bouts with chronic illness. Even if I were denied these statistics, under the concept of "maximum ignorance" (which posits that if I have no data or a priori knowledge of plausible outcomes I should assume all outcomes equally likely),[5] assuming there is a fifty-fifty chance that my life will end this way would be extremely compelling in my deliberations.

I knew that I could be very sick, with no money, occupying a small bed in some state-run hospital or nursing home. I could be lingering, dribbling food down my chin and soiling myself. I could also be demented, in great pain, and depressed. It was not a very uplifting snapshot of my "golden years." Being so dependent, so helpless, and then adding the fact of dribbling and soiling myself like a six-week-old baby is initially a depressing notion. It's as though I've devolved, gone back to not fully being human, and that's hard to accept. Then I thought about all of this again. If I faced reality, I had to acknowledge that what I found to be such an upsetting image of myself was just another phase of a process that had been going on for quite some time, aging. My body is gradually (and at times not so gradually) breaking down. Getting old is no fun. I feel strong and can hike ten miles, but I can't see six feet in front of me without glasses, have trouble hearing, ache in the morning, and have no cartilage and ligaments in one knee and so can't run a block. Seeing myself incontinent and such is just more of the same. A part of me that I must accept.[6] I'd like to die with all my faculties in order, but it is nothing I can count on. To feel degraded and ashamed is a function of an illusion, a made-up "story" of myself in which the real me is somehow perpetually 28 and sexually appealing to women of all ages.

As to being demented, I cannot begin to even guess what that would be like. Would life necessarily be intolerable? Based on my mother's experience in an Alzheimer's residence, where, though deluded, she took pleasure in her day-to-day life, I see no reason why it necessarily should be. In truth, my real concern is that my wife would have to spend a great deal of money to keep me in such a facility. And part of me would rather die than take so many resources from her to maintain a demented me. I just don't know.

On the other hand, I do know that I would not want to end my life suffering beyond reason. If I was in excruciating pain or physical-emotional misery with no end in sight except upcoming death, I'd want the option to end it. But I also do not want to have to fear that in my condition I might be coerced or that some institution would kill me against my will (particularly if I'm poor, a minority, and have no family to watch out for me in the hospital or nursing home in which I am living).

I have not been convinced by the slippery slope arguments, based on either assumptions about human nature in the context of our society or empirical studies of Oregon and the Netherlands, that assisted suicide will inevitably engender such evil that even applying it in a case such as my father's is immoral. That, however, does not mean that I do not have real concerns.[7] Whatever one may say about studies of the Netherlands, it is hard to conclude that the Dutch experience proves there are *no* problems with PAS. The Oregon experience seems more positive, but there remain many questions and ambiguities about the official state reports and reasonable concerns about the efficiency of the standards themselves. I also know something about institutions and human psychology from having lived over six decades, and the slippery slope arguments, at least in the context of our current medical delivery system, can hardly be termed frivolous.

I see our society as being in a transition in which the momentum toward PAS has slowed. As I said when discussing the concept of resilient lines, the medical profession and our society have moved rather quickly from a professed vitalist perspective to the acceptance of DNR codes, PDE, pulling plugs, acceding to the refusal of lifesaving treatment, the contextual line between ordinary and extraordinary treatment, and terminal sedation. We have also permitted all this by means of living wills and substituted judgment. But now things have stalled a bit (although the recent U.S. Supreme Court case rejecting the attorney general's attempt to block the implementation of Oregon's assisted suicide act may change that).[8] For all that remains in our repertoire of life-ending techniques is stark and direct: helping someone poison and/or suffocate themselves, or actually doing the poisoning and/or suffocating. That has made us slow down; but I do not believe that we have changed the eventual destination (acceptance of some form of PAS) provided the experience of the next decade (and we will learn a great deal over the next ten years about our health care system and resources) does not produce stories that confirm the worst fears of the anti-PAS position.

I think this slowdown phase reflects wisdom as much as skittishness. I therefore would not recommend, for example, the immediate adoption of nationwide legislation legalizing assisted suicide and euthanasia. Individual states, such as Oregon, that want to legalize physician-assisted suicide should do that. We can all study and learn. But the world of managed care is just too new, and the real medical resource crunch as the baby boomers continue to age has not yet hit full force.[9] Go slowly. This is particularly so given that there are available, though admittedly imperfect, stopgap measures that can suffice until we learn more. Thus, I am taking into account the range of available methods through which a very ill person can end his or her life, including PDE, refusing treatment, pulling the plug, and terminal sedation, and the recognition that there are doctors who will make pills available or will even conduct PAS or euthanasia, even though it is against the law.[10]

At this point, I should note that I considered a middle ground between either permitting or forbidding PAS—a form of legal defense. This would hardly have been novel,[11] such accommodation being found in the laws of other nations.[12] And, in truth, there are sympathetic cases (such as my father's) in which the suffering person could not find release from any of the currently available measures. For those cases, I considered providing a complete defense to criminal prosecution under certain circumstances. The defense would have been based on the reality of human needs and weaknesses. As such, it would take the form of a legal "excuse" (such as duress) rather than a legal "justification" (such as self-defense). The result, however, would be the same regardless of whether the action was labeled excused or justified. The defendant would be acquitted.

In the end, however, I abandoned the enterprise as ill-advised. First, most people will be able to die through such accepted methods as pulling the plug and PDE. As to someone like my father, it is hard to imagine anything but the most remote chance that, if my sister and I had helped him die, anyone would have questioned the cause of his death (unless I put a bullet in his head). After all, he was in the final stages of dying from cancer. So one must wonder whether it is worth all the cost, resources, and time that would necessarily go into first creating the system and then running it. Perhaps not. Second, it is conceivable that any such "stopgap" measure will in fact tend to impede real discussion on the issue of PAS by providing a rationale to avoid facing this complex set of issues altogether (e.g., "We don't really have to deal with this most complex issue because we have given a defense in the criminal law"). Third, the very existence of such a defense may lead to tortured interactions in which the dying, suffering person will be forced to beg another for assistance, trying to convince the needed assistant that he or she will be protected by that defense.

Finally, I had to ask myself, if such a defense had existed, would it have made any difference in my decision whether or not to help my father? I don't think so at all. I would have been just as scared of criminal prosecution. Of course, it would seem that with such a defense I at least would have been better off if I had helped Dad and somehow been caught. But even that is not necessarily true. A prosecutor (or prosecutor's office) may be antagonistic to the very fact that such a defense exists, thereby giving some legitimacy to assisting suicide. Thus, while had the legislature not provided such a defense, the prosecution might have looked at my individual case with compassion and mercy; now the prosecutor might not see me, but only the existence of the defense, and might then decide to attack the policy decision to permit such a defense by prosecuting me to the limit.

In the end, I decided not to oppose the idea of PAS. The coming years may well show that PAS is an appropriate option in end of life care and that this option is worth the risks (and/or we have found we are able to significantly mitigate those risks). If so, PAS should be available when reasonable in every state, just not today.

There is a final approach that superficially might appear to resemble the one I have just taken but is really quite different: intentionally leave things the way they are and do nothing. The reasoning underlying this approach is surprisingly intricate. First, we must understand that we are allocating a resource—the means to terminate one's life. Initially, there would seem to be a sufficiently available supply of razors, guns, bridges, poisons, drugs, DNR orders, trains, high cliffs, and such that this resource is available to everyone in the country who wishes to terminate his or her life. But, of course, to make that resource available there are other costs in terms of lost lives, lost workers, lost productivity, lost taxes, lost family support, and so forth.

Moreover, even if this resource is seen as plentiful, its allocation, as we have seen, involves tensions between certain basic values (sanctity of life, autonomy, freedom from suffering), none of which we are prepared to compromise and all of which we desire to promote. So leave things as they are, replete with rough accommodations using pulling plugs and giving fatal doses of pain medications in which we hide from questions about who is making the actual choice that results in terminating life.[13] Let all this happen, including a euthanasia "underground," letting it all coexist with a legal prohibition without meaningful enforcement, and we have an American form of pragmatic tolerance or even tacit approval. We de facto allow autonomy its place, know that suffering will be dealt with, and yet have not formally passed a law devaluing the absolute sanctity of life.

While completely rational, this is not a feasible alternative in this instance. The pressure from the now aging baby boomers, who as a generation have sought to choose how to live their lives without being constrained by prior tradition and conventions, combined with a sizable euthanasia underground[14] and a health care system (managed care and HMOs) that operates according to a business rather than a medical model, will not permit us to rely on the status quo. It is far too dangerous. Significant regulation and oversight will be required. Again, if experiments like that in Oregon function well, alleviating our fears of a slippery slope, then regulated PAS would be appropriate. If, however, the experiment fails, and other data confirm our worst fears, then law must aggressively address the euthanasia underground and any de facto practices resembling euthanasia in managed care facilities. Either way, we will not be able to leave things as they are.

Epilogue

Calling this the end of my journey probably is more rhetoric than reality. It is the end of the book, but I've come to recognize that the journey will never end for me. I am no longer haunted by what happened, but I am not at peace either. Even now, as I go back to the time surrounding the deaths of my parents, my chest constricts a little and my breath gets short. I was so much in the middle of their dying, even though the deaths were theirs alone. I think they would be proud that I cared so much about the rightness or wrongness of what happened that I wrote this book.

Notes

Introduction

1. Peter G. Filene, *In The Arms of Others: A Cultural History of the Right to Die in America* 53 (Ivan R. Dee 1999); *Physician Assisted Suicide* 34 (Robert F. Weir, ed., Indiana Univ. Press 1997); Daniel Callahan, *The Troubled Dream of Life: Living with Mortality* 141 (Simon and Schuster 1993); Win J. Deikers, "Images of Death and Dying" (paper presented at Nijimegan Conference on "Death without Suffering") (April 5–7, 2000) [hereinafter "Nijimegan Conference"].

2. Daniel Callahan, supra n. 1, at 88; "Extracts from the Report of the House of Lords Select Committee on Medical Ethics," in *Euthanasia Examined: Ethical, Clinical, and Legal Perspectives* 96 (John Keown, ed., Cambridge Univ. Press 1998) [hereinafter "Euthanasia Examined"]; Sheryl A. Russ, "Care of Older Persons: The Ethical Challenge of American Medicine," 4 *Issues in Law & Med.* 87, 88 (1988).

3. Daniel Callahan, supra n. 1, at 32–33, 47; Mary Clement and Derek Humphrey, *The Unspoken Argument: Euthanasia and the High Cost of Dying* 15 (ERGO 2002) [hereinafter "High Cost of Dying"]; Joyce Ann Schofield, "Care of the Older Person: The Ethical Challenge to American Medicine," 4 *Issues in Law & Med.* 53, 53 (1989); Sheryl A. Russ, supra n. 2, at 88; *Cruzan v. Director Missouri Dept. of Health,* 497 U.S. 261, 328–29 (1990); David Field, "Palliative Medicine and the Medicalization of Death," 3 *European J. Cancer Care* 59 (1994); "Legal Euthanasia: Ethical Issues in an Era of Legalized Dying," 18 *J. Med. & Phil.* 270–71 (1994).

4. Derek Humphrey and Mary Clement, *Freedom to Die: People, Politics, and*

the Right to Die Movement 19 (St. Martin's Griffin 2000). The same demographics of the dying also appear in Britain. See David Field, supra n. 3, at 60.

5. John M. Cooper, "Greek Philosophies on Euthanasia and Suicide," in *Suicide and Euthanasia: Historical and Contemporary Themes* 9 (Baruch M. Brody, ed., Kluwer Academic 1989) [hereinafter "Historical and Contemporary Themes"]. See also Steve Zanskas and Wendy Conduti, "Eugenics, Euthanasia, and Physician Assisted Suicide: An Overview for Rehabilitation Professionals," 72 *J. Rehab.* 27, 28 (2006) (*eu* = "good," *thanatos* = "death"); Robert I. Mishbin, *Euthanasia: The Good of the Patient, the Good of Society* 47 (University Publishing Group 1992). For Stoics and Epicureans, it was a matter of personal choice. Fr. Robert Barry, O.P., "The Development of the Roman Catholic Teaching on Suicide," 9 *Notre Dame J.L. Ethics Publ. Pol.* 449, 464 (1995); John M. Cooper, "Greek Philosophers on Euthanasia and Suicide," in "Historical and Contemporary Themes," supra, at 29 (though they still encouraged people to try to avoid suicide); Lynn Tracy Nerland, "A Cry for Help: A Comparison of Voluntary, Active Euthanasia Law," 13 *Hastings Int'l & Compar. L. Rev.* 115, 119–21 (1989). See also Michael Manning, *Euthanasia and Physician-Assisted Suicide: Killing or Caring?* 7 (Paulist Press 1998) (in making a decision, one must also consider responsibilities to others). Socrates also approved (Fr. Robert Barry, O.P., supra, at 461), though Plato expressed some reservations (John M. Cooper, "Greek Philosophers on Euthanasia and Suicide," in "Historical and Contemporary Themes," supra, at 19). Those opposed to suicide included the Pythagoreans, see Fr. Robert Barry, O.P., supra, at 461 (God values each soul), and on Aristotle, see Fr. Robert Barry, O.P., supra, at 462; and John M. Cooper, "Greek Philosophers on Euthanasia and Suicide," in "Historical and Contemporary Themes," supra, at 208 (suicide is cowardice and violates our duty to serve the state). They also included the followers of Hippocrates. See Michael Manning, supra, at 8. But also see id., at 8–9 (a minority of Hippocratic physicians in the fourth or fifth century believed they had the discretion to terminate the patient's life).

6. Stacy L. Mojica and Dan S. Murrell, "The Right to Choose: When Should Death Be in the Individual's Hands?" 12 *Whittier L. Rev.* 471, 471 (1991). Fr. Robert Barry, O.P., supra n. 5, at 463. Suicide was common among aristocrats as a response to loss of honor and shame or even something done as a whim. Id. Fr. Robert Barry, O.P., supra n. 5, at 463; Kay Redfield Jamison, *Night Falls Fast: Understanding Suicide,* 13 (Knopf 1999).

7. See Stacy L. Mojica and Dan S. Surrell, supra n. 6, at 474–75.

8. Patricia S. Mann, "Meanings of Death," in *Physician Assisted Suicide: Expanding the Debate* 25 (Margaret P. Battin, Rosamond Rhodes, and Anita Silvers, eds., Routledge 1998) [hereinafter "Expanding the Debate"]; *The Reference Shelf: Suicide* (Robert E. Long, ed., H.W. Wilson 1995); Daniel C. Maguire, *Death by Choice* 86 (Schocken Books, 1975).

9. Daniel C. Maguire, supra n. 8, at 84; Tracy Nerland, supra n. 5, at 122.

10. Wesley J. Smith, *Forced Exit: The Slippery Slope from Assisted Suicide to*

Legalized Murder 75, 81 (Times Books 1997); Ian Dowbiggen, *A Merciful End: The Euthanasia Movement in Modern America* 4, 63–65 (Oxford Univ. Press 2003); Lynn Tracy Nerland, supra n. 5, at 124–25; N.D.A. Kemp, *"Merciful Release": The History of British Euthanasia Movement* 208 (Manchester Univ. Press 2002); Shai J. Lavi, *The Modern Act of Dying: A History of Euthanasia in the United States* (Princeton Univ. Press 2005).

11. Robert I. Mishbin, supra n. 5, at 151; Harold Y. Vanderpool, "Doctors and the Dying of Patients in American History," in *Physician-Assisted Suicide* 33 (Robert Weir, ed., Indiana Univ. Press 1997) [hereinafter "Physician-Assisted Suicide"]; Ian Dowbiggin, supra n. 10, at 36, 47; N.D.A. Kemp, supra n. 10, at 205 (". . . social Darwinism and eugenics were strong themes of the euthanasia debate"). In fact, between 1907 and 1945, 40,000 U.S. citizens were subjected to eugenic sterilizations. See Steve Zanskas and Wendy Coduit, supra n. 5, at 27.

12. Barry Rosenfeld, *Assisted Suicide and the Right to Die: The Interface of Social Science, Public Policy, and Medical Ethics* 17–18 (American Psych. Assn. 2004) (doctors developed diagnostic methods from which one could predict the outcome of a disease, and anesthesia and pain medicines).

13. Ian Dowbiggin, supra n. 10, at 64, 70; Wesley J. Smith, supra n. 10, at 83; N.D.A. Kemp, supra n. 10, at 211 (. . . the British euthanasia movement could not avoid being tarred with the Nazi brush).

14. Malcolm Parker, "End Games: Euthanasia under Interminable Scrutiny," 19 *Bio Ethics* 523, 534 (2005) ("Very gradually, but inexorably, physician-assisted suicide and euthanasia are being legalized across the world"). See also id., at 534 ("Germany allows physician-assisted suicide, but not active euthanasia"); C. Gastmans, F. Van Neste, and P. Schotsmans, "Facing Requests for Euthanasia," 30 *J. Med. Ethics* 212 (2004) (Belgium law legalizing euthanasia took effect on September 23, 2002); Katy Heslop, "Euthanasia around the World," *Observer* (Sept. 19, 2004) (self-administered assisted suicide legal in Switzerland). It has been noted that in Europe, in addition to religious beliefs, moral values, and sociodemographics, perceptions on euthanasia are "probably also influenced by national traditions and history." Joachen Cohen, Isabelle Marcoux, John Bilsen, Patrick DeBroosere, Gerrit Van Der Wel, and Luc Deliens, "European Public Acceptance of Euthanasia: Socio-demographics and Cultural Factors Associated with the Acceptance of Euthanasia in 33 European Countries," 63 *Soc. Sci. & Med.* 743 (2006).

15. Annette E. Clark, "Autonomy and Death," 71 *Tulane L. Rev.* 45, 54–55 (1996); Lynn Tracy Nerland, supra n. 5, at 127 (58 percent favor euthanasia in 1988); Robert T. Hall, "Final Acts: Sorting out Ethics of Physician Assisted Suicide," 54 *Humanist* 10 (1994) (1993 Harris Poll: 73 percent favor same form of Oregon-like physician-assisted suicide); Sarah Horsfell, Christian Alcocar, C. Temple Duncan, and Jonathan Polk, "Views of Euthanasia from an East Texas University," 38 *Soc. Sci. J.* 617 (2001) (72 percent support PAS); "Knowledge, Attitudes, and Behavior: Survey Finds Majority Support Right to Euthanasia and Physician-Assisted Suicide," *AIDS Weekly* 13 (Jan. 28, 2002) (61 percent support law permit-

ting PAS). See also Linda Ganzini, Wendy S. Johnson, Bentson M. McFarland, Susan M. Tolle, and Melinda A. Lee, "Attitudes of Patients with Amyotrophic Lateral Sclerosis and Their Caregivers toward Assisted Suicide," 339 *New Engl. J. Med.* 967 (1998) (majority of patients in Washington and Oregon with amyotrophic lateral sclerosis (ALS) would consider assisted suicide); Lauren Neergaard, "How People Meet Death: A Major Study," *Seattle Post Intelligencer* (Nov. 15, 2000) (60 to 80 percent of Americans believe terminally ill people in pain should be able to end their lives); Jennifer Silverman, "Views on Physician-Assisted Suicide," 38 *Int'l Med News* (Apr. 10, 2005) (57 percent of physicians say PAS is ethical, and 41 percent would endorse legalization in a wide variety of cases); "Survey Shows Most Physicians and General Public Support Physician-Assisted Suicide," *Life Science Weekly* (Nov. 8, 2005) (62 percent of physicians and 64 percent of public believe physicians should be permitted to dispense life-ending medication); O.D. Duncan and L.F. Parmelee, "Trends in Public Approval of Euthanasia and Suicide in the U.S., 1947–2003," 32 *J. Med. Ethics* 266, 268 (2006) (". . . one might say, tentatively, [that] approval of euthanasia has leveled off at approximately two-thirds of the population"). Cf. Paul J. Zwier, "Looking for a Non-legal Process: Physician-Assisted Suicide and the Care Perspective," 30 *U. Richmond L. Rev.* 199, 204 n. 23 (in a 1981 survey, 61 percent of Christian laity surveyed approved of suicide in cases of "incurable disease").

16. Sarah Horsfall et al., supra n. 15. In contrast, the position of mental health doctors for or against PAS is strongly correlated with their individual belief systems, particularly their religious beliefs. Tony D. Pasquale and John P. Gluck, "Psychologists, Psychiatrists, and Physician-Assisted Suicide: The Relationship between Underlying Beliefs and Professional Behavior," 32 *Profess. Psych. Research & Behavior* 50 (2001).

17. See the discussion of Oregon law in chapter 4. For an analysis of why a seemingly popular PAS referendum failed, see Steven J. Zieglar, Ph.D., J.D., and Robert A. Jackson, J.D., "Who's Not Afraid of Proposal B? An Analysis of Exit-Poll Data from Michigan's Vote on Physician-Assisted Suicide," 23 *Pol. & Life Sci.* 42 (2005).

18. Felicia Cohn and Joanne Lynn, "Vulnerable People: Practical Rejoinders to Claims in Favor of Assisted Suicide," in *The Case against Assisted Suicide: For the Right to End-of-Life Care* 240 (Katheleen Foley, M.D., and Herbert Hendin, M.D., eds., Johns Hopkins Univ. Press 2002) [hereinafter "The Case against Assisted Suicide"]; Liezl Van Zyl, *Death and Compassion: A Virtue-Based Approach to Euthanasia,* 124–25 (Ashgate 2000). See also Ian Dowbiggin, supra n. 10, at 175. (Consistently in the polls one-third support PAS, one-third support PAS in isolated cases but oppose it in general, and one-third oppose PAS under all circumstances. While there is a general endorsement of the abstract right to PAS, people balk when considering the right in specific situations.)

19. J. Hegelin, T. Hilstun, J. Hau, and H.E. Carlsson, "Surveys on Attitudes towards Legalization of Euthanasia: Importance of Question Phrasing," 30 *J.*

Med. Ethics 521 (2002); Donald P. Haides-Markel and Mark R. Joslyn, "Just How Important Is the Messenger versus the Message? The Case of Framing Physician-Assisted Suicide," 28 *Death Studies* 243, 257 (2004) ("Respondents exposed to a depiction that emphasized individual rights were significantly more supportive of PAS . . ."); David W. Moore, "Three in Four Americans Support Euthanasia: Significantly Less Support for Doctor Assisted Suicide," *Gallup News Service* (May 17, 2005) (the fact that the word *suicide* is contained in the phrase "physician-assisted suicide" dramatically affected the outcome of the poll).

20. See C. Leget, "Boundaries, Borders, and Limits. A Phenomenological Reflection on Ethics and Euthanasia," 32 *J. Med Ethics* 256, 256, 259 (2006) (arguments from both sides of the debate are interrelated and logically connected).

Issue 1

1. See Malcolm Parker, supra intro. n. 14, at 530:

   i. For most people, our ultimate preferences and principles, which satisfy our conceptions of the good life, can certainly conflict with others' preferences and principles, so morality involves both the realization of our individual conceptions and attempts to harmonize them with those of others.

   ii. This kind of theory is naturalistic in that it bases morality in human needs, concerns, attitudes and preferences, but also retains deontological language in its traditional place, to refer to those widely agreed principles of which we approve and which we can commend, setting them apart from just any possibility, and reserving to them a critical edge, as well as their generality and claim to universality.

2. Guido Calabresi and Phillip Bobbitt, *Tragic Choices* 198 (Norton 1978).

3. Ronald Dworkin, *Life's Dominion: An Argument about Abortion, Euthanasia, and Individual Freedom* 11, 25 (Vintage 1994); "Submission to the Select Committee of the House of Lords on Medical Ethics by the Linacre Centre for Health Care Ethics," in *Euthanasia, Clinical Practice, and the Law* Book Two, "Euthanasia and the Law: The Case against Legalism" 118 (Luke Gormally, ed., Linacre Centre for Health Care Ethics 1994) [the volume is divided into two parts referred to as Book One and Book Two; the volume as a whole is hereinafter cited as "Clinical Practice"]; James M. Gustafson, "Mongolism, Parental Desires, and the Right to Life," in *Death, Dying, and Euthanasia* 275 (Dennis I. Moran and David Mall, eds., Univ. Publications of America 1997) [hereinafter "Death-Dying"]; Luke Gormally, "Walton, Davies, Boyd, and the Legalization of Euthanasia," in "Euthanasia Examined," supra intro. n. 2, at 128: Liezl van Zyl, supra intro. n. 18, at xix, 9 (life and death are part of the "secular sacred"). Interestingly, the notion of the sanctity of life, which seems so fundamental to us, is really of relatively

recent origin in human history. M.T. Meulders-Klein, "The Right over One's Own Body: Its Scope and Limits under Comparative Law," 6 *Bost. Col. Int. & Compar. L.R.* 29, 32, 33 (1983).

4. John Keown, *Euthanasia, Ethics, and Public Policy: An Argument against Legalization* 224 (Cambridge Univ. Press 2004); Bryan Bennett, "Letting Vegetative Patients Die," in "Euthanasia Examined," supra intro. n. 2, at 179; Robert I. Mishbin, supra intro. n. 5, at 741; Larry Goshin, J.D., "The Right to Choose Death: The Judicial Trilogy of Brophy, Bovia, and Conroy," 14 *Law, Med., & Health Care* 198, 199 (1922); John F. Kavanagh, S.J., "Ethics Notebook: Killing and Letting Die," 183 *America* 23 (Sept. 23, 2000).

5. Dennis Sullivan, M.D., "Euthanasia versus Letting Die: Christian Decision-Making in Terminal Patients," 21 *Ethics & Med* 109, 111 (2005) ("The intuitive nature of the injunction against taking [innocent] life goes beyond the Decalogue to a shared consensus of the secular community as well . . .").

6. Karen Lebacgz, Ph.D., and H. Tristram Engelhardt Jr., Ph.D., M.D., "Suicide," in "Death-Dying," supra n. 3, at 688.

7. Peter Singer, *Rethinking Life and Death: The Collapse of Our Traditional Ethics* 70, 74 (St. Martin's Griffin 1994). See also "Submission to the Select Committee of the House of Lords on Medical Ethics by the Linacre Centre for Health Care Ethics," in "Clinical Practice," supra n. 3, at 39; and Margaret P. Battin, "Is a Physician Ever Obligated to Help a Patient Die?" in *Regulating How We Die: The Ethical, Medical, and Legal Issues Surrounding Assisted-Suicide* 32 (Linda L. Emanuel, ed., Harvard Univ. Press 1998) [hereinafter "Regulating How We Die"].

8. Germain Grisez, "Suicide and Euthanasia," in "Death-Dying," supra n. 3, at 786–87; Kay Redfield Jamison, supra intro. n. 6, at 65, 88.

9. Kay Redfield Jamison, supra intro. n. 6, at 72–73; Elaine Scarry, *The Body in Pain: The Making and Unmaking of the World* 67 (Oxford Univ. Press 1985).

10. "War, Morality Of," in the *New Catholic Encyclopedia,* vol. 14, at 635 et seq. (2d ed., Gates 2002); Margaret Somerville, *Death Talk: The Case against Euthanasia and Physician Assisted Suicide* 300 (McGill-Queen's Univ. Press 2001).

11. *The New Catholic Encyclopedia,* supra n. 10, at 659.

12. Germain Grisez, "Suicide and Euthanasia," in "Death-Dying," supra n. 3, at 804; Daniel C. Maguire, supra intro. n. 8, at 83, 121.

13. A. J. Ashworth, "Self-Defense and the Right to Life," 34 *Camb. L.J.* 282, 283 (1975); Sanford H. Kadish, "Respect for Life and Regard for Rights in the Criminal Law," 64 *Cal. L. Rev.* 871, 883 (1976).

14. Joshua Dressler, *Understanding Criminal Law,* §18.07B, at 228 (Matthew Bender 1995).

15. Daniel C. Maguire, supra intro. n. 8, at 111. See also German Grisez, supra n. 12, at 786–87.

16. See Jim Dwyer, Peter Neufeld, and Barry Scheck, *Actual Innocence* (2000); Edward F. Conners, Thomas Lundregan, Neal Miller, and Tom

McEwen, *Convicted by Juries, Exonerated by Science: Case Studies in the Use of DNA Evidence to Establish Innocence after Trial* (U.S. Department of Justice 1996). See also Innocence Project, http://www.innocenceproject.org; and "Sister Helen Prejean on Death Row: Nun Author and Anti-death Penalty Movement," 127 *Commonwealth* 11 (Oct. 6, 2000).

17. Ibid.

18. Stuart Banner, *The Death Penalty: An American History* 5–23, 88–111 (Harvard University Press 2002).

19. James Boyd White, "Telling Stories in the Law and in Ordinary Life: The *Oresteia* and 'Noon Wine,'" chapter 8 of *Heracles' Bow: Essays on the Rhetoric and Poetics of Law* 176 (University of Wisconsin Press 1985).

20. Erich H. Loewy, "Harming, Healing, and Euthanasia," in "Regulating How We Die," supra n. 7, at 54; Arthur Dyck, "Beneficent Euthanasia and Benemortasia: Alternative Views of Mercy," in "Death-Dying," supra n. 3, at 352.

21. "Submission to the Select Committee of the House of Lords on Medical Ethics by the Linacre Centre for Heath Care Ethics," in "Clinical Practice," supra, n. 3, at 126 (such a belief in equality is necessary if we will have "Justice" in our society); Arthur Dyck, "Beneficent Euthanasia and Benemortasia: Alternative Views of Mercy," in "Death-Dying," supra n. 3, at 359 (no person or community can say who deserves to live or die); Luke Gormally, "Walton, Davies, Boyd, and the Legalization of Euthanasia," in "Euthanasia Examined," supra intro. n. 2, at 115 (we protect all by making all equally entitled to justice); Peter Singer, supra n. 7, at 65; Marc Stauch, "Causal Authorship and the Equality Principle: A Defense of the Acts-Omission Distinction in Euthanasia," 26 *J. Med. Ethics* 237, 240 (2000). As was the case with the sanctity of life, the notion that all lives have equal value is a recent one in human history. M.T. Meulders-Klein, supra n. 3, at 35.

22. "Introduction: A Medical, Legal, Psychosocial Perspective," in "The Case against Assisted Suicide," supra intro. n. 18, at 13; Diane Coleman, "Not Dead Yet," in "The Case against Assisted Suicide," supra intro. n. 3, at 213; John Finnis, "Misunderstanding the Case against Euthanasia: Response to Harris's First Reply," in "Euthanasia Examined," supra intro. n. 2, at 64; Peter Singer, supra n. 7, at 36, 49, 199. This concern is said to be particularly acute for the disabled given how society tends to undervalue them and limit their lifestyle choices. Jerome E. Bickenbach, "Disability and Life-Ending Decisions," in "Expanding the Debate," supra intro. n. 8, at 123; Darrel W. Amundsen, "The Significance of Inaccurate History in Legal Considerations of Physician-Assisted Suicide," in "Physician-Assisted Suicide," supra intro. n. 11, at 16; Peter Singer, supra n. 7, at 181.

23. Thomas H. Lellie and James I. Werth Jr., "End-of-Life Issues and Persons with Disabilities: Introduction to Special Edition," 16 *J. Disability Pol'y Studies* 2, 2, 3 (2005); James L. Werth Jr., "Concerns about Decisions Related to Withholding/Withdrawing Life-Sustaining Treatment and Futility for Persons with Disabilities," 16 *J. Disability Pol'y Studies* 21, 32 (2005). ("The primary concerns expressed by advocates related to assisted suicide revolve around the social deval-

uation of persons with disabilities that is present in the United States and the pos-
sibility that persons with disabilities will internalize these negative attitudes.");
Merope Pavlides, "Whose Choice Is It, Anyway? Disability and Suicide in Four
Contemporary Films," *J. Disability Pol'y Studies* 46 (2005) ("This review confirms
the hypothesis that such films underscore our cultural tendency to view disability
and illness as an experience that demands release rather than support"); Darrell
W. Amundsen and Gail Taira, "Our Lives and Ideologies: The Effect of Life
Experience on the Perceived Morality of the Policy of Physician-Assisted Suicide,"
16 *J. Disability Pol'y Studies* 53, 55 (2005) ("The very people whose job it was to care
for me believed that I would be better off dead"); id., at 56 ("The ableist's ideol-
ogy. . . : The unhappiness of 'those people' is caused by their impairments, not by
the ableist's own lack of social conscience. This is the social harm caused by
ableism and abetted by the assisted suicide movement."). But see Karen Hwang,
"Attitudes of Persons with Physical Disabilities toward Physician-Assisted Suicide: An Exploratory Assessment of the Vulnerability Argument," 16 *J. Disability
Pol'y Studies* 16, 20 (2005) (the disabled community is not monolithic in its view;
some don't think of themselves as vulnerable and resent the label). But the disabled may be more prone to consider ending their lives because of discriminatory
services that make life difficult to live, Paul K. Langmore, "Policy, Prejudice, and
Reality: Two Case Studies of Physician-Assisted Suicide," 16 J. *Disability Pol'y
Studies* 38, 44 (2005); and an unsupportive cultural environment that keeps the
disabled from seeing the potential quality and value their lives might have,
Richard Radtke, "A Case against Physician-Assisted Suicide," *J. Disability Pol'y
Studies* 58 (2005).

24. Bill Moyers, "Living with Dying," segment 1 of *On Our Own Terms:
Films for the Humanities and Science* (2000); Darrel W. Amundsen, "The
Significance of Inaccurate History in Legal Considerations of Assisted Suicide," in
"The Case against Assisted Suicide," supra intro. n. 3, at 13; Darrel W. Amundsen,
"The Significance of Inaccurate History in Legal Consideration of Physician
Assisted Suicide," in "Expanding the Debate," supra intro. n. 8, at 91; Stacie L.
Mojica and Dan S. Murel, supra intro. n. 6, at 471, 485. This opposition on the
part of African Americans, however, may be as much a function of religious belief
as concerns about racial bias. Peter G. Filene, supra intro. n. 1, at 213. Dona J.
Reese, Robin E. Ahern, Shankar Nair, Joleen D. O'Faire, and Claudia Warren,
"Hospice Access and Use by African Americans: Addressing Cultural and Institutional Barriers through Participatory Action Research," 44 *Social Work* 549, 553–54
(1999) (barriers to use of hospice include knowledge of service economic
restraints, religious views that to not pray for a miracle and fight on demonstrates
a lack of faith in God, cultural views about fighting for life and a cure versus
accepting palliative care and inevitable death, distrust of nondiverse health care
system when a recommendation for palliative care is made).

25. "Social worth" was a central criterion for decisions about who would be
given access to kidney dialysis in some programs. Twenty-nine percent of the cen-

ters definitely excluded patients with a "poor family environment, 21 percent indigency, 20 percent poor employment record." See Renee C. Fox and Judith P. Swazey, *The Courage to Fail: A Social View of Organ Transplants and Dialysis* 230 table 5 (2d ed., University of Chicago Press 1978). Further, "'marital status,' 'net worth,' 'occupation,' and 'past performance and future potential' were the types of social worth criteria that the committee member avowedly considered." Id., at 232.

An even more vivid sense of the role of social worth criteria in these life and death decisions comes from the recollections of one board member who made such decisions.

> "The choices were hard," Mr. N, a lay member of the committee, told us, "and I wasn't happy about some of the decisions I made. For example, I remember voting against a young woman who was a known prostitute. I found I couldn't vote for her, rather than another candidate, a young wife and mother who had proved her responsibility and worth. I also voted against a young man who had been a ne'er-do-well, a real playboy, until he learned he had renal failure. He promised he would reform his character go back to school, and so on, if only he were selected for treatment. But I felt I'd lived long enough to know that a person like that won't really do what he was promising at the time."

Id.; see also Paul E. Kalb and David H. Miller, "Utilitarian Strategies for Intensive Care Units," 261 *JAMA* 2389 (1989) ("such social considerations as quality of life, family preferences, and potential contribution to family and society were all important factors in physician treatment decisions"). Thus, in making decisions about who would be given dialysis the committee tended to choose people like them, the upper middle class. See Renee C. Fox and Judith P. Swazey, supra n. 25, at 230–31.

> [T]hose making microallocation decisions have a strong tendency to prefer patients with whom they identify; if the decision-makers are well-educated and well-to-do professionals, an allocation system in which the patient's social worth were a factor would be likely to prefer patients with high socio-economic status. Minority groups and the underprivileged might be underrepresented.

The preceding quotation is from Maxwell J. Mehlman, "Rationing Expensive Lifesaving Medical Treatment," 1985 *Wisc. L. Rev.* 239, 258 (n. omitted). See also Kelli D. Back, "Rationing Health Care: Naturally Unjust?" 12 *Hamline J. Pub. L. & Pol.* 245, 249 (1991) (noting that those making rationing decisions "tend to favor patients with whom they can identify"). Cf. President's Commission for the Study of Ethical Problems in Medicine and Biomedical and Behavioral Research, *Allocation of Resources for Medical Intensive Care, Securing Access to Health Care: The Ethical Implications of Differences in the Availability of Health Services* 306

(1983) (doctors consciously or unconsciously are influenced by their affinity, or lack thereof, with a patient, including whether the doctor and patient are of the same socioeconomic class).

26. Daniel C. Maguire, supra intro. n. 8, at 88, 132. For a fuller discussion of the Nazi horror, see chapter 4.

27. Helga Kuhse and Peter Singer, "For Sometimes Letting—and Helping—Die," 19 *Law, Med. & Health Care* 149, 150 (1987).

28. See *Cruzon v. Director, Missouri Dept. of Health*, 497 U.S. 261, 302 (1990). This is less surprising when one realizes that on average 80 days of the last year of one's life are spent in a hospital or nursing home. Peter G. Filene, supra intro. n. 1, at 55. See also Paul J. Zweir, supra intro. n. 5, at 224 (70 percent of these decisions will involve withdrawing treatment); George P. Smith, "Restructuring the Principles of Medical Futility," 11 *J. Palliative Care* 9.9 (1995); and Marcia Angell, "Helping Desperately Ill People to Die," in "Regulating How We Die," supra n. 7, at 12. A somewhat different estimate (though limited to hospitals) estimates that 50 percent of deaths in hospitals from nonemergency cases result from withdrawing lifesaving treatment. Robert T. Hall, supra intro. n. 15, at 10.

29. Daniel Callahan, "Self-Extinction: The Morality of the Helping Hand," in "Physician Assisted Suicide" supra intro. n. 11, at 95. If a nonphysician pulled the plug, it would be homicide. Leslie Pickerias Francis, "Assisted Suicide: Are the Elderly a Special Case?" in "Expanding the Debate," supra intro. n. 8, at 241; Peter Singer, supra n. 7, at 77. See also J.P. Bishop, "Euthanasia, Efficiency, and the Historical Distinction between Killing a Patient and Allowing a Patient to Die," *J. Med. Ethics* 220, 220 (2006) (we can't distinguish between killing and letting die because the modern view of causality wrongly focuses on effect not motives and intent like the older formulation).

30. David J. Roy and Charles-Henri Rapine, "Regarding Euthanasia," 1 *European J. Palliative Care* 57, 58 (1994).

31. George P. Smith, supra n. 28, at 10. Smith includes four concepts within the notion of futility: (1) the treatment won't cure, (2) the treatment is not beneficial, (3) the treatment is unlikely to produce benefits, and (4) the treatment is plausible but not yet validated. See also Robert I. Mishbin, supra intro. n. 5, at 144–45 (no right to use resources if "futile"). Cf. Robert I. Mishbin, supra intro. n. 5, at 127 (on "go slow" codes in hospitals). For the Catholic view on futility, see Kevin D. O'Rourke, O.P., "Pain Relief: Ethical Issues and Catholic Teaching," in *Birth, Suffering, and Death* 157, 163 (K.W. Wilder, ed., Kluwer Academic 1992); and "Nutrition and Hydration: Moral and Pastoral Reflections," 15 *J. Contemp. Health Law & Policy* 455, 466 (1999) (National Conference of Catholic Bishops Committee for Pro-life Activities) (discusses when providing water is considered futile).

32. James L. Werth, "Concerns about Decisions Relating to Withholding/ Withdrawing Life Sustaining Treatment and Futility for Persons with Disabilities," 16 *J. Disability Pol'y Studies* 31, 34 (2005) ("If Futility is to be a useful concept in practice, it must have an understandable and acceptable definition and be

applied consistently by physicians. Research indicates that this is not the case, ..."); David Rieff, "Illness as More Than Metaphor," *New York Times Magazine* (Dec. 4, 2005) (in writing about the death of his mother, Susan Sontag, her son notes, "I have found no consensus [regarding the meaning of medical futility] among the oncologists I have spoken with in the aftermath of my mother's death, and I don't believe there is one").

33. Peter Asili, "Right to Die Cases and Theology," 100–101 *Law & Justice* 58, 66 (1998) (discusses the concept of disproportionality in the Catholic moral tradition in medicine).

34. John Keown, supra n. 4, at 44; Law Reform Commission of Canada, *Protection of Life: Euthanasia, Aiding Suicide, and Cessation of Treatment* (working paper 2) 35 (1982) [hereinafter: "Canada"]. For the Catholic perspective on the ordinary versus extraordinary distinction, see, Peter Asili, supra n. 33, at 66.

35. Gillian M. Craig, "On Withholding Nutrition and Hydration in the Terminally Ill: Has Palliative Medicine Gone Too Far?" 20 *J. Med. Ethics* 139, 144 (1994).

36. Daniel C. Maguire, supra intro. n. 8, at 124–25. In fact, the Catholic application of the doctrine includes a consideration of costs and burdens on the remaining family members. Asili, supra n. 33, at 66; Joseph Boyle, "A Case for Sometimes Feeding Patients in a Persistent Vegetative State," in "Euthanasia Examined," supra intro. n. 2, at 199.

37. Peter Singer, supra n. 7, at 112; Leizl van Zyl, supra intro. n. 18, at 52; John Harris, "The Philosophical Case against the Philosophical Case against Euthanasia," in "Euthanasia Examined," supra intro. n. 2, at 33, 39; "Submission to the Select Committee of the House of Lords on Medical Ethics by the Linacre Centre of Health Care Ethics," in "Clinical Practice," supra n. 3, at 139; Robert T. Hall, supra intro. n. 15, at 12; George P. Smith, supra n. 28, at 10.

38. Margaret P. Battin, "Is a Physician Ever Obligated to Help a Patient Die?" in "Regulating How We Die," supra n. 7, at 41; Lawrence O. Gostin, supra n. 4, at 94. On the other hand, there are authors who say that one cannot easily tell whether or not morphine was the cause of a particular death. Wesley J. Smith, supra intro. n. 10, at 222. There are even some who claim that, properly administered, morphine carries no greater risk of death than aspirin. "Submission to the Select Committee of House of Lords on Medical Ethics by the Linacre Centre for Health Care Ethics," in "Clinical Practice," supra n. 3, at 79.

39. Alan Donagan, *The Theory of Morality* 57 (1997); John Keown, supra n. 4, at 20; Joseph M. Boyle Jr., "Toward Understanding the Principle of Double Effect," 90 *Ethics* 527 (1980); Kevin D. O'Rourke, G.P., supra n. 31, at 165.

40. Liezl van Zyl, supra intro. n. 18, at 127. See also Alan Donagan, supra n. 39, at 159; Joseph M. Boyle Jr., supra n. 39, at 531–32.

41. Glanville Williams, *The Sanctity of Life and the Criminal Law* 322 (Knopf 1972); Liezl van Zyl, supra intro. n. 18, at 129: Joseph M. Boyle Jr., supra n. 39.

42. Yale Kamisar, "The Reasons So Many People Support Physician Assisted

Suicide and Why Those Reasons Are Not Convincing," 12 *Issues in Law & Med.* 113, 125 (1996).

43. "Submission to Select Committee of House of Lords on Medical Ethics by the Linacre Centre for Health Care Ethics," in "Clinical Practice," supra n. 3, at 63. Cf. Robert I. Mishbin, supra intro. n. 5, at 141.

44. Craig Paterson, "On Clarifying Terms in Applied Ethics Discourse: Suicide, Assisted Suicide, and Euthanasia," 43 *Int'l Phil. Q.* 351, 351–55 (2003). ("Suicide is to be taken to mean: an act or omission whose proximate effect results in the person's own bodily death, voluntarily and knowingly undertaken, with the intended objective [whether as an end in itself or as a means to some further end] that one's bodily life be so terminated.")

45. Bernard Gert, Charles M. Culver, and K. Danner Clooser, "An Alternative to Physician-Assisted Suicide," in "Expanding the Debate," supra intro. n. 8, at 182; John D. Arras, "Tragic View," in "Expanding the Debate," supra intro. n. 8, at 294; Balfour M. Mount and Pat Hamilton, "When Palliative Care Fails to Control Suffering," 10 *J. Palliative Care* 24 (1994); Marion D. Cooper, "When Palliative Care Fails to Control Suffering," 10 *J. Palliative Care* 27 (1994); Gillian M. Craig, supra n. 35, at 139; Gillian M. Craig, "On Withholding Artificial Hydration and Nutrition from the Terminally Ill: The Debate Continues," 22 *J. Med. Ethics* 147 (1996); Stacy Diloreto, "The Complexities of Assisted-Suicide," 34 *Patient Care* 65, 65 (2000).

46. Raanan Gillon, "Palliative Care Ethics: Non-provision of Artificial Nutrition and Hydration to Terminally Ill Sedated Patients," 20 *J. Med. Ethics* 131 (1994); Judith A.C. Rietjens, Ph.D., Johannes J.M. van Delden, M.D., Ph.D., Agnes van der Deide, M.D., Ph.D., Astrid M. Vrakking, M.S., Breggie D. Onwuteaka-Philipsen, Ph.D., Paul J. van der Maas, M.D., Ph.D., and Gerrit van der Wal, M.D., Ph.D., "Terminal Sedation and Euthanasia: A Comparison of Clinical Practices," 166 *Arch. Internal Med* 749, 749 (2006).

47. David Orentlicher, "The Supreme Court and Terminal Sedation: Rejecting Assisted Suicide, Embracing Euthanasia," 24 *Hast. Const. Q.* 947, 953–58 (1997); Id., at 959 (sedation prevents saving a patient who has been misdiagnosed because he or she will die anyway from starvation); John D. Arras, "Tragic View," in "Expanding the Debate," supra intro. n. 8, at 300 (author believes that terminal sedation is even worse than PAS); David Orentlicher, "The Supreme Court and Terminal Sedation: An Ethically Inferior Alternative to Physician-Assisted Suicide," in "Expanding the Debate," supra intro. n. 8, at 301.

48. Judith A.C. Reitjens et al., supra n. 46, at 752.

Issue 2

1. H. Tristram Englehardt Jr., "Death by Free Choice: A Modern Variation on an Antique Theme," in "Historical and Contemporary Themes," supra intro. n. 5, at 260; Paul I. Mishbin, supra intro. n. 5, at 175.

2. "Limits to Moral Pluralism," in "Clinical Practice," Book One, "Euthanasia and Clinical Practice: Trends, Principles, and Alternatives (Working Party Report, 1982)," supra ch. 1 n. 3, at 45; Glanville Williams, supra ch. 1 n. 41, at 19.

3. See, for example, Melinda A. Lee, Heidi D. Nelson, Virginia P. Tilden, Linda Ganzini, Terri A. Schmidt, and Susan W. Tolle, "Legalizing Assisted Suicide: Views of Physicians in Oregon," 334 *New Engl. J. Med.* 310, 314 (1996); David W. Moore, supra intro. n. 19 (religious beliefs are most strongly correlated with opposition to PAS if the person is a weekly churchgoer and/or an evangelical Christian).

4. On one side are those who attribute the ban to a pragmatic need to prevent wholesale martyrdom. Fr. Robert Barry, O.P., supra intro. n. 5, at 471. On the other are those who find the ban an existing moral principle throughout the history of the church. Id.; Darrel W. Amundsen, "Suicide and Early Christian Values," in "Historical and Contemporary Themes," supra intro. n. 5, at 79, 130–32, 140 (Augustine condemned the Donatists).

5. Darrel W. Amundsen, "Suicide and Early Christian Values," in "Historical and Contemporary Themes," supra intro. n. 5, at 77.

6. Fr. Robert Barry, O.P., supra intro. n. 5, at 472; Darrel W. Amundsen, "The Significance of Inaccurate History in Legal Considerations of Physician-Assisted Suicide," in "Physician-Assisted Suicide," supra intro. n. 11, at 3.

7. Darrel W. Amundsen, "Suicide and Early Christian Values," in "Historical and Contemporary Themes," supra intro. n. 5, at 79, 104. See also id., at 62 (Jewish martyrs).

8. Fr. Robert Barry, O.P., supra intro. n. 5, at 470 (rape by a pagan); Darrel W. Amundsen, "Suicide and Early Christian Values," in "Historical and Contemporary Themes," supra intro. n. 5, at 79, 121; Darrel W. Amundsen, "The Significance of Inaccurate History in Legal Considerations of Physician-Assisted Suicide," in "Physician-Assisted Suicide," supra intro. n. 11, at 13, 20. But see Darrel W. Amundsen, "Suicide and Early Christian Values," in "Historical and Contemporary Themes," supra intro. n. 5, at 140 (Augustine condemned suicide by rape victims), Darrel W. Amundsen, "The Significance of Inaccurate History in Legal Considerations of Physician-Assisted Suicide," in "Physician-Assisted Suicide," supra intro. n. 11, at 12 (arrest by pagans); and Darrel W. Amundsen, "Suicide and Early Christian Values," in "Historical and Contemporary Themes," supra intro. n. 5, at 80 (torture by pagans)

9. Paul I. Mishbin, supra intro. n. 5, at 143.

10. Tom L. Beauchamp, "Suicide in the Age of Reason," in "Historical and Contemporary Themes," supra intro. n. 5, at 197; Gerald A. Larue, *Euthanasia and Religion: A Survey of the Attitudes of World Religions to the Right to Die* 3 (Hemlock Society 1985); *Basic Questions on Suicide and Euthanasia: Are They Ever Right?* Bio Basics Series, 35–36 (Gary P. Steward, ed., Kregel 1998).

11. Fr. Robert Barry, O.P., supra intro. n. 5, at 253 (Samson, Razis), 456 (Saul, Zimri, Ahithophel, Judas).

12. Id., at 45; Darrel W. Amundsen, "Suicide and Early Christian Values," in

"Historical and Contemporary Themes," supra intro. n. 5, at 127; Daniel C. Maguire, supra intro. n. 8, at 143 (Samson); Darrel W. Amundsen, "The Significance of Inaccurate History in Legal Considerations of Physician-Assisted Suicide," in "Physician-Assisted Suicide," supra intro. n. 11, at 24.

13. Fr. Robert Barry, O.P., supra intro. n. 5, at 451, 452, 456.

14. Gerald A. Larue, supra n. 10, at 24; Anthony Fisher, "Theological Aspects of Euthanasia," in "Euthanasia Examined," supra intro. n. 2, at 316; Joni Eareckson Tada, *When Is It Right to Die?* 112 (HarperCollins 1992).

15. Fr. Robert Barry, O.P., supra intro. n. 5, at 454–55 (the prophets Elijah, Jonah, Job, Moses, and Tabil wished to die), 458.

16. James F. Childress, "Religious Viewpoints," in "Regulating How We Die," supra ch. 1 n. 5, at 125; Beth Spring and Ed Laron, *Euthanasia: Spiritual, Medical, and Legal Lessons in Health Care* 109 (Multnomah 1988) (Saint Augustine's position); Joseph Boyle, "Sanctity of Life and Suicide: Tensions and Developments within Common Morality," in "Historical and Contemporary Themes," supra intro. n. 5, at 226 (author notes that the phrase "your neighbors" is not added to modify "Thou shall not kill").

17. Cf. Alan Donagan, supra ch. 1 n. 39, at 6.

18. Daniel B. Sinclair, "The Interaction between Law and Morality in Jewish Law in the Area of Feticide and Killing of a Terminally Ill Individual," 11 *Criminal Justice Ethics* 76, 80 (summer–fall 1992); H. Tristram Engelhardt Jr., "Death by Free Choice: Modern Variations on an Antique Theme," in "Historical and Contemporary Themes," supra intro. n. 5, at 257; Peter Singer, supra ch. 1 n. 7, at 218 (the threat of murder causes fear because humans can see themselves existing over time and the risk of death at the hands of another "threatens the peaceful existence on which our society depends"). See also Carl Wellman, "A Moral Right to Physician-Assisted Suicide," 38 *Am. Phil. Q.* 271, 273 (2001) (murder also harms the family and friends of the victim).

19. Daniel C. Maguire, supra intro. n. 8, at 6; Glanville Williams, supra ch. 1 n. 41, at 313–14; Karen Labacqz and H. Tristram Engelhardt Jr., M.D., "Suicide," in "Death-Dying," supra ch. 1 n. 8, at 695.

20. Glanville Williams, supra ch. 1 n. 41, at 256. Cf. also Karen Lebacqz, Ph.D., and H. Tristram Engelhardt," supra ch. 1 n. 6, at 686. ("Murder . . . is the violation of a person's 'right to life.' In suicide, there is no violation of someone's right to life, because the act is not against the victim's will.")

21. James F. Childress, "Religious Viewpoints," in "Regulating How We Die," supra ch. 1 n. 7, at 26 (author goes through Aquinas's "metaphors," i.e., gifts, loans, and such); Fr. Robert Barry, O.P., supra, intro. n. 5, at 476; Beth Spring and Ed Laron, supra n. 16, at 122.

22. Noam J. Zohar, "Jewish Deliberations on Suicide," in "Expanding the Debate," supra intro. n. 8, at 364.

23. Paul I. Mishbin, supra intro. n. 5, at 169; Baruch A. Brody, "A Historical Introduction to Jewish Casuistry on Suicide and Euthanasia," in "Historical and

Contemporary Themes," supra intro. n. 5, at 39; James F. Childress, "Religious Viewpoints," in "Regulating How We Die," supra ch. 1 n. 7, at 138; Rabbi Immanuel Jacobvit, "Some Recent Jewish Views on Euthanasia," in "Death-Dying," supra ch. 1 n. 3, at 343.

24. Fr. Robert Barry, O.P., supra intro. n. 5, at 476; Darrel W. Amundsen, "Suicide and Early Christian Values," in "Historical and Contemporary Themes," supra intro. n. 5; Thomas L. Beauchamp, "Suicide in the Age of Reason," in "Historical and Contemporary Themes," supra intro. n. 5, at 142, 190–92; Michael Manning, M.D., supra intro. n. 5, at 17; Glanville Williams, supra ch. 1 n. 4, at 264.

25. Karen Labacqz and H. Tristram Engelhardt Jr., M.D., "Suicide," in "Death-Dying," supra ch. 1 n. 3, at 695; Beth Spring and Ed Laron, supra n. 16, at 97; "The Gift of Life," in "Clinical Practice," Book One, "Euthanasia and Clinical Practice: Trends, Principles, and Alternatives (Working Party Report, 1982)," supra ch. 1 n. 3, at 51.

26. Paulo Coelho, *Veronica Decides to Die* 8 (Margaret Jull Costas, trans., HarperCollins 1998).

27. Germain Griez, "Suicide and Euthanasia," in "Death-Dying," supra ch. 1 n. 3, at 763; John Finnis, "A Philosophical Case against Euthanasia," in "Euthanasia Examined," supra intro. n. 2, at 32.

28. Paul I. Mishbin, supra intro. n. 5, at 173; "The Conditions of Our Stewardship," in "Clinical Practice," Book One, "Euthanasia and Clinical Practice: Trends, Principles, and Alternatives (Working Party Report, 1982)," supra ch. 1 n. 3, at 53; Peter Asili, supra ch. 1 n. 33, at 65. But see Glanville Williams, supra ch. 1 n. 41, at 250 (author considers a conundrum: How can you return your soul if it is destroyed at death? Yet, if it's not destroyed, God gets it back.).

29. Gerald A. Larue, supra n. 10, at 16; Tom L. Beauchamp, "Suicide in the Age of Reason," in "Historical and Contemporary Themes," supra intro. n. 5, at 203.

30. Daniel C. Maguire, supra intro. n. 8, at 61, 142.

31. Tom L. Beauchamp, "Suicide in the Age of Reason," in "Historical and Contemporary Themes," supra intro. n. 5, at 204; Kenneth Boyd, "Euthanasia: Back to the Future," in "Euthanasia Examined," supra intro. n. 2, at 73.

32. Fr. Robert Barry, O.P., supra intro. n. 5, at 150; *Basic Questions on Suicide and Euthanasia: Are They Ever Right?* Bio Series 28 (Gary P. Stewart, ed., Kregel 1998); Paul Ramsey, "The Indignity of Death with Dignity," in "Death-Dying," supra ch. 1 n. 3, at 322.

33. Darrel W. Amundsen, "Suicide and Early Christian Values," in "Historical and Contemporary Themes," supra intro. n. 5, at 712.

Issue 3

1. John Stuart Mill, "Utilitarianism," 4 (George Sher, ed., Hackett 1988) (1861).

2. *The Encyclopedia of Philosophy,* vol. 7, 207 (Paul Edward, ed. in chief, Collier Macmillan 1962) [hereinafter "Philosophy"]; interview with John Harris, Professor of Philosophy and Bioethics, Manchester University, Manchester, England, April 2001 [hereinafter "Interview"]; Standley Haverwas, "Selecting Children to Live or Die: An Ethical Analysis of the Debate between Dr. Lorber and Dr. Freeman on the Treatment of Meningomyeloclere," in "Death-Dying," supra ch. 1 n. 3, at 243; Alan Donagan, supra intro. n. 39, at 192; John Stuart Mill, "Utilitarianism," supra n. 1, at vii, 16.

3. John Stuart Mill, "Utilitarianism," supra n. 1, at 21.

4. "Philosophy," supra n. 2, at 206; "Clinical Practice," Book One, "Euthanasia and Clinical Practice: Trends, Principles, and Alternatives (Working Party Report, 1982)," supra ch. 1 n. 3, at 28 (generally people seek happiness; variously defined). See also John Stuart Mill, "Utilitarianism," supra n. 1, at 8–13, 34.

5. John Stuart Mill, "Utilitarianism," supra n. 1, at 35.

6. "Philosophy," supra n. 2, at 208.

7. Id.

8. Id., at 209. See, generally, David Lyons, *Forms and Limits of Utilitarianism* (Clarendon 1965).

9. Derek Humphrey, *Final Exit: The Practicalities of Self-Deliverance and Assisted Suicide for the Dying* xv (published by Hemlock Society; distributed by Carol Pub. 1991); Katy Redfield Jamison, supra intro. n. 6, at 24; John Wesley Smith, supra intro. n. 6, at xvi.

10. Kay Redfield Jamison, supra intro. n. 6, at 24.

11. David Lyons, supra n. 8, at 69–72.

12. Karen Lebacqz and H. Tristram Engelhardt Jr., M.D., "Suicide," in "Death-Dying," supra ch. 1 n. 3, at 676–79. Cf. Glanville Williams, supra ch. 1 n. 41, at 272 (laws against suicide may deter some at the margins).

13. David Lester, "Suicide among the Elderly in the World: Covariation with Psychological and Socio-economic Factors," in *Suicide and Euthanasia in Older Adults: A Trans-cultural Journey* 7, 12 (Daniel DeLeo, ed., Horgrefe and Huber 2001) [hereinafter "Older Adults"].

14. Kay Redfield Jamison, supra intro. n. 6, at 24; Karen Lebacqz and H. Tristram Engelhardt Jr., M.D., "Suicide," in "Death-Dying," supra ch. 1 n. 3, at 675; Margaret A. Dickerson, Melinda A. Lee, and Linda Ganzini, "Practical Issues in Physician Assisted Suicide," 126 *Annals of Internal Med.* 146, 149 (1997). But cf. "Grief Eased for Euthanasia Families," *Times* (London) (July 25, 2003) ("Families whose loved ones die as a result of euthanasia suffer less harrowing grief and fewer symptoms of stress than do those whose relations die of natural causes according to Dutch study").

15. Harvey Max Chochinov, M.D., and Keith G. Wilson, Ph.D., "The Euthanasia Debate: Attitudes, Practices, and Psychiatric Considerations," 40 *Can. J. Psych.* 593, 598–99 (25 percent of cancer patients show depressive symptoms, with 6 to 10 percent exhibiting "major" depression, which is significant because of

the correlation between depression and the desire for death); Linda Ganzini and Melinda A. Lee, "Psychiatry and Assisted Suicide in the United States," 36 *New Engl. J. Med.* 1824, 1825 (1997) (80 percent of cancer patients who killed themselves had "depressive syndrome"); Harvey M. Chochinov, M.D., Ph.D., and Leonard Schwartz, LL.B, LL.M, M.D., "Depression and the Will to Live in the Psychological Landscape of Terminally Ill Patients," in "The Case against Assisted Suicide," supra intro. n. 18, at 261, 264; Robert G. Twycross, "Where There Is Hope, There Is Life: A View from Hospice," in "Euthanasia Examined," supra intro. n. 2, at 145; Leslie Pickering Frances, "Assisted Suicide: Are Elderly a Special Case?" in "Expanding the Debate," supra intro. n. 8, at 82–83 (depression can affect choices); Michael Teitelman, "Not in the House: Arguments for a Policy of Excluding Physician-Assisted Suicide from the Practice of Hospital Medicine," in "Expanding the Debate," supra intro. n. 8, at 208–9 (it is difficult to evaluate depression in the terminally ill). Cf. also Kay Redfield Jamison, supra intro. n. 6, at 81 (the overwhelming majority of suicides are linked to psychological illness [the book focuses on those under 40]).

However, "interest" in suicide and the "desire for hastened death" were better correlated with hopelessness than depression. Zeehan A. Butt, James C. Overholser, and Carla Kmett-Danielson, "Predictors of Attitudes towards Physician-Assisted Suicide," 47 *Omega* 107, 114 (2003); Malcolm Parker, supra intro. note 14, at 524; Barry Rosenfeld, supra intro. n. 12, at 86.

16. Jean Amery, *On Suicide: A Discourses on Voluntary Death* 114 (John D. Barlow, trans., Indiana Univ. Press 1995).

17. Linda Ganzini and Melinda A. Lee, supra n. 15, at 1825 (no effect on mild to moderate depression); Linda Ganzini, Melinda A. Lee, Robert T. Hintz, Joseph D. Bloom, and Darien S. Fenn, "The Effect of Depression Treatment on Elderly Patients' Preferences for Life-Sustaining Medical Treatment," 151 *Am. J. Psych.* 1631 (1994).

18. Harry M. Chochinov, M.D., Ph.D., and Leonard Schwartz, LL.B, LL.M, M.D., "Depression and the Will to Live in the Psychological Landscape of Terminally Ill Patients," in "The Case against Assisted Suicide," supra intro. n. 18, at 268 (the correlation between suicidal ideation and hopelessness was greater than that between suicidal ideation and depression). But see N. Gregory Hamilton, M.D., and Catherine A. Hamilton, M.A., "Competing Paradigms of Response to Assisted Suicide Requests in Oregon," 162 *Am. J. Psych.* 1060, 1060 (2005) ("Although physical illness may be a precipitation cause of despair, these patients usually suffer from treatable depression and are always ambivalent about their desire for death").

19. Mark Sullivan, Linda Ganzini, and Stuart J. Young, "Should Psychiatrists Serve as Gatekeepers for Physician-Assisted Suicide?" 28 *Hastings Center Report* 24, 28 (1998).

20. Yale Kamisar, "Some Non-religious Views against Proposed 'Mercy Killing' Legislation," in "Death-Dying," supra ch. 1 n. 3, at 432–33; John Keown,

supra ch. 1 n. 4, at 73: Wesley J. Smith, supra intro. n. 10, at 166; "Canada," ch. 1 n. 34, at 461; Gerald A. Larue, supra ch. 2 n. 10, at 16; Kathy Doyle and Alex Carroll, "The Slippery Slope," 146 *New Law J.* 759 (May 1996) (story of a patient who recovered after being diagnosed as PVS).

21. "Canada," supra n. 20, at 46; Yale Kamisar, "The Reasons So Many People Support Physician-Assisted Suicide and Why Those Reasons Are Not Convincing," 12 *Issues in Law and Med.* 115, 132, 143 (1996); Gerald A. Larue, supra ch. 2 n. 10, at 16; Yale Kamisar, "Some Non-religious Views against Proposed 'Mercy Killing' Legislation," in "Death-Dying," supra ch. 1 n. 3, at 435–42.

22. See, generally, Robert Finn, *Cancer Clinical Trials: Experimental Treatments and How They Can Help You* (O'Reilly 1999); *The Reference Shelf: Suicide* 127 (Robert Emmett Long, ed., H.W. Wilson 1995).

23. Peter J. Filenes, supra intro. n. 1, at 75; Wesley J. Smith, "The Right to Die, the Power to Kill," 46 *Nat'l Rev.* 38 (1994); John F. Kavanagh, S.J., "Ethics Notebook: Killing and Letting Die," 183 *America* 23 (Sept. 23, 2000).

24. Peter G. Filenes, supra intro. n. 1, at 39 (would it have been worth it to keep Karen Ann Quinlan alive if the chances for her recovery were "one in a million"?).

25. Ronald Dworkin, supra ch. 1 n. 3, at 197–98; Gerald Dworkin, R.G. Frey, and Sissela Bok, *Euthanasia and Physician Assisted Suicide: For and Against* 77–88 (Cambridge Univ. Press 1998); Helga Kuhse, "Killing a Poor Philosophical Argument against Euthanasia," *Aust. Fin Rev.* 16 (March 28, 1995).

26. Leon R. Kass, M.D., Ph.D., "I Will Give No Deadly Drug," in "The Case against Assisted Suicide," supra intro. n. 18, at 25–26; Yale Kamisar, supra ch. 1 n. 42, at 116.

27. Leon R. Kass, M.D., Ph.D., "I Will Give No Deadly Drug," in "The Case against Assisted Suicide," supra intro. n. 18, at 25–26.

28. Paul J. Zwier, supra intro. n. 15, at 242.

29. Linda Ganzini and Steven K. Dobscha, "Clarifying Distinctions between Contemplating and Completing Physician Assisted Suicide," 15 *J. Clinical Ethics* 119 (2004) ("Physicians [in Oregon] reported that 46 percent of the patients who requested PAS changed their minds following a substantive intervention by a physician"); Zeesham A. Butt, James C. Overholser, and Carla Kmett Danielson, "Predictors of Attitudes towards Physician-Assisted Suicide," 47 *Omega* 107, 115 (2003) (instability of PAS request was prevalent in elderly patients who were both terminally and nonterminally ill); Ronald Dworkin, supra intro. n. 3, at 46; Robert G. Turycross, "Where There Is Hope There Is Life: A View from the Hospice," in "Euthanasia Examined," supra intro. n. 2, at 141, 155; "Assisted Suicide and the Fluctuating Will to Live," 17 *Med. Health Letters* (Oct. 1, 2000). Cf. also Margaret Somerville, supra ch. 1 n. 10, at 123 (significant difference between a person "asking to die," and "asking to be killed").

30. Margaret Somerville, supra ch. 1 n. 10, at 262; Jos M.V. Welie, *In the Face*

of Suffering: The Philosophical-Anthropological Foundations of Clinical Ethics 163 (Creighton Univ. Press 1998); Liezl van Zyl, supra intro. n. 18, at 181 (the paradigm 1850s American masculine view was that you must be tough in the face of pain and indifferent to suffering).

31. Yale Kamisar, "Some Non-religious Views against Proposed Mercy Killing Legislation," in "Death-Dying," supra ch. 1 n. 3, at 427; Liezl van Zyl, supra intro. n. 18, at 164; Richard A. McCormick, "Bioethic: A Moral Vacuum?" 180 *America* 8, 10 (May 1, 1999); Sara R.S. Bryce, "Appropriate Care of the Incompetent Older Person," 4 *Issues in Law & Med.* 69, 81 (1988).

32. Yale Kamisar, "Some Non-religious Views against Proposed Mercy Killing Legislation," in "Death-Dying," supra ch. 1 n. 3, at 427; Liezl van Zyl, supra intro. n. 18, at 164. See also Thomas R. Cole, "The Enlightened View of Aging: Victorian Morality in a New Key," 13 *Hastings Center Report* 34 (1983); Sara R.S. Bryce, "Appropriate Care of the Incompetent Older Person," 4 *Issues in Law & Med.* 69, 81 (1988) (sequestering of the elderly away from the mainstream of life results from our society's inability to reconcile the reality of their dependence with its wish to believe in autonomy).

33. John Keown, supra ch. 1 n. 4, at 276; Helga Kuhse, supra n. 25, at 166. Cf. also the concern that the "right to die" may become perceived as a "duty to die" on the part of the patient. Liezl van Zyl, supra intro. n. 18, at 43; David J. Mayo and Martin Gunderson, "Physician Assisted Suicide and Hard Choices," in "Legal Euthanasia: Ethical Issues in an Era of Legalized Dying," 18 *J. Med. & Phil.* 329, 335 (1993) (Margaret P. Battin and Thomas J. Bole III, issue eds.).

34. Allen Verhey, "A Protestant Perspective on Ending Life: Faithfulness in the Fact of Death," in "Expanding the Debate," supra intro. n. 8, at 350; Robert I. Mishbin, supra intro. n. 5, at 199.

35. Gerald Dworkin, R.G. Frey, and Sissela Bok, supra ch. 3, n. 25, at 67–69.

Issue 4

1. See Amicus Brief of Surviving Family Members in Support of Oregon's Death with Dignity Act, filed in *Oregon v. Ashcroft* (No. CV01–1647–JO); Liezl van Zyl , supra intro. n. 18, at 57; Timothy E. Quill, M.D., *Death and Dignity: Making Choices and Taking Charge* (Norton 1994); Phil Such, "Why I'm Starving Myself to Death," *Daily Mail* (Feb. 21, 2002). Cf also Derek Humphrey (with Ann Wickets), *Jean's Way* (Hemlock Society 1978); and Juliet Cassuto Rothman, *Saying Goodbye to Daniel: When Death Is the Best Choice* (Continuum 1995) (withdrawal of life support).

2. Liezl van Zyl, supra intro. n. 18, at 47.

3. Robert I. Mishbin, supra intro. n. 5, at 17. Gerald Dworkin, R.G. Frey, and Sissela Bok, supra ch. 3 n. 25, at 44–45; Thomas St. Martin, "Euthanasia: The Three-in-One Issue," in "Death-Dying," supra ch. 1 n. 3, at 600.

4. Gerald Dworkin, R.G. Frey, and Sissela Bok, supra ch. 3 n. 25, at 58–59.

5. David W. Louiselle, "Euthanasia and Biathanesia: On Dying and Killing," in "Death-Dying," supra ch. 1 n. 3, at 389.

6. Debra M. Bryan, "It's My Body and I'll Die if I Want to: A Plan for Keeping Personal Autonomy from Spinning out of Control," 8 *J. Med. & Law* 45, 53 (2004); Mary A. Fisher, "To Live or to Die," *Reader's Digest* 107, 112 (May 2003). See also "Assisted Suicide and Euthanasia, Part I," Testimony to Senate Judiciary Committee on Civil Rights, Constitutional and Property Rights, Congressional Testimony of Wesley J. Smith, Senior Fellow, Discovery Institute, at 6 (May 26, 2006, congressional testimony) (Smith "extrapolates" from the Dutch experience that if PAS were legalized in the United States there would be 170,000 instances of it each year, with 85,000 being involuntary).

7. Daniel C. Maguire, supra intro. n. 8, at 140–41.

8. Margaret F. Battin, "Is a Physician Ever Obligated to Help a Patient Die?" in "Regulating How We Die," supra ch. 1 n. 7, at 19–34. Cf. Joel Feinberg, vol. 3: *The Moral Limits of the Criminal Law: Harm to Self* 34 (Oxford Univ. Press 1984–88).

9. Gerald Dworkin, R.G. Frey, and Sissela Bok, supra ch. 3 n. 25, at 45.

10. Daniel C. Maguire, supra intro. n. 8, at 88, 132; Leo Alexander, M.D., "Medical Science under Dictatorship," in "Death-Dying," supra ch. 1 n. 3, at 571; Wesley J. Smith, supra intro. n. 10, at 70; Ian Dowbiggin, supra intro. n. 10, at 62–66.

11. Wesley J. Smith, supra intro. n. 10, at 75 (350,000 people).

12. Wesley J. Smith, supra intro. n. 10, at Id. 78–79 (this eventually resulted in 275,000 deaths). See also Leo Alexander, M.D., "Medical Science under Dictatorship," in "Death-Dying," supra ch. 1 n. 3, at 574.

13. David C. Thomasama, "When Physicians Choose to Participate in the Death of Their Patients: Ethics and Physician Assisted Suicide," 24 *Law, Med. & Ethics* 183, 191 (1996).

14. Wesley J. Smith, supra intro. n. 10, at 74.

15. Id., at 7; Leo Alexander, M.D., "Medical Science under Dictatorship," in "Death-Dying," supra ch. 1 n. 3, at 571.

16. Fredric Wertham, M.D., "The Geranium in the Window: The 'Euthanasia' Murder," in "Death-Dying," supra ch. 1 n. 3, at 602. See also Wesley J. Smith, supra intro. n. 10, at 79.

17. Wesley J. Smith, supra intro. n. 10, at 78.

18. Id., at 79.

19. Daniel C. Maguire, supra intro. n. 8, at 133; Robert I. Mishbin, supra intro. n. 5, at 18–19.

20. Karl Binding and Alfred Hoche, M.D., "Permitting Destruction of Life Not Worth of Life: Its Extent and Form" (Liepzig 1920), reprinted in 8 *Law & Med.* 23 (1992); Ian Dowbiggin, *A Concise History of Euthanasia* 77–80 (Rowman and Littlefield 2005) (author places Binding and Hoche in their historical con-

text); David C. Thomasama, supra n. 13, at 191; Wesley J. Smith, supra intro. n. 10, at 73.

21. *Buck v. Bell,* 274 U.S. 200 (1927); Wesley J. Smith, supra intro. n. 10, at 81.

22. Robert I. Mishbin, supra intro. n. 5, at 49.

23. Derek Humphrey and Mary Clement, supra intro. n. 4, at 21; Robert I. Mishbin, supra intro. n. 5, at 33. See also *The Reference Shelf: Suicide* 129 (Robert Emmett Long, ed., H.W. Wilson 1995) (doctors are revolted by death and leave it to nurses). In fact, it has only been since the beginning of the twentieth century that doctors could really heal. See Peter G. Filenes, supra intro. n. 1, at 20.

24. Derek Humphrey and Mary Clement, supra intro. n. 4, at 22; Robert I. Mishbin, supra intro. n. 5, at 92; Annette E. Clark, supra intro. n. 15, at 126; Herbert Hendin, "Selling Death and Dignity," 25 *Hastings Center Report* 19, 23 (1995).

25. John Keown, supra ch. 1 n. 4, at 165.

26. Daniel Callahan, supra intro. n. 1, at 58, 72.

27. Linda L. Emanuel, "A Question of Balance," in "Expanding the Debate," supra intro. n. 8, at 256, 257; Peter E. Filenes, supra intro. n. 1, at 4; Ira R. Byock, "Physician-Assisted Suicide Is Not an Acceptable Practice for Physicians," in "Physician Assisted Suicide," supra intro. n. 11, at 109.

28. Susan M. Wolf, "Facing Assisted Suicide and Euthanasia in Children and Adolescents," in "Expanding the Debate," supra intro. n. 8, at 106–7; Annette E. Clark, supra intro. n. 15, at 88.

29. Annette E. Clark, supra intro. n. 15, at 88.

30. Nelson Lund, "Two Precipices, One Chasm: The Economics of Physician-Assisted Suicide and Euthanasia," 24 *Hastings Const. Q.* 903, 909 (1997). See also Annette E. Clark, supra intro. n. 18, at 88.

31. Rein Janssen and Zbigniew Zylicz, "Articulating the Concept of Palliative Care: Philosophical and Theological Perspectives," 15 *J. Palliative Care* 38, 38 (1999); Nelson Lund, supra n. 30, at 908.

32. Nelson Lund, supra n. 30, at 908.

33. Rein Janssen and Zbigniew Zylicz, supra n. 31, at 39; Michael J. Hyde, *The Call of Conscience: Heidegger and Levinas and the Euthanasia Debate* 128 (Univ. South Carolina Press 2001).

34. Robert I. Mishbin, supra intro. n. 5, at 33–34; David C. Thomasama, supra n. 13, at 193. But see Robert T. Hall, supra intro. n. 15, at 16 (patients are more likely to trust a doctor if they know that the doctor will stay to the end, help them die); "Euthanasia Wouldn't Kill Patients' Trust, Survey Says," *Akron Beacon Journal* (Ohio) (Dec. 6, 2005) (in a survey by Wake Forest University researchers interviewees were asked if they agreed or disagreed with the statement "If doctors were allowed to help patients die, you would trust your doctor less." Fifty-eight percent of the adults questioned disagreed with the statement.). The outcome of a patient survey may be different, however, in the managed care/HMO environment, where a patient may wonder whether a doctor's suggestion of PAS is motivated by concern for the patient or for his or her employer's bottom line. See Steve

P. Calandrillo, "Corralling Kevorkian: Regulating Physician-Assisted Suicide in America," *Virg. J. Soc. Pol'y & L.* 41, 82 (1999).

35. Gary P. Stewart, ed., *Basic Questions on Suicide and Euthanasia: Are They Ever Right?* Bio Basics Series 61 (Kregel 1998) (patients indicated that they would lose trust if a doctor brought up PAS). But see Margaret P. Battin, "Is a Physician Ever Obligated to Help a Patient Die?" in "Regulating How We Die," supra ch. 1 n. 7, at 40 (patients who believe that doctors will help them die tend to hold on to the end); and Paul Van Der Maas and Linda L. Emanuel, "Factual Findings," in "Regulating How We Die," supra ch. 1 n. 7, at 168 (most patients would not lose trust if they knew their doctor was involved in PAS or euthanasia).

36. "The possibility that persons may get comfort from having the medication (and never using it) should not be minimized. . . . In fact, this may be one of the most important findings from the Oregon experience and is consistent with the data showing that control is one of the key factors in why people want to use the Act." Howard Weinberg and James L. Werth Jr., "Physician-Assisted Suicide in Oregon: What Are the Key Factors?" 27 *Death Studies* 501, 512–13 (2002). Cf. Linda Ganzini and Steven K. Dobscha, supra ch. 3 n. 29, at 120 (only one out of 100 patients who consider PAS die after ingesting a lethal prescription); Noelle Knox, "An Agonizing Debate over Euthanasia," *USA Today* (Nov. 23, 2005) ("In Europe, Physicians and others have found that many people ask about euthanasia or assisted suicide but don't pursue the option. The reason may be more effective pain medications and peace of mind that comes from knowing euthanasia is an option.").

37. Nelson Lund, supra n. 30, at 530–31.

38. Yale Kamisar, supra ch. 1 n. 42, at 114.

39. Cicely Saunders, "A Hospice Perspective," in "The Case against Assisted Suicide," supra intro. n. 18, at 283; Richard Lamerton, M.D., "How Hospices Cope," in "Death-Dying," supra ch. 1 n. 3, at 550; Liezl van Zyl, supra intro. n. 18, at 198; Cicely Saunders, "The Philosophy of Terminal Care," in *The Management of Terminal Malignant Disease* 232 (Cicely Saunders, ed., Edward Arnold 1978); Cicely Saunders, "Forward," in *Oxford Textbook of Palliative Medicine* (C.D. Doyle, G.F.W. Hanks, and N. MacDonald, eds., Oxford Univ. Press 1998); "Palliative Medicine: A Time for Definition?" (editorial), 7 *Palliative Med.* 253 (1993).

40. Sanford Levinson, "Assisted Suicide Should Be Legalized," in *Euthanasia: Contemporary Issues Companion* 69 (Linda Yount, ed., Greenhaven 2002); Harvey M. Chochinov and Leonard Schwartz, "Depression and the Will to Live in the Psychological Landscape of Terminally Ill Patients," in "The Case against Assisted Suicide," supra intro. n. 18, at 272, 275, 298–302; Daniel Callahan, supra intro. n. 1, at 100–101; Nathan I. Cherny and Russell K. Portenoy, "Sedation in the Management of Refractory Symptoms: Guidelines for Evaluation and Treatment," 10 *J. Palliative Care* 31 (1994); Stacy Diloreto, "The Complexities of Assisted Suicide," 34 *Patient Care* 65 (2000); Zbiginew Zylicz, "Ethical Considerations in the Treatment of Pain in a Hospice Setting," 41 *Patient Educ. & Counseling* 47

(2000); Herbert Hendin, "Suicide, Assisted Suicide, and Mental Illness," 16 *Harv. Mental Health Letter* (Jan. 1, 2000).

41. David Orentlicher, supra ch. 1 n. 47, at 453–54.

42. "Introduction," in "Expanding the Debate," supra intro. n. 8, at 4; Margaret P. Battin, "Is a Physician Ever Obligated to Help a Patient Die?" in "Regulating How We Die," supra ch. 1 n. 7, at 24; Paul Van Der Maas, "Factual Findings," in "Regulating How We Die," supra ch. 1 n. 7, at 157 (10 percent of cancer patients are in "untreatable pain"); Derek Humphrey and Mary Clement, supra intro. n. 4, at 57 (10 percent of cancer patients in untreatable pain). But see Ira R. Byock, "Physician-Assisted Suicide Is Not an Acceptable Practice for Physicians," in "Physician-Assisted Suicide," supra intro. n. 11, at 115 (author cites authorities that some pain cannot be controlled but disagrees with these authorities, though recognizes that in the current reality pain is not controlled).

43. Presentation by Zbigniew Zylicz, "Ethical Issues in Pain Management in Hospice Care," in "Nijimegan Conference," supra intro. n. 1.

44. Forty-two percent of U.S. hospitals offer a formal pain management program, and 23 percent offer formal hospice programs. Debra M. Bryan, "It's My Body and I'll Die if I Want to: A Plan for Keeping Personal Autonomy from Spinning out of Control," 8 *J. Law & Med.* 45, 62; Margaret P. Battin, "Safe, Legal, Rare? Physician-Assisted Suicide and Cultural Change in the Future," in "Older Adults," supra. ch. 3, n. 13 ". . . about 50% of dying hospitalized patients were reported to have experienced moderate to severe pain at least 50% of the time in their last three days of life"); id., at 203, 204 n. 1. Most studies have failed to find a significant relationship between pain and requests for PAS. See Barry Rosenfeld, supra intro. n. 12, at 96, 98. However, this may be misleading:

> Although a superficial reading of this literature might lead one to conclude that pain is not a significant predictor of interest in assisted suicide (because the two were significantly associated in only one of five published studies), several alternative explanations also exist. First, as noted earlier in this volume (chap. 4), there is ample reason to believe that pain would be more relevant as a predictor of interest in assisted suicide in some medically ill populations than in others. Pain may be a less salient factor in patients with HIV/AIDS, MS, or ALS, compared to patients with cancer. Thus, the failure to observe a relationship between pain and interest in assisted suicide might reflect the populations studied, not the importance of pain as a trigger. Only one of the studies described above focused squarely on cancer-related pain (M. Sullivan et al., 1997), although most of the patients studied by E.J. Emanuel et al. (2000) also had a primary diagnosis of cancer. Thus, in both studies of cancer patients, some relationship between pain (either expectancies or severity) has been noted, and the strongest relationship by far was observed in Emanuel et al.'s much larger, and far more methodologically sound study. (Id., at 98–99)

45. Kathleen Foley, M.D., "Compassionate Care, Not Assisted Suicide," in "The Case against Assisted Suicide," supra intro. n. 18, at 298–99; Kristi L. Kirschner, Carrol J. Gill, and Christine K. Cassel, "Physician-Assisted Death in the Context of Disability," in "Physician-Assisted Suicide," supra intro. n. 11, at 154; Peter G. Filenes, supra intro. n. 1, at 216; Annette E. Clark, supra intro. n. 15, at 105, 131, 134; Stuart Coates, "Spiritual Components in Palliative Care," 2 *European J. Palliative Care* 37 (spring 1995).

46. Derek Humphrey and Mary Clement, supra intro. n. 4, at 63; Liezl van Zyl, supra intro. n. 18, at 33; Annette E. Clark, supra intro. n. 15, at 105. But see lawsuits in civil cases for not relieving pain. Liezl van Zyl, supra intro. n. 18, at 184; Anne Helm, "Voluntary Euthanasia: An International Perspective," 17 *Law/Technology* 300, 302 (1984).

47. Derek Humphrey and Mary Clement, supra intro. n. 4, at 63 (fear of prosecution); Kathleen Foley, M.D., "Compassionate Care, Not Assisted Suicide," in "The Case against Assisted Suicide," supra intro. n. 18, at 304 (fear of a Drug Enforcement Administration investigation and license revocation). See, also Professor Sandra Johnson, Saint Louis School of Law, "End of Life Decisions," speech delivered at the Seattle University School of Law, Seattle, Washington (Oct. 7, 2002).

48. Gerald Dworkin, R.G. Frey, and Sissela Bok, supra ch. 3 n. 25, at 118–20 (discusses a 1994 study that concluded that palliative care in American hospitals was deplorable). Cf. also, regarding similar problems in Canada, Harvey Max Chochinov, M.D., and Keith G. Wilson, Ph.D., "The Euthanasia Debate: Attitudes, Practices, and Psychiatric Considerations," 40 *Can. J. Psychiatry* 593, 597 (1995) (a significant percentage of patients die in unnecessary pain).

49. Derek Humphrey and Mary Clement, supra intro. n. 3, at 63–65; Anne Helm, supra n. 46, at 302.

50. Derek Humphrey and Mary Clement, supra intro. n. 4, at 65.

51. Kathleen Foley and Herbert Hendin, "Conclusion: Changing the Culture," in "The Case against Assisted Suicide," supra intro. n. 18, at 328–32; C.D. Doyle, G.F.W. Hanks, and N. MacDonald, "Introduction," in *The Oxford Textbook of Palliative Medicine* (C.D. Doyle, G.F.W. Hanks, and N. MacDonald, eds., Oxford Univ. Press 1998). But cf. Annette E. Clark, supra intro. n. 15, at 120–22 (even after intensive training, only one-third of hospital staff accessed advance directives in patient's files).

52. Robert G. Twycross, "Where There Is Hope, There Is Life: A View from Hospice," in "Euthanasia Examined," supra intro. n. 2, at 141, 165; Howard Brody, "Assisting in Patient Suicides Is an Acceptable Practice for Physicians," in "Physician-Assisted Suicide," supra intro. n. 11, at 138; Paul Van Deer Mass and Linda L. Emanuel, in "Regulating How We Die," supra ch. 1 n. 7, at 156; Liezl van Zyl, supra intro. n. 18, at 146.

53. Michael M. Burgess, "The Medicalization of Dying," in "Legal Euthanasia: Ethical Issues in an Era of Legalized Dying," 18 *J. Med. & Phil.* 269 (1993)

(Margaret P. Battin and Thomas J. Boyle III, issue eds.); Kathleen Foley and Herbert Hendin, "Conclusion: Changing the Culture," in "The Case against Assisted Suicide," supra intro. n. 18, at 311.

54. Ezekiel J. Emanuel, Diane Fairclough, Brian C. Claridge, Diane Blum, Eduardo Bruera, W. Charles Penley, Lowell E. Schnipper, and Robert J. Mayer, "Attitudes and Practices of U.S. Oncologists regarding Euthanasia and Physician-Assisted Suicide," 133 *Annals of Internal Med.* 527 (October 2000); Harvey Max Chochinov, M.D., and Keith G. Wilson, Ph.D., supra ch. 3 n. 15, at 595.

55. Noelle Knox, supra note 36 ("Kimsa, the family doctor in the Netherlands who has helped people end their lives, said he found the experience 'shattering'"); Steven K. Dobscha, M.D., Ronald T. Heinz, M.D., Nancy Press, Ph.D., and Linda Ganzini, M.D., M.P.H., "Oregon Physicians' Responses to Requests for Assisted Suicide: A Qualitative Study," 7 *J. Palliative Med.* 451, 453–54 (2004) ("Requests for assisted suicide carried both apprehension and discomfort"). Yet, "[d]espite discomfort at many levels, physicians reported that going through the assisted suicide decision making process had a positive impact on them personally, and on their ability to speak with patients about the end of life" (id., at 459).

56. Paul Starr, *The Social Transformation of American Medicine: The Rise of a Sovereign Profession and the Making of a Vast Industry* 420, 420 (Basic Books 1982); Gerald Dworkin, R.G. Frey, and Sissela Bok, supra ch. 3 n. 25, at 126–27; Richard A. McCormick, supra ch. 3 n. 31, at 11; Nelson Lund, supra ch. 4 n. 30; Mary Clement and Derek Humphrey, "High Cost of Dying," supra intro. n. 3, at 27.

57. Mary Clement and Derek Humphrey, supra n. 56, "High Cost of Dying," supra intro. n. 3, at 38; Margaret Somerville, supra ch. 1 n. 10, at 233.

58. Mary Clement and Derek Humphrey, "High Cost of Dying," supra intro. n. 3, at 9–10.

59. Noelle Knox, supra. n. 36 ("As members of the baby boom generation age, their increasing frailty will strain health care and welfare systems, not to mention their families").

60. Beth Spring and Ed Laron, *Euthanasia: Spiritual, Medical, and Legal Lessons in Terminal Health Care* 23 (Multnomah 1988). We spend three and a half times more on their health care than the remainder of the population. See *The Reference Shelf: Suicide* 95 (Robert Emmet Long, ed., H.W. Wilson 1995).

61. Merrill Matthews Jr., "Would Physician-Assisted Suicide Save the Healthcare System Money (or Is Jack Kevorkian Doing All of Us a Favor)?" in "Expanding the Debate," supra intro. n. 8, at 315; Mary Clement and Derek Humphrey, "High Cost of Dying" supra intro. n. 3, at 7.

62. "Thus, when one couples America's aging population with the fact that Medicare enrollment in managed care organizations is rapidly rising, a conflict is brewing that will directly determine the amount of (and whether) care will be given to chronically ill, elderly patients in the future. This problem is particularly acute given that 40 percent of total Medicare expenditures come in the last few months of life, making it fertile area in which HMO's will try desperately to slash

costs, perhaps even encouraging P.A.S. to inappropriate candidates." Steve P. Calandrillo, supra n. 34, at 74 [nn. omitted]).

63. Wesley J. Smith, supra intro. n. 8, at 141, 147–48; John Keown, supra ch. 1 n. 4, at 275–76; Paul Starr, supra n. 56, at 447–48 (doctors are losing their "professional autonomy" and becoming tied to "profit centers"). Cf. id., at 448 (77 percent of nursing homes are proprietary). But see those contending that, in fact, the cost savings from PAS for hospitals and nursing homes would be far less than people believe. "Notes," in "Regulating How We Die," supra ch. 1 n. 7, at 266, note 9; Paul Starr, supra n. 56, at 171 (less aggressive life sustaining would only save 3.3 percent of the health care budget); Felicia Cohn and Joanne Lynn, "Vulnerable People: Practical Rejoinders to Claims in Favor of Assisted Suicide," in "The Case against Assisted Suicide," supra intro. n. 18, at 240; Merrill Matthews Jr., "Would Physician-Assisted Suicide Save the Healthcare System Money? (or, is Jack Kevorkian doing us all a favor)," in "Expanding the Debate," supra. intro. n. 8, at 320–21.

64. Steve P. Calandrillo, supra n. 34, at 44 ("HMOs know all too well that elderly and terminally ill patients run up huge medical bills in their last months of life [40 percent of Medicare expenditures are made in the last year of life], and it is not unimaginable that PAS—in the absence of regulation—will be introduced as one very haunting method to control those costs"); id., at 73–74, 75 ("Put simply, managed care organizations have a direct financial incentive to limit care and control costs because every dollar patients pay into the plan that is not spent on care [or on administrative costs] remains in the plan's coffers"). See also Steve Zanskas and Wendy Coduti, supra intro. n 5, at 31–32 (authors discuss PAS and the economics of managed care). One gets little solace from the revelation that an organization that supports Kaiser Permanente and lobbies for "groups practicing in the managed care model" have strongly advocated to the California legislature in support of passing an assisted suicide bill. See "Flashback 2002; Kaiser Shops for Doctors Willing to Prescribe Assisted Suicide Drugs in Oregon," *Obesity, Fitness and Wellness Week* (April 14, 2007).

65. See Herbert Hendin, supra n. 24, at 19; Dr. Timothy E. Quill, M.D., supra ch. 4 n. 1, at 122–24; David Rieff, "Illness as More than Metaphor," *New York Times,* supra ch. 1, n. 32 (". . . the doctor's power to influence those [terminal] patients, one way or the other, is virtually complete."); Steve P. Calandrillo, supra n. 34, at 83 ("There is abundant empirical evidence indicating that physicians exert a great deal of control over the 'independent' choices of their patients merely by presenting them with information and suggestions").

66. Dieter Giesen, "Dilemmas at Life's End: A Comparative Legal Perspective, in "Euthanasia Examined," supra intro. n. 2, at 212; Paul Starr, supra n. 56, at 378; Margaret Somerville, supra ch. 1 n. 10, at 13; Nelson Lund, supra n. 30, at 939–40; Sheryl A. Russ, "Care of the Older Person: The Ethical Challenge of American Medicine," 4 *Issues in Law & Med.* 87, 88 (1988).

67. See supra intro. n. 28. See also Yale Kamisar, supra ch. 1 n. 42, at 125.

68. Gerald Dworkin, R.G. Frey, and Sissela Bok, supra ch. 3, n. 25, at 57. Cf. Robert S. Magnusson and Peter H. Ballis, *Angels of Death: Exploring the Euthanasia Underground* (Yale Univ. Press 2002).

69. The *Leeowarden* (1973) case. For a very detailed, case by case discussion of the series of Dutch court cases involving euthanasia, see Raphael Cohen-Almager, *Euthanasia in the Netherlands: The Policy and Practice of Mercy Killing* 39–49 (Kluwer Academic 2004). See also Wesley J. Smith, supra intro. n. 10, at 95; and Julia Belian, "Deference to Doctors in Dutch Euthanasia Law," 10 *Emory Int'l L.J.* 255, 262 (1996). For a novel that portrays the Dutch system gone mad, see Ian McEwan, *Amsterdam* (Anchor 1999).

70. Julia Belian, supra n. 69, at 259.

71. Wesley J. Smith, supra intro. n. 10, at 95; John Keown, "Some Reflections on Euthanasia in the Netherlands," in "Clinical Practice," supra ch. 1 n. 3, at 211 (author questions leaving legal decision to the standards of practice of the medical profession); Julia Belian, supra n. 69, at 262.

72. Wesley J. Smith, supra intro. n. 10, at 95.

73. Carlos F. Gomez, M.D., *Regulating Death: Euthanasia and the Case of the Netherlands* 37–38 (Free Press 1991); B. Sluyters, "Euthanasia in the Netherlands," 57 *Medico-Legal J.* 34 (1988).

74. Bert Gordian, "New Developments in Dutch Legislation concerning Euthanasia and Physician Assisted Suicide," 26 *J. Med. & Phil.* 299, 300 (2000) [hereinafter "New Developments"]; Julia Belian, supra n. 69, at 265–69.

75. Liszl van Zyl, supra intro. n. 18, at 51–52; John A. Robertson, "Involuntary Euthanasia of Defective Newborns: A Legal Analysis," in "Death-Dying," supra ch. 1 n. 3, at 165; Joshua Dressler, supra ch. 1 n. 14, at § 22.01, p. 261.

76. Julia Belian, supra n. 69, at 265–69.

77. Wesley J. Smith, supra intro. n. 10, at 96.

78. Julia Belian, supra n. 69, at 255.

79. Id.

80. See Raphael Cohen-Almager, supra n. 69, at 58.

81. Bert Gordijn, "Regulating Moral Dissent in an Open Society: The Dutch Experience with Pragmatic Tolerance," 26 *J. Med. & Phil.* 225, 230 (2001) [hereinafter "Pragmatic Tolerance"]. See also Herbert Hendin, "The Dutch Experience," in "The Case against Assisted Suicide," supra intro. n. 18, at 98; and Robert I. Mishbin, supra intro. n. 5, at 183, 187.

82. Bert Gordijn, "Pragmatic Tolerance," supra n. 81, at 229.

83. Id., at 232 (concept arose in the sixteenth century); Herbert Hendin, M.D., *Seduced by Death: Doctors, Patients, and Assisted Suicide* 163 (Norton 1998) [hereinafter "Seduced by Death"].

84. Bert Gordijn, "Pragmatic Tolerance," supra n. 81, at 232; Herbert Hendin, "The Dutch Experience," in "The Case against Assisted Suicide," supra intro. n. 18, at 97.

85. Kenneth Culp Davis, *Police Discretion* (West 1975).

86. John Keown, "Further Reflections on Euthanasia in the Netherlands in Light of the Remmelink Report and the Van Der Maas Survey," in "Clinical Practice," supra ch. 1 n. 3, at 219, 236.

87. Carlos F. Gomez, M.D., supra n. 73, at 122; John Keown, supra ch. 1 n. 4, at 132.

88. David C. Thomasama, Thomasine Kimborough-Kushner, Gerrit K. Kimsma, and Chris Ciesielski-Carlucci "Part II: Living with Euthanasia: Physicians and Families Speak for Themselves," in *Asking to Die: Inside the Dutch Debate about Euthanasia*, 275 (Kluwer Academic 1998) [hereinafter "Asking to Die"]; John Keown, supra ch. 1 n. 4, at 132. Half of Dutch doctors do not report because it is "too much trouble." See Keith B. Richburg, "Netherlands Struggling with Right to Die Law: In the First Nation to Legalize Euthanasia Some Applaud Death with Dignity, Others Are Dubious," *Chicago Tribune* (Jan. 18, 2004); Tony Sheldon, "Only Half of Dutch Doctors Report Euthanasia, Study Says," http://bmjjournals.com/cgi/content/full/326/7400/1164?etoc (May 31, 2003). On the other hand, there is a noted increase in the percentage of general practitioners [GPs] reporting. See id. (level of GPs reporting increased from 44 to 60 percent).

89. See David C. Thomasama et al., "Asking to Die," supra n. 88, at 275, 290. Cf. also id., at 317 (author discusses those working in a hospital that does not approve of VAE); John Keown, supra ch. 1 n. 4, at 132. Cf. Jurgen Woretschafer and Matthias Borgers, "The Dutch Procedure for Mercy Killing and Assisted Suicide by Physicians in a National and International Perspective," 2 *Maastricht J. European and Compar. Law* 4, 17 (1995) (authors discuss the international law analogue to our Fifth Amendment, nemo tenetur).

90. Julia Belian, supra n. 69, at 278–79 (e.g., five-month suspended sentence and such).

91. John Keown, supra ch. 1 n. 4, at 133.

92. Id., at 85.

93. Id., at 85–86; Bert Gordijn, "New Developments," supra n. 74, at 302, 303.

94. Carlos F. Gomez, M.D., supra n. 73, at 117 (2 percent, 2 to 4 percent, 6 percent).

95. Id., at 130.

96. John Keown, supra ch. 1 n. 4, at 144.

97. Bert Gordijn, "New Developments," supra n. 74, at 306–7.

98. Id., at 303.

99. Id., at 305.

100. Carlos F. Gomez, M.D., supra n. 73, at 96.

101. Id., at 130; Herbert Hendin, M.D., "Seduced by Death," supra n. 83, at 136; John Keown, supra ch. 1 n. 4, at 83; Wesley J. Smith, supra intro. n. 10, at 83.

102. John Keown, supra ch. 1 n. 4, at 83.

103. Herbert Hendin, M.D., "Seduced by Death," supra n. 83, at 214.

104. John Keown, supra ch. 1 n. 4, at 109; Robert I. Mishbin, supra intro. n. 5, at 72–73; Julia Belian, supra n. 69, at 297 (discusses Dr. Chabot). But see Stephanie van den Berg, "Dutch Supreme Court Rules against Widening Euthanasia Guidelines," *Agence-France Presse* (Dec. 4, 2003) (Dutch Supreme Court upheld the conviction of a doctor who euthanized a healthy 86-year-old

patient solely because patient was "sick of living"); Raphael Cohen-Almagar, supra n. 69, at 167.

105. John Keown, supra ch. 1 n. 4, at 85, 88–89.

106. Id.

107. Herbert Hendin, M.D., "Seduced by Death," supra n. 83, at 162. But cf. Johanna H. Groenewould et al., "Physician Assisted Death in Psychiatric Practice in the Netherlands," 336 *New Engl. J. Med.* 1795 (1997) (psychiatrists get many requests for AVE, but "very few" are granted).

108. John Keown, supra ch. 1 n. 4, at 91, 125.

109. Herbert Hendin, "The Dutch Experience," in "The Case against Assisted Suicide," supra intro. n. 18, at 103; Wesley J. Smith, supra intro. n. 10, at 101.

110. Herbert Hendin, "The Dutch Experience," in "The Case against Assisted Suicide," supra intro. n. 18, at 103. When physicians report VAE, 99 percent of the doctors reporting say that they have engaged in consultation; among those not reporting, only 18 percent consult with another doctor. John Keown, supra ch. 1 n. 4, at 132. Moreover, when death is the result of nonvoluntary active euthanasia (NVAE), 97 percent do not consult with another doctor. Herbert Hendin, "The Dutch Experience," in "The Case against Assisted Suicide," supra intro. n. 18, at 103; John Keown, supra ch. 1 n. 4, at 132.

111. Herbert Hendin, "The Dutch Experience," in "The Case against Assisted Suicide," supra intro. n. 18, at 111.

112. John Keown, supra ch. 1 n. 4, at 87.

113. Bregje D. Onwutteaka-Philipsen and Gerrit Van der Wal, "A Protocol for Consultation of Another Physician in Cases of Euthanasia and Assisted Suicide," 275 *Med. Ethics* 331 (2001).

114. See Raphael Cohen-Almager, supra n. 69, at 170.

115. Herbert Hendin "The Dutch Experience," in "The Case against Assisted Suicide," supra intro. n. 18, at 102: Rein J.P.A. Janssen, Henk A.M.J. Tenhave, and Zbigniew Zylicz, "Hospice and Euthanasia in the Netherlands: An Ethical Point of View," 25 *J. Med. Ethics* 408, 408 (1999) (in the mid-1990s palliative care in the Netherlands was "in its infancy").

116. Herbert Hendin, "The Dutch Experience" in "The Case against Assisted Suicide," supra intro. n. 18, at 121 ("... the Dutch experience suggests that engaging physicians in palliative care is much harder when the easier option of euthanasia is available. . . .").

117. Bert Gordijn and Rein Janssen, "The Prevention of Euthanasia through Palliative Care: New Developments in the Netherlands," 41 *Patient Educ. & Counseling* 35, 38 (2000); Bert Gordijn and Adraan Visser, "Issues in Dutch Palliative Care: Readjusting a Distorted Image," 41 *Patient Educ. & Counseling* 3 (2000).

118. Bert Gordijn and Rein Janssen, supra n. 117, at 38.

119. Herbert Hendin, "The Dutch Experience," in "The Case against Assisted Suicide," supra intro. n. 18, at 120–21. Cf., for example, E.P. Tross, "Too Big for Their Wooden Shoes," 27 *Human Life Rev.* 53 (2002) (formerly pro-euthanasia physicians said in an interview that if they had been familiar with palliative care they would not have killed some of the patients they euthanized).

120. Herbert Hendin, "The Dutch Experience," in "The Case against Assisted Suicide," supra intro. n. 18, at 120–21. Still, the critics do not believe the care is good at this point of time. See id., at 123, 143; and John Keown, supra ch. 1 n. 4, at 112, 141.

121. Robert I. Mishbin, supra intro. n. 5, at 62; John Keown, supra ch. 1 n. 5, at 112 (the commission characterized this large-scale NVAE as "care for the dying").

122. Robert I. Mishbin, supra ch. 1 n. 5, at 62. Yet it is common for the seriously ill to ask for VAE one day and wish to live the next. Herbert Hendin, M.D., "Seduced by Death," supra n. 83, at 34–36, 159. See also Margaret Sommerville, supra ch. 1 n. 10, at 123 (even if patients say they want to die, that does not mean they are asking to be killed).

123. Robert I. Mishbin, supra intro. n. 5, at 62.

124. David C. Thomasama et al., "Asking to Die," supra n. 88, at 13.

125. John Keown, supra ch. 1 n. 4, at 105.

126. Herbert Hendin, M.D., "Seduced by Death," supra n. 83, at 95.

127. David C. Thomasama et al., "Asking to Die," supra n. 88, at 13.

128. Id. (87 percent); Robert I. Mishbin, supra intro. n. 5, at 62 (70 percent).

129. Robert I. Mishbin, supra intro. n. 5, at 62; John Keown, supra ch. 1 n. 4, at 105.

130. John Keown, supra ch. 1 n. 4, at 105.

131. Id., at 126. See, generally, Liezl van Zyl, supra intro. n. 18, at 60 (the practice of NVAE may be more widespread than believed since the society as a whole is valued over the individual).

132. John Keown, supra ch. 1 n. 4, at 96.

133. Id., at 96, 97–98, 106. A total of 6,250 were given drugs with the partial intent of causing death, 5,000 without a specific patient request. Id., at 96, 97–98.

134. Id., at 126.

135. David C. Thomasama, supra ch. 4, n. 13, at 185. Note that in the United States, in cases in which life-sustaining treatment was withdrawn, 35 percent was without the patient's consent. Annette E. Clarke, supra intro. n. 15, at 119.

136. Helga Kubse, "Killing a Poor Philosophical Argument against Euthanasia," *Aust. Finan. Rev.* 16 (Mar. 28, 1995). See also Peter Singer, supra ch. 1 n. 7, at 153; and David C. Thomasama et al., "Asking to Die," supra n. 88, at 58 (no evidence that NVAE is on the rise). But see John Keown, "Euthanasia in the Netherlands: Sliding down the Slippery Slope?" in "Euthanasia Examined," supra intro. n. 2, at 287 (even without pre-1990 data, the Dutch experience supports the slippery slope argument). In fact, according to a more recent article, the number of

those euthanized has decreased. "Number of Declared Euthanasia Cases in Netherlands Declining," *Agence-France Presse* (Apr. 29, 2003).

137. "Nearly two years after the Netherlands became the first country to legalize euthanasia and doctor-assisted suicide, an estimated 2,000–3,000 lives end that way there each year. . . . There is some dispute about the number of mercy killings performed in the Netherlands, but both sides agree there has been no surge in reported cases since the law took effect in April 2002." Keith B. Richburg, supra n. 88.

138. John Keown, supra ch. 1 n. 4, at 79 (author discusses the expansion of the concept of "unbearable suffering").

139. See Raphael Cohen-Almager, supra n. 69, at xii, 103 et seq.

140. Sixty-six percent of those living independently were opposed to legalizing euthanasia. Cynthia M. Bumgardener, "Euthanasia and Physician-Assisted Suicide in the United States and the Netherlands: Paradigms Compared," 10 *Ind. Int'l & Comparative L. Rev.* 387, 415 (2000). Ninety-five percent of those living in nursing homes were opposed. Id. Fifty to 60 percent of seniors in another survey indicated that they feared involuntary euthanasia. Julie A. Di Camillo, "A Comprehensive Analysis of the Right to Die in the Netherlands and the United States after Cruzan: Reassessing the Right of Self-Determination," 7 *Am. U.J. Int'l Law & Policy* 807, 819–20 (1992). In a general medical survey, 10 percent gratuitously added that they feared being involuntarily killed. "Euthanasia in the Netherlands," *International Anti-Euthanasia Task Force* 4 (2000).

141. Robert I. Mishbin, supra intro. n. 5, at 102.

142. Wesley J. Smith, supra intro. n. 10, at 94; Peter Singer, supra ch. 1 n. 7, at 158; Robert I. Mishbin, supra intro. n. 5, at 97; Ute Angelique Joas, "Physician-Assisted Lethal Injection versus the Plastic Bag: Will Euthanasia Ever Come? A Comparison of Standards in the Netherlands and the United States," 6 *Temple Int'l & Comparative L. J.* 365, 387 (1992). But see David C. Thomasama et al., "Asking to Die," supra n. 88, at 502 (the tradition that everyone has a family doctor is changing as the Dutch population becomes increasingly transient).

143. Liezl van Zyl, supra intro. n. 18, at 107.

144. Wesley J. Smith, supra intro. n. 10, at 93; Peter Singer, supra ch. 1 n. 7, at 158; Robert I. Mishbin, supra intro. n. 5, at 99; David C. Thomasama et al., "Asking to Die," supra n. 88, at 319, 503.

145. Wesley J. Smith, supra intro. n. 10, at 109.

146. David C. Thomasama et al., "Asking to Die," supra n. 88, at 319, 503.

147. Carlos F. Gomez, M.D., supra n. 73, at 21.

148. Herbert Hendin, M.D., "Why the Netherlands? Why the United States," in "Seduced by Death," supra ch. 4 n. 83, at 163, 171 ("The common [Dutch] attitude was that the doctor may have been mistaken, but that he was entitled to his judgment on the matter. . . . [This is] consistent with . . . the Dutch lack of moral passion and unwillingness to assign individual responsibility.").

149. John Keown, supra ch. 1 n. 4, at 167.

150. Id.; Wesley J. Smith, supra intro. n. 10, at 117.

151. *Lee v. Oregon,* 107 F.3d. 1382 (9 Cir., 1997); Annette E. Clark, supra intro. n. 15, at 61; Wesley J. Smith, supra intro. n. 10, at 126.

152. Derek Humphrey and Mary Clement, supra intro. n. 4, at 274.

153. Id., at 294. With this perspective, the attempt of U.S. Attorney General Ashcroft to undermine the act by taking away the ability of Oregon doctors to use any federally controlled drug to conduct euthanasia is ironic. See Nelson Lund, "Why Ashcroft Is Wrong on Assisted Suicide," 113 *Commentary* 50 (2002).

154. John Keown, supra ch. 1 n. 4, at 176, 172, 179.

155. Id., at 176 (for 1998), 177 (for 1999), 179 (for 2000).

156. *New York Times* (Mar. 6, 2003).

157. The number of suicides was 46 in 2006 (Steve Geissinger, "To the North, Euthanasia Up," *Oakland Tribune,* local section [March 9, 2007]), 42 in 2003, 30 in 2002, 21 in 2001, 27 in 2000, 27 in 1999, and 16 in 1998. "Assisted-Suicide Numbers Increase," *Statesman Journal* (Mar. 10, 2004). Interestingly, while it is estimated that nationally 1 in 250 deaths is really disguised PAS, in Oregon all evidence indicates that the death by PAS rate is far lower—1 in 1,000. Linda Ganzini and Steven K. Dobscha, supra ch. 3 n. 29, at 121. In fact, "a very small percentage of terminally ill Oregonians seem determined to request lethal medication." Howard Wineberg and James L. Weith Jr., "Physician-Assisted Suicide in Oregon: What Are the Key Factors?" 27 *Death Studies* 501, 501 (2003). This is consistent with national data indicating that "Only a small minority of terminally ill people seek to hasten their own deaths." "Few Ponder Euthanasia, Study Says," *Globe and Mail* (Toronto) (Nov. 15, 2000), A-19. See also Robyn Leigh and Brian Kelly, "Family Factors in the Wish to Hasten Death and Euthanasia," in "Older Adults," supra n. ch. 3 n 13, at 185; ("[T]he over whelming majority of terminally ill patients fight for life to the end and only 2–4 percent of suicides occur in the setting of terminal illness").

158. John Keown, supra ch. 1 n. 4, at 177.

159. There were 69 in 1998 and 71 in 2000. Id., at 176–77.

160. Linda Ganzini, Heidi D. Nelson, Terri A. Schmidt, Dale F. Kraemer, and Molly A. Delorist, "Physicians' Experiences with the Oregon Death with Dignity Act," 342 *New Engl. J. Med.* 557, 563 (2000).

161. "People Requesting Assisted Suicide Reportedly Do So to Keep Control," *Oregonian* (Aug. 22, 2003) [hereinafter "Oregon Hospice"]; Linda Ganzini, Heidi D. Nelson, Melinda A. Lee, Dale F. Kraemer, Terri A. Schmidt, and Molly Delorit, "Oregon Physicians' Attitudes about the Experience with Dignity Act," 18 *JAMA* 2363, 2363 [hereinafter "Attitudes about Dignity Act"].

162. "Oregon Hospice," supra n. 161; Kathleen Foley and Herbert Hendin, "The Oregon Experiment," in "The Case against Assisted Suicide," supra intro. n. 18, at 171.

163. Linda Ganzini et al., "Attitudes about Dignity Act," supra n. 161, at 2363.

164. Timothy E. Quill, "Kevorkian: Hero, Villain, or Somewhere in Between?" in *Euthanasia: Contemporary Issues Companion* 61 (Lisa Yount, ed., Greenhaven 2002).

165. Barry Rosenfeld, supra intro. n. 12, at 159 (". . . a referral for more adequate palliative care was the most common physician response to requests for lethal medications . . ."). Cf. Howard Weinberg and James L. Werth Jr., supra ch. 4 n. 36, at 511 ("Oregonians do not appear to be taking medications to end their lives because of lack of end-of-life care, given that 80% of those using PAS were enrolled in hospice with the other 20% declining hospice"); Pamela J. Miller, "Life after Death with Dignity: The Oregon Experience," 45 *Social Work* 263, 268 (2000) ("Oregon has the lowest in-hospital mortality rate in the country, admission rates into hospice have increased 20 percent, and the use of medical morphine has increased 70 percent. Oregon has developed comfort care teams that specifically address pain management.").

166. "Oregon Hospice," supra n. 161.

167. John Keown, supra ch. 1 n. 4, at 178; "Oregon's Death with Dignity Act: Three Years of Legalized Physician-Assisted Suicide," report, Department of Human Services, Oregon Health Division, Center for Disease Prevention and Epidemiology 12, 13 (Feb. 22, 2001).

168. John Keown, supra ch. 1 n. 4, at 176, 178, 179. Cf. Bert Gordijn, "New Developments," supra ch. 4 n. 74, at 40 (for those seeking euthanasia in the Netherlands, pain is not the most important reason).

169. John Keown, supra ch. 1 n. 4, at 172; Daniel Callahan and Margot White, "The Legalization of Physician Assisted Suicide: Creating a Regulatory Potemkin Village," 30 *U. Richmond L. Rev.* 1, 44 (1996).

170. John Keown, supra ch. 1 n. 4, at 72. Cf. Yale Kamisar, "The 'Right to Die': On Drawing (and Erasing) Lines," 35 *Duq. L. Rev.* 418, 504 (1996).

171. John Keown, supra ch. 1 n. 4, at 171.

172. Id., at 172; Kathleen Foley and Herbert Hendin, "The Oregon Experiment," in "The Case against Assisted Suicide," supra intro. n. 18, at 145; id., at 166 (anonymous study found that 43 percent of those requesting PAS were in pain).

173. John Keown, supra ch. 1 n. 4, at 191–96.

174. Id., at 172, 175.

175. Kathleen Foley and Herbert Hendin, "The Oregon Experiment," in "The Case against Assisted Suicide," supra intro. n. 18, at 150.

176. John Keown, supra ch. 1 n. 4, at 172, 175.

177. Id., at 175; Linda Mancini, Darrin S. Fenn, Melinda A. Lee, Robert Heinz, and Joseph D. Bloom, "Attitudes of Oregon Psychiatrists towards Physician-Assisted Suicide," 153 *Am. J. Psych.* 1469, 1469 (1996).

178. Tony D. Pasquale and John P. Gluck, supra intro. n. 16, at 504.

179. John Keown, supra ch. 1 n. 4, at 175. See also Kathleen Foley and Herbert Hendin, "The Oregon Experiment," in "The Case against Assisted Suicide," supra intro. n. 18, at 151 (60 percent were depressed).

180. "The Case against Assisted Suicide," supra intro. n. 18, at 145, 172. In 2005, only two of 38 patients who ended their lives through PAS had a "psychiatric referral." "Physicians for Compassionate Care Analyzes Oregon's Assisted

Suicide Law: The 'Medical Killing' of Vulnerable Patients Continues," 33 *Right to Life News* (Apr. 1, 2006).

181. Kathleen Foley and Herbert Hendin, "The Oregon Experiment," in "The Case against Assisted Suicide," supra intro. n. 8, at 166.

182. John Keown, supra ch. 1 n. 4, at 177.

183. Id., at 179.

184. Steven White, "Euthanasia Jurisprudence and Physician-Assisted Suicide: What Did *Glucksberg* Teach Us?" 75 *J. Ala. Acad. Sci.* 214, 222, (2004) ("No law can be 'abuse proofed.' But no abuses of the Oregon law have been reported since its activation in 1997."); Linda Ganzini and Steven K. Dobscha, supra ch. 3 n. 29, at 121 ("Whatever the reason, these data do not support a slippery slope of increasing death-hastening acts—within or outside the law"); Barry Rosenfeld, supra intro. n. 12, at 154 ("Hence, most commentators have continued to suggest that [the Oregon act] has been utilized in an appropriate and thoughtful manner, without evidence of either abuse or misuse, and that fears of a growing reliance on assisted suicide over time have simply not been realized this far [n. omitted]"); B. Steinbeck, "The Case for Physician Assisted Suicide: Not (Yet) Proven," 31 *J. Med. Ethics* 235 (2005) (". . . fears that legalizing PAS [by means of the Oregon law] might lead to overuse do not seem to have been realized"). Nonetheless, anti-PAS constituencies point to two cases in which they claim the standards of the act were clearly violated. B. Steinbeck, supra, at 42–43; N. Gregory Hamilton, M.D., and Catherine A. Hamilton, M.A., supra ch. 3 n. 18, at 1061–62. However, in each of these cases, "there are two ways to see the story" (B. Steinbeck, supra, at 39), one of which supports the pro-PAS position that the safeguards of the act are working as envisioned. Id., at 39–40.

In fact, in criticizing the Dutch guidelines as inadequate, the author of an extensive study of the Dutch practice repeatedly cited to various sections of the Oregon guidelines as examples of appropriate guidelines, contrasting the Oregon regime with that of the Dutch. Raphael Cohen-Almager, supra ch. 4 n. 69, at 181, 182, 184, 185.

185. Michael Manning, M.D., supra intro. n. 6, at 47.

186. *In re Dinnerstein,* 6 Mass. App. 466, 380 NE2d. 134 (1978); *Superintendent of Bekhartown State School et al. v. Saikiewitz,* 373 Mass. 728, 370 NE2d. 412 (1977).

187. *In re Conroy,* 98 N.J. 321, 486 A.2d 1209 (1985); William F. May, Ph.D., "Ethical Considerations in Life and Death Decisions," in *Life and Death Issues* 62 (James E. Hammer III, D.D.S., Ph.D., and Barbara J. Sax Jacobs, J.D., eds., Univ. of Tenn. 1986); George J. Annas, "The Right to Die in America: Sloganeering from Quintin and Cruzan to Quill and Kevorkian," 34 *Duq. L. Rev.* 875, 883 (1986); Yale Kamisar, "When Is There a Constitutional Right to Die? When Is There a Constitutional Right to Live?" 25 *Ga. L. Rev.* 1139, 1222 (1991). But see Beth Spring and Ed Laron, supra ch. 2 n. 16, at 16 (food and hydration were previously considered "natural support"); "Submission to the Select Committee of

the House of Lords on Medical Ethics by the Linacre Centre for Health Care Ethics," in "Clinical Practice," supra ch. 1 n. 3, at 142 (food and hydration are not considered medical treatment).

188. Margaret Somerville, supra ch. 1 n. 10, at 47 (the nature of marker events is that those on one side of the line are different from those on the other side, particularly with regard to avoiding precedent).

189. Marvin Harris, *Cows, Pigs, Witches, and Wars* 107, 196, 206–7 (Vintage 1975); Pennethorne Hughes, *Witches* (Penguin 1965) (author attributes the general elimination of witchcraft practice in Europe to purges by the church and state and also as the result of economics, culminating in the Industrial Revolution, during which peasants, who practiced the "old ways," were brought in contact with the new ideas of the urban population).

190. Pennethorne Hughes, supra n. 189, at 172–73.

191. Marvin Harris, supra n. 189, at 207 (500,000 killed); Pennethorne Hughes, supra n. 189, at 195 (nine million killed).

192. Pennethorne Hughes, supra n. 189, at 213–15. Cf. also Marvin Harris, supra n. 189, at 243 (author details the resurgence of the occult in modern American life).

193. Pennethorne Hughes, supra n. 189, at 164. Cf. also Exodus 7:8, in *Tanakh: A New Translation of the Holy Scriptures according to the Traditional Hebrew Text* (Jewish Publ. Society 1985) (Moses has a competition with the pharaoh's court magicians).

194. Pennethorne Hughes, supra n. 189, at 164.

195. Carlos Castenada, *The Teachings of Don Juan* (University of California Press 1968).

196. Pennethorne Hughes, supra n. 189, at 197.

197. Id., at 184.

198. Id., at 190.

199. Id., at 184.

200. Marvin Harris, supra n. 189, at 238.

201. Id.

202. Pennethorne Hughes, supra n. 189, at 202–5; Marvin Harris, supra n. 189, at 213.

203. Pennethorne Hughes, supra n. 189, at 202.

204. Id., at 198.

205. Id., at 206–7.

206. Len Doyl, "Why Active Euthanasia and Physician Assisted Suicide Should Be Legalized," 323 *BMJ* 1079, 1080 (2001).

207. Daniel Callahan and Margot White, supra ch. 4 n. 169, at 61.

208. Id., at 58–59.

209. See, generally, Daniel Callahan, "Self-Extinction: The Morality of the Helping Hand," in "Physician-Assisted Suicide," supra intro. n. 11, at 82 ("There is no way, even in principle, to write or enforce a meaningful law that can guar-

antee effective procedural safeguards [for PAS]"). See also Gerald Dworkin, R.G. Frey, and Sissela Bok, supra ch. 3 n. 25, at 46–47.

210. See, for example, Michael M. Burgess, "The Medicalization of Dying," in "Legal Euthanasia: Ethical Issues in an Era of Legalized Dying," 18 *J. Med. & Phil.* 269, 274 (Margaret P. Battin and Thomas J. Bole III, issue eds.) (1993).

211. See Steve P. Calandrillo, supra ch. 4 n. 34, at 91 (describes "a Model Act to Authorize and Regulate Physician-Assisted Suicide"). See also Charles H. Baron et al., "A Model State Act to Authorize and Regulate Physician-Assisted Suicide," 33 *Harv. J. on Legis.* 1 (1996).

212. "If the law is too bureaucratic, too intrusive, or gives insufficient legal shelter to doctors acting in good faith, it will be ignored in practice and will fail in its objective of re-regulating PAS/AE. The challenge for those interested in minimizing harm is to design a regime that is robust, but which is also more attractive than the stresses and risks of illicit action. Locating this middle ground is all the more controversial because of the feared consequences of 'unsafe' law." R.S. Magnusson, "Euthanasia: Above Ground, below Ground," 30 *J. Med. Ethics* 441, 444 (2004).

213. See, generally, Daniel Callahan and Margot White, supra ch. 4 n. 169.

Issue 5

1. Derek Humphrey and Mary Clement, supra intro. n. 4; Sue Woodman, *Last Rights: The Struggle over the Right to Die* (Perseus 1998). See also Wesley J. Smith, supra intro. n. 10, at 6; Margaret Somerville, supra ch. 1 n. 10, at 312; Bernadette-Tobin, "Did You Think about Buying Her a Cat? Reflections on the Concept of Autonomy," 11 *J. Contemp. Health Law & Pol'y* 417 (1991); and Steve P. Calandrillo, supra ch. 4 n. 34, at 65 (". . . autonomy has thus become something of a trump card in the debates of recent years . . ."). Cf. Brian Clark, *Whose Life Is It Anyway?* (Bard 1978).

2. The first argument ties autonomy to sanctity of life. "Submission to the Select Committee of the House of Lords on Medical Ethics by the Linacre Centre for Health Care Ethics," in "Clinical Practice," Book Two, "Euthanasia and the Law: The Case against Legalization," supra ch. 1 n. 3, at 132. This argument posits that the principle of sanctity of life is what makes the notion of autonomy coherent. Why should we respect *your* individual choices? Why do we give you equal value regardless of whether you're rich or poor, brilliant or stupid? The answer, as already discussed, is the commitment of our society to the right and principle of equal justice. The right and principle, in turn, ultimately are based on the notion that all lives have equal value because they are equally sacred. As such, autonomy cannot be relied on to justify a denial of life's absolute sanctity through taking that life through suicide since our very respect for autonomy is dependent on accepting the sacredness of life.

I do not find this argument persuasive. The commitment to equal justice does not necessarily require reliance on notions such as sacredness. While admittedly having a moral flavor, equal justice can equally be based on a political philosophy, which reflects the conception of the individual in a modern, liberal society (exemplified by the Western democracies). It is a concept that gives high value to the individual creation of ideas and identity and serves as a form of insurance against the risk that any of us could have had an unlucky draw at birth in the social lottery (e.g., in the distribution of brains, wealth, status, health, and support). But it is just one vision of a society. Some societies do not focus on the individual but on the broader unit, and in that effort they have even discouraged individuality (e.g., in Maoist China or ancient Sparta). Even in America, the land of the rugged individual, movements appear from time to time that ask us to think not as individuals but as a community.

Moreover, the argument does not follow on its own terms. In the context of considering autonomy, it is true that the concept is underlain by the notion that my life has as much value as anyone else's and that my right to choose for myself merits the same respect as another's right to choose. All that said, it still is not clear to me why *I* can't make the choice to end *my* life. Someone making that choice for me against my desires based on their assessment of my comparative value would assuredly violate the principle of equal justice. But that is not what we are talking about here, at least not on a theoretical level (admittedly, on a pragmatic plane, there are concerns about coercion by family members and doctors, which I considered when addressing the slippery slope).

The second argument posits that autonomy cannot logically coexist with self-destruction. See Luke Gormally, "Walton, Davies, Boyd, and the Legalization of Euthanasia," in "Euthanasia Examined," supra intro. n. 2, at 118–19; "Submission to the Select Committee of the House of Lords on Medical Ethics by the Linacre Centre for Health Care Ethics," in "Clinical Practice," Book Two, "Euthanasia and the Law: The Case against Legalization," supra ch. 1 n. 3, at 131 (autonomy is meant to be used so that we might "flourish"); and Michael J. Hyde, supra ch. 4 n. 33, at 165. The purpose of autonomy is to fulfill oneself as a person, to give an individual the full ability to exercise his or her capacity for growth and self-definition. Self-destruction, thus, is antithetical to the very enterprise underlain by autonomy.

I agree with this argument as a descriptive matter. Generally, we do use our autonomy to make choices based on what we believe (sometimes mistakenly) will be a greater fulfillment of our potential as a human being. But it does not follow that self-death is *never* an appropriate choice under *any* circumstances. Someone in the circumstances of my father is beyond the niceties of elevating his being as a full person. He was dying, every function in his body was breaking down, and he was miserable. Under the circumstances, suicide may have been an appropriate choice as a means of protecting the self from further torture while that self existed in any coherent sense and in fulfilling the final destiny of that self in its earthly journey. Thus, I do not find this position convincing.

3. John Harris, "Euthanasia and the Value of Life," in "Euthanasia Examined," supra intro. n. 2, at 12; Dan W. Brock, "Physician-Assisted Suicide Is Sometimes Morally Justified," in "Physician-Assisted Suicide," intro. n. 11, at 8. But see Richard A. McCormick, supra ch. 3 n. 31.

4. Ronald Dworkin, supra ch. 1 n. 3, at 16.

5. Peter G. Filene, supra intro. n. 1, at 173–74; Anthony Fisher, "Theological Aspects of Euthanasia," in "Euthanasia Examined," supra intro. n. 2, at 319 (extreme autonomy is antisocial); Wesley J. Smith, supra intro. n. 10, at 6; Robert I. Mishbin, supra intro. n. 5, at 174–75; Liezl van Zyl, supra intro. n. 18, at 125; Margaret Somerville, supra ch. 1 n. 10, at 343; Ira R. Block, "Physician-Assisted Suicide Is Not an Acceptable Practice for Physicians," in "Physician-Assisted Suicide," supra ch. 1 n. 2, at 112–13. See also Patricia S. Mann, "Meanings of Death," in "Expanding the Debate," supra intro. n. 8, at 19. Cf. Liezl van Zyl, supra intro. n. 8, at iv (death can provide the opportunity for social connection).

6. Bernadette Tobin, supra n. 1, at 422–25.

7. For a discussion of how experts use cognitive modes and structures in developing problem representations and solutions, see Marilyn Berger and John Mitchell, "Rethinking Advocacy Training," 16 *Am. J. Trial Adv.* 821, 822–28 (1993); and James Voss et al., *Problem-Solving Skill in the Social Sciences,* 17 *Psychol. Learning & Motivation* 165, 191–212 (1983).

Further elaboration of the basic cognitive processes of making meaning through interpretive frameworks, generally referred to as "schema theory," can be found in Richard C. Anderson, "The Notion of Schemata and the Educational Enterprise: General Discussion of the Conference," in *Schooling and the Acquisition of Knowledge* 415, 419 (Richard C. Anderson et al., eds., Lawrence Erlbaum Associates 1977); Robert Glaser, "Education and Thinking the Role of Knowledge," 39 *Am. Psychol.* 93 (1984); John B. Mitchell, "Current Theories on Expert and Novice Thinking: A Full Faculty Considers the Implications for Legal Education," 39 *J. Legal Educ.* 275, 277–83 (1989); and David D. Rumelhart, "Schemata: The Building Blocks of Cognition," in *Theoretical Issues in Reading Comprehension* 33 (Rand J. Spiro et al., eds., Lawrence Erlbaum Associates 1980). See also Jean Piaget, *The Language and Thought of the Child* (3d ed., Humanities Press 1959) (presents a cognitive, as opposed to behavioral, theory regarding child development). See also Michael J. Hyde, supra ch. 4 n. 33, at 28; and Jos M.V. Welie, supra ch. 3 n. 30, at 145 (philosophers such as Heidegger recognized that every description reflects the stance of the describer).

8. Ronald Dworkin, supra ch. 1 n. 3, at 27, 199–200, 205 (controlling one's narrative maintains "integrity" in that life); John Harris, "Euthanasia and the Value of Life," in "Euthanasia Examined," supra intro. n. 2, at 14.

9. Steve P. Calandrillo, supra ch. 4 n. 34, at 65 ("Contrary to Dworkin, Professor Rebecca Dresser believes that most of us do not have the strong sense of critical interest, autonomy, and continuity of the person necessary to adopt

Dworkin's thesis. . . . She asserts that there is no evidence to support the claim that people want narrative coherence, . . .").

Issue 6

1. Carl Wellman, "A Moral Right to Physician Assisted Suicide," 38 *Am. Phil. Q.* 271 (2000); Karen Lebacqz and H. Tristram Engelhardt Jr., M.D., "Suicide," in "Death-Dying," supra ch. 1 n. 3, at 692, 693.

2. Todd Goldberg, "A Doctor Looks at Assisted Suicide," 1 *Navigator* 35 (1998).

3. Id.

4. Margaret Somerville, supra ch. 1 n. 10, at 317–20.

5. Daniel Callahan and Margot White, supra ch. 4 n. 169, at 43; Joel Feinberg, supra ch. 4 n. 8, at 29. Cf. David C. Thomasama, supra ch. 4 n. 13, at 289 (author questions the possibility of a "rational" suicide).

6. Mark Sullivan, Linda Ganzini, and Stuart J. Young, "Should Psychiatrists Serve as Gatekeepers for Physician Assisted Suicide?" 28 *Hastings Center Report* 24, 25 (1998) (the modern medical model is that suicide is never the choice of a rational agent but a symptom of mental illness); Malcolm Parker, supra intro. n. 14, at 526 ("Australian researchers claiming a new psychiatric diagnosis, Demoralization Syndrome (DS), rule out the possibility of a rational suicide, finding the desire to die being symptomatic of the detectable pathology, n. omitted]"). See also D. Clarke and D. Kissare, "Demoralization: Its Phenomenology and Importance," 36 *Aust N.Z. Psychiatry* 733 (2002); and Timothy H. Lillie and James L. Werth Jr., "Introduction to Special Issues: End-of-life Issues and Persons with Disabilities," 16 *J. Disability Pol'y Studies* 2, 2 (2005) ("Let me be clear here: I do not agree with the concept of rational suicide, especially as applied to people with disabilities, primarily because of social and cultural concerns"). But see Kyriaki Mystakidou, Efi Parpa, Elini Tsikila, Emmanuela Katsouda, and Lambors Vlahos, "The Evolution of Euthanasia and Its Perceptions in Greek Culture and Civilization," 48 *Perspectives Bio. & Med.* 95 (2005) ("Though suicide is generally viewed to be a pathological state of mind, most often linked to depression, some professionals hypothesize that suicide in some circumstances can be quite rational"); Malcolm Parker, supra intro. n. 14, at 527 (author sees the fact that those refusing to accept that someone can rationally choose PAS but do not make the same claim about the rationality of those who refuse life-sustaining treatment "suggest that a particular moral view about assisted dying is helping to demonstrate the clinical disorder [undermining the capacity for rational suicide]"); James G. Adams, "Life or Death: Physician-Assisted Suicide and Emergency Medicine," 3 *Academic Emergency Med.* 909, 909 (1996) (61 percent of primary care physicians believe that suicide can be rational); and Derek Humphrey and Mary Clement, supra intro. n. 4, at 80 (suicide can be a totally rational response to a particular situation).

7. Kay Redfield Jamison, supra intro. n. 5; *Reference Shelf: Suicide* (Robert Emmet Long, ed., H.W. Wilson 1995) (reprints from various magazine articles).

8. Mark Sullivan, Linda Ganzini, and Stuart J. Young, supra n. 6, at 27; Linda Ganzini and Melinda Lee, "Psychiatry, and Assisted Suicide in the United States," 336 *New Eng. J. Med.* 1795, 1825 (1997); Joel Feinberg, supra ch. 4 n. 8, at 358.

9. Barry Rosenfeld, supra intro. n. 12, at 122–23. But see N. Gregory Hamilton, M.D., and Catherine A. Hamilton, M.A., supra ch. 3 n. 18, at 1061 (". . . the majority of forensic Psychiatrists . . . believe that the presence of a major depressive disorder should result in an automatic finding of incompetence to make decisions about assisted suicide").

10. Elaine Scarry, supra ch. 1 n. 9, at 29, 35; Liezl van Zyl, supra intro. n. 18, at 72.

11. Linda Ganzini, Melinda A. Lee, Robert T. Heintz, Joseph D. Bloom, and Darien S. Fenn, "The Effect of Depression Treatment on Elderly Patients' Preference for Life-Sustaining Medical Therapy," 151 *Am. J. Psych.* 1631, 1635 (1994).

12. Edmund D. Pellegrino, "The False Promise of Beneficent Killing," in "Regulating How We Die," supra ch. 1 n. 7, at 81; Yale Kamisar, "Some Non-religious Views against Proposed 'Mercy Killing' Legislation," in "Death-Dying," supra ch. 1 n. 3, at 414, 423–25.

13. Joel Feinberg, supra ch. 4 n. 8, at 29.

14. Joyce Anne Schofield, "Care of the Older Person: The Ethical Challenge to American Medicine," 4 *Issues in Law & Med.* 53, 64 (1988); Liezl van Zyl, supra intro. n. 18, at 63 (there do not exist undisputed criteria); Margaret Sommerville, supra ch. 1 n. 10, at 300–309 (some of the evaluation is "intuitive"); Mark Sullivan, Linda Ganzini, and Stuart J. Younger, "Should Psychiatrists Serve as Gatekeepers for Physician Assisted Suicide?" supra n. 6, at 26; Linda Ganzini, Gregory P. Leong, Darien S. Fenn, J. Aurturo Silva, and Robert Weinstock, "Evaluation of Competence to Consent to Assisted Suicide: View of Forensic Psychiatrists," 157 *Am. J. Psych.* 595, 599 (competency is not really a scientific concept but represents the balancing of autonomy against paternalism).

Issue 7

1. Paul J. Zwier, supra intro. n. 15, at 228.

2. *Basic Questions on Suicide and Euthanasia: Are They Ever Right?* Bio Basics Series 26 (Kregel 1998); Gerald Dworkin, R.G. Frey, and Sissela Bok, supra ch. 3 n. 25; Margaret P. Battin, "Is a Physician Ever Obligated to Help a Patient Die?" in "Regulating How We Die," supra ch. 1 n. 7, at 23; Daniel Callahan, "Self-Extinction: The Morality of the Helping Hand," in "Physician-Assisted Suicide," supra intro. n. 11, at 83 ("The two standard motives for euthanasia and assisted-suicide are said to be our right of self-determination and our claim upon mercy of others, especially doctors to relieve our suffering. These two motives are typically spliced together as a single justification.").

3. *Schoelendorff v. Society of New York Hosp.*, 211 N.Y. 125, 105 N.E. 92 (1914) (Cardoro, J.). See also *Bovia v. Superior Court*, 225 Cal. Rptr. 297, 179 Cal. App. 3d. 1127 (1986); *In re Conroy*, 98 N.J. 321, 486 A.2d. 1209 (1985).

4. *Bovia v. Superior Court*, 225 Cal. Rptr. 297, 179 Cal. App.3d. 1127 (1986); Barbara A. Blackmond, J.D., "Legal Aspects in Prolonging Life," in *Life and Death Issues* 67 (James E. Hammer III, D.D.S., Ph.D., and Barbara Sax Jacobs, eds., Univ. of Tenn. 1986).

5. Robert Finn, *Cancer Clinical Trials: Experimental Treatments and How They Can Help You* 41–42 (O'Reilly 1999); Derek Humphrey and Mary Clement, supra intro. n. 4, at 40–41; Robert I. Mishbin, supra intro. n. 5, at 108; Liezl van Zyl, supra intro. n. 18, at 35; William F. May, "Ethical Considerations in Life and Death Decisions," in *Life and Death Issues* 56 (James E. Hammer III, D.D.S., Ph.D., and Barbara Sax Jacobs, eds., Univ. of Tenn. 1986); Annette E. Clark, supra intro. n. 15, at 117.

6. Jos V.M. Welie, supra ch. 3 n. 30, at 71. Cf. Carl E. Schneider, *The Practice of Autonomy: Patients, Doctors, and Medical Decisions* 18 (Oxford Univ. Press 1998) (only I will truly protect my interests).

7. Jos V.M. Welie, supra ch. 3 n. 30, at 74, 115; Paul J. Zwier, supra intro. n. 15, at 228–29, 230 (author offers a "care perspective"); Liezl van Zyl, supra intro. n. 18, at 192–93.

8. Carl E. Schneider, supra n. 6, at 51, 94.

9. Id., at 49, 51.

10. Raymond S. Duff, M.D., "Neonatology Life and Death Issues," in *Life and Death Issues* 94 (James E. Hammer III, D.D.S., Ph.D., and Barbara Sax Jacobs, eds., Univ. of Tenn. 1986).

11. Carl E. Schneider, supra n. 6, at 41.

12. Id., at xiv.

13. Id., at 49.

14. Id., at xiv.

15. Liezl van Zyl, supra intro. n. 18, at 165; David C. Thomasama, supra ch. 4 n. 13, at 193; Annette E. Clark, supra intro. n. 15, at 115–16.

16. Jessica Cooper, "The Justification for Imprisoning Kevorkian," in *Euthanasia: Contemporary Issues Companion* 64 (Linda Yount, ed., Greenhaven 2002); Luke Gormally, "Walton, Davies, Boyd, and the Legalization of Euthanasia," in "Euthanasia Examined," supra intro. n. 2, at 132; Leon R. Kass, "I Will Give No Deadly Drug: Why Doctors Must Not Kill," in "The Case against Assisted Suicide," supra intro. n. 18, at 25, 29–30; John Keown, supra ch. 1 n. 4, at 78; Nelson Lund, supra ch. 4 n. 30, at 919.

17. See J.P. Bishop, "Framing Euthanasia," *J. Med. Ethics* 225, 227 (2006) (author uses experience with DNR codes to demonstrate how doctors can totally influence their patients' choices by the specific word choices they use in presenting options). See also Daniel Callahan and Margot White, supra ch. 4 n. 169, at 28 (can't really assess the adequacy of a particular patient's consent for PAS

because the patient will be dead); and Raphael Cohen-Almadar, supra, ch. 4 n. 69, at 97–98 (in fact, by raising the topic of euthanasia as a just "medical" option, doctors can influence their patients' decisions).

18. David C. Thomasama, supra ch. 4 n. 13, at 189; Frances M. Kamm, "Physician Assisted Suicide, Euthanasia, and Intending Death," in "Expanding the Debate," supra intro. n. 8, at 35 (assisted suicide and euthanasia are permissible when death is a "lesser evil"). But see Arthur J. Dyck, "Beneficient Euthanasia and Benemortasia: Alternative Views of Mercy," in "Death-Dying," supra ch. 1 n. 3, at 348, 355 (*mercy* means don't kill and do provide care).

19. Gerald Dworkin, R.G. Frey, and Sissela Bok, supra ch. 3 n. 25.

20. Beth Spring and Ed Laron, supra ch. 2 n. 16, at 131. As a deontological counterargument to the idea that patient autonomy mixed with mercy can justify PAS, some have pointed out that relieving suffering necessarily implies the existence of a formerly suffering person who is now relieved. If you kill someone, you may end them and their suffering with it, but no one will exist who will be relieved. It is an interesting argument (in the genre of if a tree falls in the forest and there is no one to hear it), but ultimately I believe it begs the real question. Is there a time when stopping suffering is more important than life itself so that assisted suicide is morally justified?

21. James V. Lavery, Joseph Boyle, Bernard M. Dickenson, Helen Maclean, and Peter A. Singer, "Origins of the Desire for Euthanasia and Assisted Suicide in People with HIV–1 or Aids: A Qualitative Study," 338 *Lancet* 362 (2001) (principal source of suffering includes loss of community, loss of self, and existential misery).

22. Daniel Callahan, supra intro. n. 1, at 109, 110; Nelson Lund, supra ch. 4 n. 30, at 918–19; Daniel Callahan, Ph.D., "Reason, Self-Determination, and Physician-Assisted Suicide," in "The Case against Assisted Suicide," supra intro. n. 18, at 64–65; Edmund D. Pellegrino, M.D., "Compassion Is Not Enough," in "The Case against Assisted Suicide," supra intro. n. 18, at 41, 48.

For example, one author interprets the situation in the Netherlands as one in which physicians can abrogate one of the two foundational principles of the Dutch law—patient consent (i.e. autonomy) and unbearable suffering (i.e., mercy)—and still be found sympathetic in carrying out euthanasia if the remaining principle (i.e., autonomy *or* mercy) is sufficiently compelling in the individual case. See Raphael Cohen-Almager, supra ch. 4 n. 69, at 169.

Issue 8

1. Yale Kamisar, supra ch. 1 n. 42, at 133–34. See also Larry I. Palmer, *Endings and Beginnings: Law, Medicine, and Society in Assisted Life and Death* (Praeger 2000) (contending that PAS is an issue for the legislature, too complex for the courts, as it is a product of institutional arrangements among law, medicine, and such).

2. Kay Redfield Jamison, supra intro. n. 6, at·15.

3. Id.

4. Id.

5. Id.

6. Id.

7. Beth Spring and Ed Laron, supra ch. 2 n. 16, at 64; Steven Miles, Demetra M. Pappas, and Robert Koepp, "Considerations of Safeguards Proposed in Laws and Guidelines to Legalize Assisted Suicide," in "Physician-Assisted Suicide," supra intro. n. 11, at 270; Glanville Williams, supra ch. 1 n. 41, at 257; Lawrence Gostin, supra ch. 1 n. 4, at 95.

8. Beth Spring and Ed Laron, supra ch. 2 n. 16, at 64; Steven Miles, Demetra M. Pappas, and Robert Koepp, "Considerations of Safeguards Proposed in Laws and Guidelines to Legalize Assisted Suicide," in "Physician-Assisted Suicide," supra intro. n. 11, at 210; Glanville Williams, supra ch. 1 n. 41, at 261.

9. U.S. Const. Art I, § 9(3); Stacy L. Mojica and Dan S. Murrel, supra intro. n. 5, at 482.

10. Steven Miles, Demetra M. Pappas, and Robert Koepp, "Considerations of Safeguards Proposed in Laws and Guidelines to Legalize Assisted Suicide," in "Physician-Assisted Suicide," supra intro. n. 11, at 210; Glanville Williams, supra ch. 1 n. 41, at 262; Stacy L. Mojica and Dan S. Murrel, supra intro. n. 5, at 95.

11. Yale Kamisar, "Physician Assisted Suicide: The Last Bridge to Active Voluntary Euthanasia," in "Euthanasia Examined," supra intro. n. 2, at 229.

12. Stacy L. Mojica and Dan S. Murrel, supra intro. n. 5, at 473, 500.

13. Sanford H. Kadish, supra ch. 1 n. 13, at 863.

14. Wesley J. Smith, supra intro. n. 10, at 5; in "Clinical Practice," Book One, "Euthanasia and Clinical Practice: Trends, Principles, and Alternatives (Working Party Report, 1982)," supra ch. 1 n. 3, at 30. See also *Washington v. Glucksberg* 521 U.S. 702, 710–11 (1997); *Vacco v. Quill*, 521 U.S. 793, ante 740–41 (1997) (Stevens, concurring); and *Cruzan v. Missouri Department of Health*, 497 U.S. 261, 335 (1990).

15. See Joshua Dressler, *Understanding Criminal Law* 13, § 2.03 [D] (2d ed., Matthew Bender 1995) ("Why is denunciation desirable [as a purpose of criminal punishment]? First, it's educative. We inform individuals that the community considers specific conduct improper.").

16. Liezl van Zyl, supra intro. n. 18, at 75. See also *Cruzan v. Missouri Department of Health*, 497 U.S. 261, 335 (1990); *Sue Rodriguez v. Attorney General Canada and Attorney General British Columbia*, 3 Can. Sup. Ct. Reps. 603 (Part 4, 1993). But see *Washington v. Glucksberg*, 521 U.S. 702, 752 (Stevens, concurring) (implies that government cannot interfere with constitutional rights solely for educative or symbolic value: "'. . . unqualified interest in the preservation of human life' . . . is not sufficient to outweigh the interest in liberty that may justify the only possible means of preserving a dying person's dignity and alleviate her intolerable suffering").

17. Daniel Callahan, supra intro. n. 1, at 110; Liezl van Zyl, supra intro. n. 18, at 103. Cf. Margaret P. Battin, "Is a Physician Ever Obligated to Help a Patient Die?" in "Regulating How We Die," supra ch. 1 n. 7, at 191–25 (most sick people cannot kill themselves without help).

18. A theoretical argument has also been put forth that suicide and assisted suicide are matters protected by the First Amendment. Ronald Dworkin has written that the current debate over assisted suicide reflects a difference in beliefs over the meaning of what constitutes the "sacredness/sanctity of life." As this debate, over which the country is divided fundamentally, takes the form of opposing religious values, this essentially involves First Amendment freedom of religion guarantees. Under these circumstances, the Constitution forbids the state the right to intrude. See Ronald Dworkin, supra ch. 1 n. 3, at 157, 164–65. See also David McKenzie, "Church, State, and Physician-Assisted Suicide," 46 *J. Church & State* 787, 809 (2004). While it is intriguing, there appear to be two fundamental problems with this contention. First, there are those who oppose PAS on totally non-religious grounds. See Yale Kamisar, "Some Non-religious Views against Proposed 'Mercy Killing' Legislation," in "Death-Dying," supra ch. 1 n. 3, at 411; Yale Kamisar, supra ch. 1 n. 42, at 118; and Phillip Berry, "Euthanasia: A Dialogue," 26 *J. Med. Ethics* 370 (2000) (author posits dialogue between a patient who desires euthanasia and an atheist physician who refuses to supply it). Second, the court has distinguished religious "belief" (which is constitutionally protected as an absolute) with religious "activity" (which can be regulated). See, for example, *Employment Division v. Smith,* 494 U.S. 872 (1990) (court permits application of drug laws to Native American peyote ceremony); and *Reynolds v. United States,* 98 U.S. (8 Otto) 145 (1878) (even though polygamy is part of the Mormon religious tradition, it may be prohibited under the general law prohibiting polygamy).

Finally, some have posited a constitutional right to assisted suicide for elderly, terminally ill persons based upon the Lockean social contract theory undergirding the American Constitution, see, John B. Mitchell, "My Father, John Locke, and Assisted Suicide: The Real Constitutional Right," 3 *Ind. Health L. Rev* 47 (2006), or upon the "cruel and unusual" punishment prohibition of the 8th Amendment of the United States Constitution, see Seth F. Kreimer, "The Second Time as Tragedy: The Assisted Suicide Cases and the Heritage of Roe v. Wade," 24 *Hasting Const. L. Q.* 863, 893 (1998).

19. *Washington v. Glucksberg,* 521 U.S. 702 (1997).

20. *Vacco v. Quill,* 521 U.S. 793 (1997).

21. Alan Ides and Christopher N. May, *Constitutional Law: Individual Rights* 200 (2d ed., Aspen Law and Business 2001); Ronald Dworkin, supra ch. 1 n. 3, at 104.

22. Alan Ides and Christopher N. May, supra n. 21, at 205–9 ("narrowly tailored to meet a compelling need").

23. *Planned Parenthood v. Casey,* 505 U.S. 833, 928 (1992) (Stevens, J., dissenting).

24. M.T. Meulders-Klein, supra ch. 1 n. 3, at 29, 56, 61, 78 (1983).

25. M.T. Meulders-Klein, supra ch. 1 n. 3, at 44. See also Frances M. Kamm,

"Physician-Assisted Suicide, Euthanasia, and Intending Death," in "Expanding the Debate," supra intro. n. 8, at 36; and Rosamond Rhodes, "Physicians, Assisted Suicide, and the Right to Live or Die," in "Expanding the Debate," supra intro. n. 8, at 167. But cf. "Clinical Practice," Book One, "Euthanasia and Clinical Practice: Trends, Principles, and Alternatives (Working Party Report, 1982)," supra ch. 1 n. 3, at 40 (the right involved is really the right "not to be killed").

26. See, for example, Rule 11, 18 U.S.C.A. Fed. R. Crim. Pro. (West 1986); and *Boykin v. Alabama,* 395 U.S. 238 (1969) (U.S. Supreme Court specifies the required content of the plea ritual).

27. M.T. Meulders-Klein, supra ch. 1 n. 3, at 38 (one cannot consent to a battery and thereby waive one's right not to be harmfully touched unless battery is part of a violent sport such as boxing or football); *Witmore v. Arkansas,* 495 U.S. 149, 175 n. 1 (1990) (Marshall, J., dissenting) (the justice cites to 13 states prohibiting a waiver by the defendant of a direct appeal in death penalty convictions); Daniel Callahan, supra intro. n. 1, at 105 (one can't waive the right not to be sold into slavery).

28. Todd Goldberg, supra ch. 6 n. 2, at 41. See also the view of philosopher John Stuart Mill in J.S. Mill, *On Liberty* 101 (Elizabeth Rappaport, ed., Hackett 1978) (1859).

29. See the opinions in *Washington v. Glucksberg,* 521 U.S. 702 (1992) of Justices O'Connor (737, 738), Stevens (742), Ginsberg (789), Breyer (790), and Souter (791, 792). See also Yale Kamisar, "The Rise and Fall of the 'Right' to Assisted Suicide," in "The Case against Assisted Suicide," supra intro. n. 18, at 78–79, 80; and James F. Breshnahan, "Assisted Suicide Should Be Illegal," in *Euthanasia: Contemporary Issues Companion* 76–77 (Lisa Yount, ed., Greenhaven 2002).

30. Margaret Somerville, supra ch. 1 n. 10, at 31; Daniel Callahan, supra intro. n. 1, at 36–37, 150 (one can't control everything in life and some richness can be achieved by not doing so).

31. Daniel Callahan and Margot White, supra ch. 4 n. 169, at 20; Martin Gunderson and David J. Mayo, "Altruism and Physician Assisted Death," in "Legal Euthanasia: Ethical Issues in an Era of Legalized Dying," 18 *J. Med. & Phil.* 281, 284–87 (Margaret P. Battin and Thomas J. Bole III, issue eds.) (1993) (we want loved ones to remember us as vital, etc.).

32. Germain Grisez, "Suicide and Euthanasia," in "Death-Dying," supra ch. 1 n. 3, at 782; John Finnis, "Misunderstanding the Case against Euthanasia: Response to Harris's First Reply," in "Euthanasia Examined," supra intro. n. 2, at 69; Luke Gormally, "Walton, Davies, Boyd, and the Legalization of Euthanasia," in "Euthanasia Examined," supra intro. n. 2, at 115; Fr. Robert Barry, O.P., supra intro. n. 5, at 498; Margaret Somerville, supra ch. 1 n. 10, at 255. Cf. Margaret Somerville, supra ch. 1 n. 10, at 267 (historically, dignity dealt with honor and inequality of attributes; only in the modern view do all persons have equal dignity).

33. Alan Donagan, supra ch. 1 n. 39, at 237.

34. Daniel Callahan, supra intro. n. 1, at 147; Paul Ramsey, "The Indignity of Death with Dignity," in "Death-Dying," supra ch. 1 n. 3, at 307; Margaret

Somerville, supra ch. 1 n. 10, at 257 (this notion of dignity should be thought of as "social dignity").

35. Daniel Callahan, supra intro. n. 1, at 12 et seq.; Margaret Somerville, supra ch. 1 n. 10, at 258–59.

36. The right must be: (1) carefully described, (2) "deeply rooted" in our culture and its traditions, and (3) "implicit in ordered liberty." *Washington v. Glucksberg*, 521 U.S. 702, 720–21 (1997). Generally, the court requires a "careful description" and "deeply rooted," or, "implicit in ordered liberty," but a few cases have suggested the need for both deeply rooted and implicit in ordered liberty. Cf. *Washington v. Glucksberg*, supra n. 2, at 521 U.S. at 720; and *Bowers v. Hardwick*, 478 U.S. 186, 191–92 (1986).

37. *Griswold v. Connecticut*, 381 U.S. 479 (1965).

38. *Eisenstadt v. Baird*, 405 U.S. 438 (1972).

39. *Bowers v. Hardwick*, 478 U.S. 186, 192–93 (1986). See also Id., at 196 (In concurring, Justice Berger defines the right involved as "homosexual sodomy").

40. Stephen W. Wise, "Euthanasia Jurisprudence, and Physician-Assisted Suicide: What Did Glucksberg Teach Us?" 75 *J. Ala. Acad. Sci.* 214, 221 (2004):

> What is important is this: how one "frames" the "liberty right" determines whether support for it can be found in the history and traditions of the nation. If one frames it narrowly and in negatively charged emotive language, little support will be found. If framed broadly, much support will often be found.

41. *Bowers v. Hardwick*, 478 U.S. 186, 190–91 (1986). In 2003, the Supreme Court found a fundamental right to "engage in private sexual conduct between consenting adults in one's home" and reversed *Bowers v. Hardwick* in *Lawrence v. Texas*, 539 U.S. 558, 123 S. Ct. 2472, 156 L. Ed. 2d 508 (2003).

42. *Washington v. Glucksberg*, 521 U.S. 702, 724 (1997).

43. Id.

44. Id., 726, 727, quoting *Planned Parenthood v. Casey*, 505 U.S. 833, 851 (1992).

45. Lance K. Stell, "Physician-Assisted Suicide: To Decriminalize or Legalize, That Is the Question," in "Expanding the Debate," supra intro. n. 8, at 225; Ronald Dworkin, Thomas Nagel, Robert Nozick, John Rawls, Thomas Scanlon, and Judith Jarvis Thomson, "The Philosophers' Brief [in *Washington v. Glucksberg*]," in "Expanding the Debate," supra intro. n. 8, at 431; Paul J. Zwier, supra intro. n. 15, at 7.

46. *Vacco v. Quill*, 521 U.S. 793 (1997). The Supreme Court found that the state law barring assisted suicide is "evenhanded" (id., at 799–800) and meets the "minimum rationality" standard (id., at 801) (distinguishing between PAS and withdrawing treatment is "clearly rational").

47. *City of Cleburne v. Cleburne Living Center*, 473 U.S. 432, 445–46 (1985) ("[I]t would be difficult to find a principled way to distinguish a variety of other groups who have perhaps immutable disabilities setting them off from others,

who cannot themselves mandate the desired legislative responses, and who can claim some degree of prejudice from at least part of the public at large. One need mention in this respect only the aging, the disabled, the mentally ill, and the infirm. We are reluctant to set out on that course, and we decline to do so."). See also Alan Ides and Christopher N. May, supra n. 21, at 246; Yale Kamisar, "The Rise and Fall of the 'Right' to Assisted Suicide," in "The Case against Assisted Suicide," supra intro. n. 18, at 86 notes 67, 68.

48. See, *Brown v. Board of Education,* 347 U.S. 483 (1952) (the court rejected "separate but equal").

49. *Frontiero v. Richardson,* 411 U.S. 677, 688 (1973); *Michael M. v. Superior Court,* 450 U.S. 464, 468–69 (1981) (the standard of review requires that the law reflects no gender "stereotypes," that it serve an "important" governmental objective, and that the objectives be "genuine").

50. Dana Elizabeth Hirsch, "Euthanasia: Is It Murder or Mercy Killing? A Comparison of the Criminal Laws in the United States, the Netherlands, and Switzerland," 12 *Loy. L.A. Int'l & Compar. L.J.* 820, 825 n. 22 (1990) (author collects applicable cases). Interestingly, as of 1995, withdrawal of food and hydration was more accepted in acute care hospitals than nursing homes. Alan Meisel, "Barriers to Forgoing Nutrition and Hydration in Nursing Homes," 21 *Am. J.L. & Med.* 335 (1995).

51. John A. Robertson, "Involuntary Euthanasia of Defective Newborns: A Legal Analysis," in "Death-Dying," supra ch. 1 n. 3, at 163 note 149; Daniel C. Maguire, supra intro. n. 8, at 31, 49; Dana Elizabeth Hirsch, supra n. 50, at 833–34. Cf. Gerald Dworkin, R.G. Frey, and Sissela Bok, supra ch. 3 n. 25, at 24, 29.

52. David Orentlicher, supra ch. 1 n. 47, at 445. Cf. Ronald Dworkin, supra ch. 1 n. 3, at 9.

53. Liezl van Zyl, supra intro. n. 18, at 91–133; Yale Kamisar, supra ch. 4 n. 170, at 495.

Issue 9

1. John Rawls, *A Theory of Justice* (Belknap 1971).

2. John Mitchell, "Redefining the Sixth Amendment," 67 *So. Cal. L. Rev.* 1215, 1249 n. 115 (1994). Cf. Clifford Orwin and James R. Stoner Jr., "Neoconstitutionalism? Rawls, Dworkin, and Noziak," in *Confronting the Constitution: The Challenge to Locke, Montesquieu, Jefferson, and the Federalists from Utilitarianism, Historical Marxism, Freudianism, Pragmatism, and Existentialism* 437 (Allan Bloom, ed., AEI Press 1990).

3. Alan Donagan, supra ch. 1 n. 39, at 22; Norman Daniels, "Introduction," in *Reading Rawls: Critical Studies on Rawls' A* Theory of Justice xviii (Norman Daniels, ed., Basic Books 1974).

4. John Rawls, supra n. 1, at 146–52; Alan Donagan, supra ch. 1 n. 39, at 22.

5. The concept of maximum ignorance in probability theory is attributed by some to the French scientist Pierre-Simon Laplace (1749–1827). Under this con-

cept, if one is attempting to calculate the probability of a certain event (about which little or nothing is known a priori about the relative possibilities of the outcomes) and there have been no prior trials testing whether or not the event will occur, the probability at this point of maximum ignorance is fifty-fifty. See "Pierre-Simon Laplace" at en.wikipedia.org. In other sources, the concept of maximum ignorance is attributed to Rev. Thomas Bayes. See "Stephen D. Unwin" at en.wikipedia.org. This is not surprising since "[Bayes's] friend, Richard Price, edited and presented the work in 1763, after Bayes's death, . . . [and] Pierre-Simon Laplace replicated and extended these results in an essay of 1774, apparently unaware of Bayes's work." See "Bayes' Theorem" at en.wikipedia.org.

6. Ronald Dworkin, supra ch. 1 n. 3, at 47.

7. Yale Kamisar, "The Rise and Fall of the 'Right' to Assisted Suicide," in "The Case against Assisted Suicide," supra intro. n. 18, at 88; Lance K. Still, "Physician-Assisted Suicide: To Decriminalize or to Legalize, That Is the Question," in "Expanding the Debate," supra intro. n. 8, at 246; *Sue Rodriguez v. Attorney General Canada and Attorney General British Columbia,* 3 Can. Sup. Ct. Reps. 603 (Part 4, 1993).

8. *Gonzalez v. Oregon,* 546 U.S. 243, 126 S. Ct. 904, 163 L. Ed. 2d 748

9. B. Steinbock, supra ch. 4 n. 36, at 253 (the author takes the consequentialist position balancing the current "need" for PAS with the currently perceived "risks"). Cf. Steve P. Calandrillo, supra ch. 4 n. 34, at 100 ("The crucial point to take away from the valuable anti-PAS research is not that the practice should be banned outright, but that it must be carefully scrutinized and regulated").

10. Annette E. Clark, supra intro. n. 15, at 109; Yale Kamisar, supra ch. 1 n. 42, at 119.

11. Gerald Dworkin, R.G. Frey, and Sissela Bok, supra ch. 3 n. 25, at 65; Lynn Tracy Nerland, supra intro. n. 5, at 129–31 (the Japanese give doctors a defense for mercy killing); N.D.A. Kemp, supra intro. n. 10, at 219 (the author discusses the "good faith assistance" defense, which was presented to Parliament in 1985 and defeated by a margin of 48 to 15).

12. Julie A. Di Camillo, supra ch. 4 n. 140, at 808 n. 10; Gerald Dworkin, R.G. Frey, and Sissela Bok, supra ch. 2 n. 25, at 65; Dana Elizabeth Hirsch, supra ch. 8 n. 50, at 841; "Canada," 25; Mustafa D. Sayid, "Euthanasia: A Comparison of the Criminal Laws of Germany, Switzerland, and the United States," 6 *Bost. Coll. Inter. & Compar. L. Rev.* 533 (1983). Cf. Daniel C. Maguire, supra intro. n. 8, at 39 (mercy killing is different in nature than most homicides).

13. See Guido Calibresi and Phillip Bobbitt, supra ch. 1 n. 2.

14. The size of the euthanasia underground appears to be significant. See Samia A. Hurst, M.D., "'Agreed Boundaries': Are We Asking the Right Questions?" 166 *Arch. Intern. Med.* 126 (2006) (nearly 10 percent of doctors surveyed reported having conducted euthanasia). See also R.S. Magnusson, "Euthanasia: Above Ground, below Ground," 30 *J. Med. Ethics* 441, 441 (2004) (we can never make PAS completely safe but must consider risks posed by an unregulated underground carrying out an unlawful practice).

Index

AARP. *See* American Association of Retired Persons

abortion, 68, 77, 100, 145, 146, 147

advocacy, patient, 72–73

age considerations
  aging process, acceptance of, 156
  baby boomers, 5, 68, 71–72, 102, 158, 160
  equal protection under law, 149
  health costs of elderly, 75, 187n60, 187n62
  lack of political force of elderly, 66
  median age of requested suicide, 91
  stereotypes, 149
  teenagers, 37, 47, 96

AIDS, 92, 142, 185n44

ALS. *See* sclerosis, amyotrophic lateral

Alzheimer's disease, 73–74

American Association of Retired Persons (AARP), 103, 149

American culture
  death, changes in perception of, 3
  dissent, value placed on, 89

  vs. Dutch culture, 88–89, 193n148
  equal worth of all lives, 18, 19, 169n22–23
  euthanasia debates, 3–5
  independence, value placed on, 55, 62, 70, 160, 181n32
  individual rights, value placed on, 64–65, 108–9
  religious faith, diversity of, 30
  risk-taking, 62
  sanctity of life. *See* sanctity of life, absolute

antidepressants, 50

assisted-living facilities, 74

autonomy
  individual
    in American culture, 64–65, 108–9, 198n2
    interrelationships with other issues, 6, 107, 140, 198n2, 204n20
    vs. laws protecting individual life, 137, 141–42, 198n2, 205n15, 205n16, 207n27